LIFE IN OIL

MICHAEL L. CEPEK

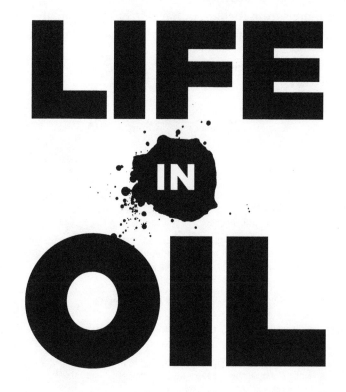

LIFE IN OIL

COFÁN SURVIVAL IN THE PETROLEUM FIELDS OF AMAZONIA

Photographs by
BEAR GUERRA

UNIVERSITY OF TEXAS PRESS
Austin

Support for this book comes from an endowment for environmental studies made possible by generous contributions from Richard C. Bartlett, Susan Aspinall Block, and the National Endowment for the Humanities.

♾ The paper used in this book meets the minimum requirements of ANSI/NISO Z39.48-1992 (R1997) (Permanence of Paper).

Unless otherwise identified, all photographs © Bear Guerra.

LIBRARY OF CONGRESS CATALOGING-IN-PUBLICATION DATA

Names: Cepek, Michael, author. | Guerra, Bear, photographer.
Title: Life in oil : Cofán survival in the petroleum fields of Amazonia / Michael L. Cepek ; photographs by Bear Guerra.
Description: First edition. | Austin : University of Texas Press, 2018. | Includes bibliographical references and index.
Identifiers: LCCN 2017025366| ISBN 978-1-4773-1507-1 (cloth : alk. paper) | ISBN 978-1-4773-1508-8 (pbk. : alk. paper) | ISBN 978-1-4773-1509-5 (library e-book) | ISBN 978-1-4773-1510-1 (nonlibrary e-book)
Subjects: LCSH: Cofán Indians—Ecuador—Dureno. | Cofán Indians—Ecuador—Dureno—Social conditions. | Oil spills—Environmental aspects—Amazon River Region. | Oil spills—Social aspects—Amazon River Region. | Dureno (Ecuador)—Environmental conditions. | Amazon River Region—Environmental conditions. | Petroleum industry and trade—Environmental aspects—Amazon River Region.
Classification: LCC F3722.1.C67 C438 2018 | DDC 986.6/412—dc23
LC record available at https://lccn.loc.gov/2017025366

doi:10.7560/35071

To Amy, who saved my life and brought me back to health, and to my father, John, and my friend Antonio, who remain so important to my life even now that they are gone.

CONTENTS

A NOTE ON THE PHOTOGRAPHS

Unless otherwise noted, all photographs in this book were taken by Roberto "Bear" Guerra, a photographer affiliated with the Fonografia Collective and Homelands Productions, during a trip to Amazonian Ecuador in February and March 2016. In the houses, gardens, and forest of the village of Dureno—as well as in the oil fields and urbanizing landscapes that surround it—Bear and I worked with indigenous Cofán collaborators to capture images that depict the Cofán's struggle to survive an era defined by oil extraction. We stayed in the house of Alejandro Criollo and Lucia Quenamá, but we worked with multiple families.

With some individuals, we went hunting and fishing. With others, we watched them cook meals, make handicrafts, and tend to their gardens. Although most of our work occurred in Dureno, we also visited oil wells, settler farms, and the provincial capital Lago Agrio, the historical center of Ecuador's oil industry. During all of the activities, I spoke to people in A'ingae, the Cofán language, as Bear took photos of them and their surroundings. In order to compensate people for our obtrusive presence and to share the material resources I had secured for my fieldwork, I paid families for their participation. All of them were willing and enthusiastic partners in the process. All of them also preferred to have their names attached to the images, where appropriate.

Bear and I worked together to select the photographs that appear

—

in the book. We wanted them to convey the open-ended quality of Cofán people's contemporary lives in the midst of petroleum extraction. For practical reasons, I have attempted to position the photographs in locations that make sense relative to the text. Readers can use them to deepen their experience of the narrative as it unfolds, but I also urge them to return to the images at multiple moments before and after they read the book—they are aesthetic objects unto themselves, as open to interpretation as their subjects.

In the future, Bear and I hope to produce an exhibition of the photographs alongside textual, audio, and video supplements that include direct Cofán commentaries on the images. More of Bear's work is posted at bearguerra.com and fonografiacollective.com.

A NOTE ON CORPORATE ACTORS

I use "Texaco" (Texas Petroleum Company) as the name of the corporate entity that explored for and produced oil in the territory of the indigenous Cofán people of Dureno, Ecuador, from 1964 through 1990. The actual corporate structure, however, was more complicated. In Ecuador, Texaco worked in a consortium with Gulf Oil until 1977. In 1974, Ecuador's state oil company, whose original name was Corporación Estatal Petrolera Ecuatoriana, obtained a 25 percent share in the consortium. In 1977, Gulf transferred its share to the state company, which became the majority owner. In 1989, the state company changed its name to Petroecuador. In 2007, the state company again changed its name to Petroamazonas.

Importantly, Texaco was the main operator in the consortium's concession. As the environmental lawyer Judith Kimerling has methodically noted in a 2006 journal article, Texaco was responsible for the design, construction, and maintenance of the petroleum-related infrastructure, including the pipelines, oil wells, roads, and waste disposal system. In 1990, Texaco transferred the operator role to Petroecuador and left the country entirely in 1992. In 2001, Texaco merged with Chevron. For a short while, the company was called ChevronTexaco. Now, it is simply Chevron.

IMPORTANT INDIVIDUALS

Alejandro Criollo: An elder and shaman (husband of Lucia, father of Roberto)

Arturo Ortiz: An accomplished hunter (neighbor of Alejandro, half-brother of Deji and Silvio)

Aurelio Quenamá: An elder and past leader (son of Yori'ye)

Bobbie Borman: A US-born missionary-linguist and health care worker who moved to Dureno in 1955 (wife of Bub, mother of Randy)

Bub Borman: A US-born missionary-linguist who moved to Dureno in 1955 (husband of Bobbie, father of Randy)

Deji Criollo: One of the author's main research assistants (half-brother of Arturo and Silvio)

Eduardo Mendua: President of Dureno from 2012 through 2015 (son of Florinda)

Emeregildo Criollo: A leader and activist involved in the Chevron lawsuit (father of Martin)

Florinda Vargas: An elder (mother of Eduardo)

Gregorio Quenamá: A leader and shaman who founded the community of Duvuno (cousin of Yori'ye, nephew of Santos)

Laura Mendua: An elder (wife of Silvio)

Lucia Quenamá: An elder (wife of Alejandro, mother of Roberto)

Martin Criollo: One of the author's main research assistants (son of Emeregildo)

—

Randy Borman: A genealogically Euro-American man who grew up in Dureno, identifies as Cofán, and became an important Cofán leader (son of Bobbie and Bub)

Roberto Criollo: A Cofán youth (son of Alejandro and Lucia)

Santos Quenamá: A shaman and leader (father of Yori'ye, uncle of Gregorio)

Silvio Chapal: An elder and past community leader (husband of Laura, half-brother of Arturo and Deji)

Toribio Aguinda: A leader responsible for organizing many anti-oil actions

Valerio Mendua: An elder (Alejandro's best friend)

Yori'ye (Guillermo Quenamá): A leader and shaman who founded Dureno (son of Santos)

LIFE IN OIL

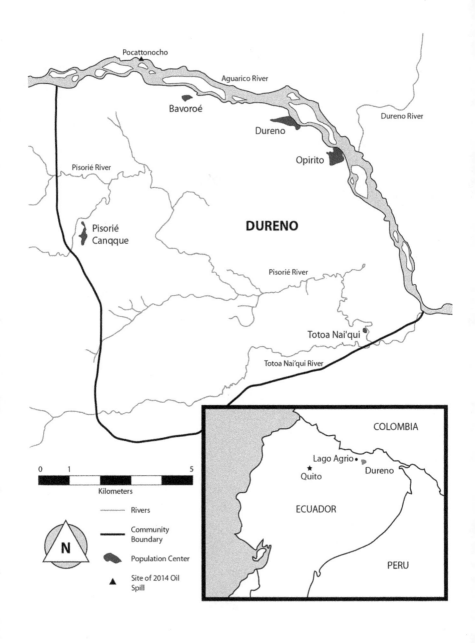

MAP O.1. *Present-day Dureno territory and settlements. Map by Leah McCurdy.*

·

CHAPTER 1

BLACK WATER

I sometimes feel like an imposter when I tell people that I'm an anthropologist of Amazonia. No one would mistake me for a courageous explorer—an image the public still associates with the vocation. My personality tends toward the anxious and the compulsive. During my childhood and teenage years in suburban Chicago, I constantly washed my hands, checked my home's door locks, and monitored my ever-growing array of nonexistent illnesses. With its geographical remoteness and army of pests, predators, and pathogens, Amazonia was an ironic choice for fieldwork. When I step back and realize how much of my life has come to revolve around the region, I have a hard time understanding how it happened. Over the past two decades of working with indigenous Cofán people in eastern Ecuador, the one thing that has kept me sane is a daily routine. While doing research for this book, I tried to begin each morning in the Cofán village of Dureno, my main field site, in exactly the same way.

–

I shared a house with my adoptive family and ritual relatives: Alejandro, Lucia, and Roberto. Every day, Alejandro woke well before dawn. Barefoot and in a traditional tunic, he walked silently into the forest toward his stash of *yoco* (*Paullinia yoco*), a vine that he grated and mixed with water to create a bitter, caffeinated drink. By 6 a.m., Lucia had started to boil ripe, sweet plantains to make *cui'ccu*,[1] a beverage that provides the caloric bulk of the Cofán diet. A stubborn teenager, Roberto tried to stay in bed as long as possible.

As soon as I heard Lucia mashing the plantains, I emerged from my mosquito net. Covered only by a pair of loose briefs, my pale flesh and soft frame were on full display. Cofán people smiled at my odd appearance and strange ways. They expected less of me than they would of a normal person, for which I was grateful given that part of a day's work might include carrying a sixty-pound peccary carcass over a five-mile forest trek. After I put on a shirt and pants, Lucia gave me a bowl of meat stew left over from dinner the night before. She also handed me a cup of hot water, into which I poured an obscene amount of instant coffee. When the coffee, the lukewarm meat, and the *cui'ccu* mingled in my stomach, my bowels kicked into high gear. On most days, I had only a few minutes to reach the makeshift latrine next to Alejandro's house.

After I finished my business in the *ccopa chango* (shit hole, in A'ingae, the Cofán language), I walked a couple hundred feet north to the south bank of the Aguarico River, along which most Cofán people live. Families from neighboring homes watched my stroll. A roll of toilet paper conspicuously bulged from one pocket and a bar of soap jutted out of the other. I waded a few feet into the river to wash my hands and face. Cleansed, I was ready to head back to Alejandro's house. From there, a typical day could go in a number of directions: writing up field notes, conducting interviews, or hunting, gardening, and socializing with friends and collaborators.

My morning ritual was deeply comforting, which is one reason the first hours of July 2, 2014, were so troubling. After I ate my breakfast and emptied my gut, I headed to the river. There was a strange sheen on its surface. Cofán people have a word for the condition: *tena'tssi*. It refers to the appearance of a liquid covered with small pools of

—

2

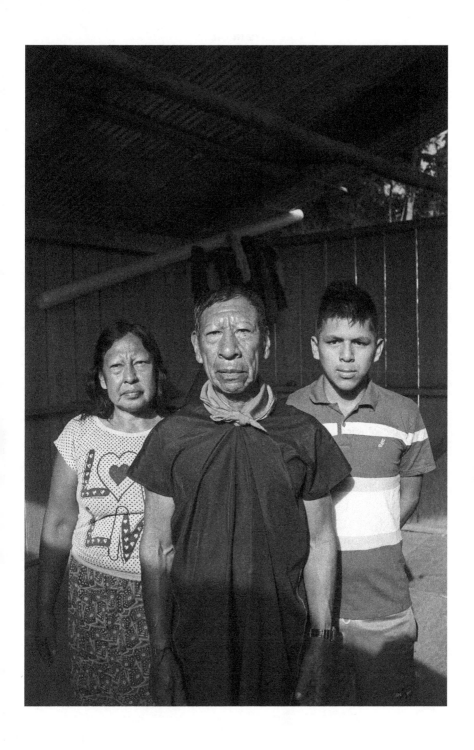

FIGURE 1.1. *Lucia, Alejandro, and Roberto*

grease or fat, much like the top layer of the tortilla soup I often enjoy at home in San Antonio, Texas. Annoyed that dirty water might jeopardize my routine, I looked upriver to see if a Cofán woman was cleaning dishes. I saw no one. Upon closer inspection, the sheen was thicker than I first thought. It smelled like gasoline. I guessed that a man might have been working on his outboard motor, but no one was tending to a canoe that morning. The further I scanned, the more viscous liquid I saw. Large patches were drifting my way. On the stones, sticks, and canoes that lined the riverbank, globules of the stuff began to form. It no longer appeared to be gasoline. It looked instead like a massive spill of thick, black, crude oil, which is exactly what it was.

I had been studying the relationship between the Cofán nation and the oil industry for twenty years, but I had never witnessed a spill of that magnitude. As perverse as it sounds, I felt lucky to see what so many Cofán people had described to me in painful detail. My closest collaborators told me they were happy I got to experience such an important part of their history. Ever since Texaco began searching for oil on their land in the 1960s, Cofán people have been living in a petroleum-soaked environment. For the past five decades, the social, ecological, medical, and political problems that accompany oil have plagued their lives. Spills of crude and other toxic wastes have covered their streams and rivers. Black ash from burning well pits and gas flares has rained down on their gardens, homes, and bodies. The colonizing farmers who followed the oil roads have stripped the Cofán of nearly all their traditional territory. The people of Dureno are now fearful, unwelcome strangers on much of their own land.

My Cofán friends asked me to take pictures of the disaster. They wanted to record and publicize the event so that other people, in other lands, could see what was happening. I sent photos and reports to contacts in the United States and Ecuador's capital, Quito. They passed the information along social media and activist networks. I filmed a Cofán leader's impromptu remarks beside the oil-covered river. In A'ingae, he talked about how often such things had happened to his people. He said the spill meant they would have nowhere to bathe, fish, or wash clothes and dishes. In the nearby town of Lago

Agrio, I worked with a young Cofán man to edit a video that included the community leader's remarks, a selection of my photos and film clips, and subtitles in English and Spanish. He uploaded it to his YouTube channel, and it traveled across the world.[2]

Although national newspapers and television crews reported the spill, the estimates for the number of barrels that reached the Aguarico River, and Dureno, were far too small. The government publicly claimed that only two hundred barrels had escaped from the spill site to the main body of the river. Covert estimates from corporate, media, and activist contacts put the number as high as twenty thousand barrels. The spill occurred after a mudslide ruptured a pipeline along a nearby road. Texaco contractors constructed the tube nearly four decades earlier. By 2014, it had become rusty and weak. Although workers from Ecuador's state oil company, Petroamazonas, tried to minimize the damage—an effort that distinguished them from Texaco employees, who, according to my Cofán collaborators, usually ignored past spills—the oil rushed into a nearby stream. Nonnative locals call the waterway the Parahuaico River. Cofán people know it as Pocattonocho, the "stream near the rock that resembles the shell of a giant river turtle." Unfortunately, the break was only a few kilometers from the Aguarico, into which the tainted water flowed. It then traveled past Dureno, other native and non-native settlements, and into Peru, where it reached the Amazon River. Along the way, it left a thick, black residue on every object it touched.

Over the next month, life was difficult in Dureno, and it was impossible to return to my routine. Soon, I noticed something strange. No one denied the tragedy, but a few older Cofán individuals said it was a relatively minor affair. In the 1960s, 1970s, and 1980s, they claimed, the layer of crude on the Aguarico was sometimes as thick as a fist. The river was unusable for weeks or months at a time. A few people said the 2014 spill reminded them of what the river looked like when it was safe to swim and fish again. They described how they used to push away pools of floating oil with their bare hands. In the small, clear-looking pockets they uncovered, they bathed, washed dishes, butchered game, and gathered water for cooking and drinking. Even on the night of July 2, one man jumped straight into the

FIGURE 1.2. *The 2014 oil spill on the Aguarico River. Photo by Michael Cepek.*

Aguarico for his daily bath. It was dark, but I could still see the crude, and the gasoline-like stench was overpowering.

Other confusing things happened after July 2. State officials declared the river to be unusable for six months. A couple weeks later, the government sent a doctor to Dureno. She told me it was OK to bathe in the water as long as I could not see the oil. But, she added, being a gringo might increase my susceptibility to the river's generally contaminated state. Supposedly, I was not as accustomed to its impurities as were the Cofán. No public health officials arrived to give a full explanation of the dangers. Elected leaders and Petroamazonas representatives delivered small packages of food, water, and other supplies to replace riverine resources. Their donations, however, were pathetic: a couple gallons of bottled water, a few tins of tuna and sardines, and bags of rice, salt, oatmeal, noodles, and sugar. Ironically, they gave people soap even though there were few places to use it. We were in a dry stretch, and the tanks people used to collect rainwater were nearly empty. Dureno has a pumping system that transports relatively clean water from a forest stream, but it had been broken for months. A few hundred dollars would have repaired the pump, but no one offered it. The funds the government did provide went to Cofán people willing to work on the cleanup. The Cofán are desperately poor. Many were happy to drive motorized canoes and collect crude-covered rocks, sticks, sand, and vegetation for "safe disposal." The work lasted for months. It was a significant economic boom.[3]

Three weeks passed before I overcame my fears and started washing in the Aguarico again. The single water spigot from a well in the village center was too crowded, and cleaning my sweat-covered body had become a nearly impossible chore. Most Cofán people were much less patient. Within three days of the spill, Alejandro was bathing in the river, Roberto was brushing his teeth in its water, and Lucia was washing dishes and gutting game on its shore. I watched groups of children play next to crude-stained vegetation. Some cleaned sugarcane in the river and placed it directly into their mouths. In small eddies, remnants of the spill were visible next to the muddy-looking sand with which the children covered their bodies. I told them the river was dirty, but they ignored me.

—

During the days after the 2014 spill, I was angry and worried. More than anything, though, I was frustrated. My instinct was to convince everyone in the village to stay as far away from the river as possible. Its contaminated state was beyond scientific doubt. I discussed the matter with many people, but my words never aroused an impassioned response or a significant shift in action. I felt impotent. The more I failed, the more I realized I was playing the familiar role of the clueless, patronizing gringo. Cofán people are not in search of saviors, and they do not trust individuals who present themselves as such. Over the past three decades, hundreds of outsiders have come to Dureno and said the same things I did. The Cofán could never figure out what their motives were: Why did they care about people they did not know? Why did they produce dozens of articles and films that had few if any results? And why did they fail to provide real material goods—and money—rather than verbal lessons that were repetitious, scripted, and out of touch with the reality of Cofán lives?

The 2014 spill confirmed my basic finding: life in oil may be deadly, but it is also a subtle, ambivalent, and contradictory condition. It offers few moments of spectacular, outrage-inducing crisis. Instead, Cofán people have gradually learned, and often forgotten, what the petroleum industry has done to their bodies, lands, and lives. The main lessons are typically far from people's conscious minds. Although visible disasters come and go, Dureno's situation has never truly changed. The companies remain. The petroleum emerges from Cofán land, crosses the Andes, and heads to the United States, China, and other countries via tankers that traverse the Pacific Ocean.

Oil's most brutal consequences are shaped so deeply by the vagaries of time, space, and chance that connections are hard to make. Nearly all Cofán territory has fallen into the hands of outsiders. But the process of dispossession has been uneven and uncertain, and most Cofán people never imagined the newcomers would stay forever. A surprising number of Dureno residents have died of cancer. But many more have not—at least not yet. Everyone knows that oil wastes exist inside their bodies, and many believe contamination will one day kill them. But the questions of who will be the next victim, when their demise will occur, and whether something else will get them first are

—

impossible to answer. In short, life in oil is a form of slow, confusing, and ultimately unknowable violence.[4] Its dangers are assumed, but they are unavoidable and unpredictable. Fatalism and resignation are central sentiments in Dureno. Many older people believe the damage is already done, which is why bathing in a crude-tinged river on the night of an oil spill does not appear to be such a crazy idea.

Despite how depressing their condition seems, the people of Dureno are poor examples of the "suffering savage."[5] The fact that they are not constantly, passionately, and tearfully opposed to oil is one thing. Even more jarring is the joy and meaning they find in their lives. They are poor, sick, and unable to maintain many of their most valued traditions. Their sense of themselves, though, remains strong. Unlike many indigenous Amazonians, they continue to use their native language as their main means of communication. Shamans regularly cure people with the aid of hallucinogenic drugs, visionary dreams, and supernatural allies. Nearly all middle-age and older Dureno residents are familiar with a pharmacopeia of medicinal plants that they deem effective against a diverse array of ailments. And even though their tiny island of forest lies in a sea of oil infrastructure, settler farms, and colonist towns, the people of Dureno manage to hunt, garden, and fish for much of their food.

Perhaps the most striking sign of Dureno residents' subtle confidence is the constant laughter one hears in their homes. No one smiles at the sickness or death of a friend or relative, but everything else is fair game for comedy. Alejandro's Spanish nickname is Payaso (Clown). In his house, people tell bawdy, belly-laugh-inducing stories well into the night. When people walk along the path in front of his home, Alejandro manages to elicit at least a giggle from them. "Co'feye atesu'cho," they say—"He is one who knows how to play." Any people who smile and laugh as much as the Cofán do must be convinced that life can always offer joy no matter how painful and precarious it becomes.

Some Cofán people are even optimistic about the future of petroleum production on their land. Although no one in Dureno has a positive opinion of Texaco, which worked in Ecuador until 1992 and oversaw the construction of the original oil infrastructure, some

—

residents express approval of the state company, Petroamazonas, the main operator in their territory. During my fieldwork, Petroamazonas's true chief was Rafael Correa, Ecuador's president from 2007 to 2017. The left-leaning economist committed to increasing resource extraction in Amazonia and dedicated millions of dollars in government spending to social, medical, and educational projects in places like Dureno. In one of the most extreme examples of oil-enabled largesse, the Correa government funded the construction of a "millennium community" in Dureno, one of a few such projects to house indigenous populations in Amazonian Ecuador. The housing complex provides a $45,000 home for each Cofán family. The structures are hybrids of the modern and the traditional. They have stilt legs and bamboo walls, but they are equipped with potable water and safe sewage systems. For a people with little money and quickly dwindling stocks of forest resources, the millennium community seems like a dream come true. None of the Cofán's environmentalist allies have given them a fraction of the resources Correa marshaled. Nevertheless, as many Cofán people realize, anything they accept from Ecuador's government is an implicit promise to allow even more oil development on their land. They hope for safer, cleaner technology, but they have learned to distrust everyone. Many also doubt they have the power to say no to any company that is truly determined to extract oil from their territory. The inequalities are simply too obvious and too extreme.

Such is the paradoxical condition of life in Dureno. The transnational petroleum industry has hit the community harder than any other indigenous village in the Americas. Dozens of observers have predicted the Cofán's extinction since Texaco made Cofán territory the epicenter of its Ecuadorian operations. The Cofán, however, have refused to be destroyed. Dureno residents seek justice and reparation for the losses they have experienced, but they do not believe they will disappear.

The concurrent confidence, suffering, and fear combine into a complicated message. The Cofán are victims of history who deserve material compensation for oil's assault on their lives. Simultaneously, they want the world to know they are committed survivors with a

—

11

language, a culture, and a way of life they are determined to maintain. Their political balancing act is a challenge. If they stress the former part of the message too much, outsiders write them off as sad, dying relics with no home in the modern world. If they stress the latter, others wonder if oil has hurt them at all. The West demands too much of contemporary native peoples, the Cofán included. It hopes to make them into tragic symbols of its worst crimes while portraying them as wise beacons who offer a superior and authentic way of life, even today.

Few outsiders hear Cofán people's message in the terms they favor. The wrongs they have experienced at the hands of the oil industry have made them famous, but non-Cofán people have produced the best-known accounts of Cofán struggles against oil. The most highly publicized derive from the Cofán's role as plaintiffs in a transnational lawsuit against Chevron, which acquired Texaco in 2001. First filed by an international legal team in 1993, the case has moved back and forth between Ecuador and the United States for more than two decades. In 2011, an Ecuadorian court awarded the Cofán and other residents of Amazonian Ecuador roughly $19 billion for the damages Texaco had done to them. Although multiple layers of Ecuador's judicial system have reviewed and affirmed the ruling, Chevron has spent more than a half-billion dollars fighting it. In 2014, the company's lawyers convinced a US federal judge that the Ecuadorian verdict was the product of fraud. In 2016, the US Court of Appeals for the Second Circuit upheld the judge's decision in favor of Chevron. The case's next stop might be the US Supreme Court. No one knows when the legal battle will finally end. Meanwhile, the plaintiffs' lawyers are trying to collect the Ecuadorian court's judgment by having Chevron property seized in courts across the world, including in Canada, Brazil, and Argentina. By 2007, Chevron had pulled its assets out of Ecuador, making it immune to judgments in that country.[6]

The Cofán are the most striking symbols of the tragedies the suit seeks to address. Their faces, lands, and translated words appear in a mountain of articles, books, films, and websites about the case. Its complexities and never-ending timeline confuse and depress them. They would appreciate any outcome that would give them better

FIGURE 1.3. *Petroleum-filled sludge from an abandoned waste pit in Cofán territory*

health care, a remediated environment, sustainable income sources, and enough money to buy back as much of their homeland as possible. But many doubt that compensation from the lawsuit will ever reach their community. Outsiders have failed them so many times. They expect little from the lawyers who fight on their behalf, although they would love to be proven wrong.

This book is not about the legal war with Chevron. It dedicates few pages to dissecting the stereotypical images the press, the activists, and the lawyers compose of the Cofán and their damaged lives. In it I seek instead to share the largely unknown stories Cofán people create themselves—the ones they tell in their own language, in their own communities, to each other and the few outsiders they know and trust. I am one of a handful of non-Cofán people who speak A'ingae, which allows me to communicate with all Dureno residents. I did all my fieldwork in the language so I could collect the most accurate information from the largest number of people. Although I have been visiting Dureno since 1998, my most concentrated period of research for this book occurred over the summers of 2012, 2013, and 2014. I lived with Alejandro, Lucia, and Roberto, and I worked with individuals from many households. I visited oil wells, attended community meetings, and accompanied Cofán people employed in the petroleum industry. I conducted interviews with thirty-four men and women on eight sets of oil-related topics, and I collaborated with Cofán assistants to make sure my translations were correct. I also coordinated the production of economic diaries with fourteen Dureno families. The records gave me quantitative information on a year's worth of daily activities, which helped me understand how community residents continue to eke a living out of a radically transformed environment.

The story of oil is incredibly important. Scholars from many disciplines have told us how essential the substance has been to the historical emergence and potential demise of the modern world.[7] Although few deny the troubling role oil plays in contemporary political, economic, and ecological orders, the story of its relationship to Cofán people can tell us new things about its qualities and consequences. As we struggle to grasp the costs of an oil-based existence, we should try to understand the experiences of people who reside on the lands from which the substance comes. After five decades of encounters with the petroleum industry, the Cofán of Dureno know an impressive amount about what oil has done to their bodies, their way of life, and the Amazonian environment. Their ability to reflect on oil from a culturally distinct viewpoint offers the possibility of reimagining the omnipresent commodity from a novel, provocative perspective.

Such is the aim of anthropology: to open our minds and increase our knowledge by making the familiar strange and the strange familiar. By assuming we do not know the logic of our collaborators' perspectives at the outset of our investigations, we try to be as intellectually flexible and self-critical as possible. Only with much time and effort can we understand even a small part of what it means to live in a particular cultural context, with a particular set of political struggles, historical experiences, and visions for the future. Effectively communicating that particularity to both academic and nonacademic audiences is even more challenging. If successful, our studies do not fix people in their difference and thereby isolate or caricature them. Rather, in the words of Edward Said, good anthropology fosters "coexistence and enlargement of horizons."[8] At its best, anthropology creates the conditions for dialogue—and even alliance—across cultural, political, and historical lines.

In all likelihood, the people who read this book also use oil that comes from Cofán territory. I believe we have an obligation to know what our dependence on petroleum means for the earth's most marginalized inhabitants. Across the world, people like the Cofán live on top of the resources that have become essential to our lives. The least we can do is hear what Cofán people have to say, whether they are college-educated individuals who speak English and Spanish or impoverished elders who have never left their homeland. My hope is that learning about the impact of oil on Cofán lives will motivate us to rethink and transform our own relationship to the substance. There is still time to make this planet a more just and sustainable home for all its residents. Understanding the challenges posed by oil, in Dureno and elsewhere, is essential to that mission.

—

FIGURE 2.1. *Alejandro in his shamanic ornamentation*

·

CHAPTER 2

DURENO

Alejandro Criollo is almost as old as Ecuador's oil industry.[1] He was born in Dureno in the late 1940s as Royal Dutch Shell conducted seismic exploration along the Aguarico River. Shell never found significant reserves in the area. A decade and a half later, Texaco succeeded where its predecessor failed. In 1967, it discovered a large petroleum field upriver from Dureno. When Alejandro married Lucia Quenamá in 1972, Texaco began extracting commercial quantities of crude. Soon thereafter, Ecuador joined the Organization of Petroleum Exporting Countries (OPEC), and a dense system of roads, wells, pipelines, and production facilities encircled Dureno. By the time Alejandro and Lucia had Roberto in 2002, Ecuador was producing approximately a half-million barrels of oil a day.

Despite his awareness of the harm the petroleum industry had done to his people, Alejandro decided to begin working for an oil company in 2013. Desperate to find money for daily necessities and his son's schooling, he took a position with the Chinese National Petroleum Corporation as a guard at a seismic camp inside Dureno's territory. After decades of opposition, the community had finally decided to allow oil exploration on their land. Alejandro, like so many other Dureno residents, no longer saw the possibility or wisdom of standing in oil's way.

I do not remember when I first met Alejandro. It might have been in 1998 when I arrived in Dureno to explore the idea of studying the relationship between oil and the community. Or it might have been in 2001 when I was conducting doctoral research in the Cofán village of Zábalo, far downriver from Dureno. Alejandro's face, however, was familiar to me before I set eyes on him. He is one of the best-known members of the Cofán nation. If you Google "Alejandro Criollo Cofan," you will find dozens of pictures of him on the Internet. There are stock photos, photos from blogs and websites, and photos from newspaper and magazine articles. Most depict Alejandro in his favored ornamentation: a tall, circular crown of green and yellow parrot feathers; long plumes from macaws and other birds stuck through his nose and ears; layer upon layer of shining beaded necklaces; strings of carefully arranged peccary, jaguar, and ocelot teeth over his chest and shoulders; bunches of fragrant leaves tied to his upper arms; and intricately drawn, bright red dots and lines of achiote (*Bixa orellana*) paint on his cheeks and forehead. He is always in a blue or black *ondiccu'je*, the long tunic that is the traditional form of male Cofán dress. And he usually finds a way to tie a red bandana above the ornaments that cover his neck.

It is easy to see why Alejandro is so popular with outsiders. His colorful difference is an intriguing sight for Western eyes. Also, unlike many older Cofán people, he is the picture of strength and vitality. His body is long and sinewy. He has surprisingly thick hands, and his broad feet are usually bare. Bunched muscles on his arms and legs betray the many years he has spent making a life in the forests of western Amazonia. His facial expressions hint at his quick wit and energetic demeanor. Some photographers have even captured Alejandro smiling, which is an uncommon gesture for Cofán people in front of a camera. Below his triangular nose, his wide lips—stained

18

dark after years of applying purple plant dye to his teeth and mouth—
curve into a sly grin. His brown eyes sit below a brow with hardly a
hair on it. (Since he was a child, Alejandro has plucked his face bare
to create a perfect canvas for painting.) Although he seems extraordinarily "other" to outsiders, he looks invitingly friendly. Alejandro's
image offers the stirring hope of a world where cultural diversity is
alive, well, and eager to be met. It is a powerful image, one that non-
Cofán people cannot resist attempting to document and share. That
is why Alejandro appears so often in tourist brochures, coffee-table
books, and documentary films about northeastern Ecuador's places
and peoples.

I became friends with Alejandro and Lucia after they requested
my help in 2002. For my dissertation, I was studying a set of environmental projects that joined the people of Zábalo to the Cofán activists
at work with the Foundation for the Survival of the Cofán People,
an organization based in Ecuador's capital city, Quito, high in the
Andes. The head of the foundation had ties to Ecuador's evangelical
Christian community, including a Quito orphanage named For His
Children. Despite years of trying, Alejandro and Lucia had failed to
produce a child of their own. The foundation asked the head of the
orphanage if they had a boy whom Alejandro and Lucia could adopt.
The foundation did have an infant, less than a year old, whom they
had already named Roberto.

Roberto was not Cofán, however. The social workers wanted to
familiarize the child with the Cofán lifestyle and his prospective
parents before arranging a first meeting. My contacts at the foundation asked me to travel from Quito to Dureno to record the voices
of Alejandro and Lucia and to take pictures of them as they went
about their daily routine: making *cui'ccu*, hunting animals, weeding
gardens, and weaving palm fiber into string for hammocks, necklaces,
and bags. They also asked me to bring back an unwashed tunic from
Alejandro and a dirty skirt and blouse from Lucia. They wanted
Roberto to learn his new parents' smells before meeting them. Alejandro went along with the idea, but he thought it was comically
demeaning. "What? Do they think we are animals or something?" he
laughed after I gave him the instructions.

—

In November 2002, Alejandro and Lucia traveled from Dureno to Quito to meet Roberto. If all went well, they would bring him home with them. On the day they met the boy, the social worker placed the pictures of Alejandro and Lucia along with their clothes in front of Roberto as he crawled on the foundation's carpeted floor. After he played with the objects for a while, Alejandro and Lucia walked in and sat next to him. There were no tears of joy, but it was clear that the relationship would work. I have a framed photo from that first meeting on my wall. Lucia is picking up Roberto and placing him into her cotton carrying sling just as he is sliding his finger into his nose. The unfortunate timing adds a bit of humor to a touching image. The care of Lucia and the comfort of Roberto are impossible to miss.

The only remaining challenge was to get the adoption approved by a court in Ecuador's Ministry of Social Welfare. As I soon learned, it was the first case in which an indigenous Amazonian couple sought to adopt a child through official Ecuadorian channels. There was a specific concern that Roberto was not a member of his parents' ethnic group. Cofán leaders who were working with the foundation asked me to testify on Alejandro and Lucia's behalf at the court hearing. I was an anthropological specialist on Cofán culture—a supposedly trustworthy and impartial expert.

A few days later, I went to the ministry with Alejandro, Lucia, Roberto, and their allies. The panel of judges asked me a long series of questions about Alejandro and Lucia's suitability as parents. I had to make a case that even though they were illiterate, monolingual, unemployed, and believers in a cosmological and medical system very different from the Ecuadorian norm, they could provide Roberto with a safe and supportive home. In other words, my job was to argue that being a "traditional" Cofán person is just as valuable and fulfilling as being any other kind of person. The task was especially daunting given my assumption that the judges were upper-class Ecuadorians marked by their country's long history of anti-indigenous racism. Somehow, they already knew Alejandro was a curer. They had a few especially pointed questions about shamanism. They asked whether Alejandro would force Roberto to drink hallucinogenic drugs at a young age. Thankfully, he said no. Apart from that small moment of drama, the judges were surprisingly supportive and kind.

After a short discussion among themselves, the judges decided to approve Roberto's adoption. Everyone was elated. Immediately after the hearing, we walked outside to the building's lobby. Alejandro told me how much he appreciated my help. He then asked me to become Roberto's ritual father. As a new relative, I would address Alejandro as Comba, an A'ingae rendition of "compadre." I would address Lucia as Inise, the A'ingae word for "name." Both Alejandro and Lucia would call me Comba, and I would call Roberto Du'su, which also means "son-in-law." He would refer to and address me as Opi'su Quitsa, "carrying father."[2] A few weeks later, I traveled to Dureno and made the relationship official through a short ritual and a long party filled with manioc beer and deep drags off one of Alejandro's homegrown tobacco cigars. From then on, Alejandro, Lucia, Roberto, and I were family. I promised to support them in any way I could, and they committed to hosting me whenever I was in Dureno. The mutual obligation is lifelong.

Since 2002, I have spent many months in Dureno. It is the most populous of Ecuador's thirteen Cofán communities that line the banks of the Aguarico, Bermejo, and San Miguel Rivers. The San Miguel forms much of the border between Ecuador and Colombia. Cofán people live in Colombia, too. In 2014, Roberto Aguinda, then-president of the Cofán ethnic federation, told me that according to the most recent census, more than 500 people lived in Dureno. He said that Ecuador's total Cofán population was close to 1,400, with approximately the same number living in Colombia along the San Miguel, Guamués, and Putumayo Rivers. The Colombian Cofán have experienced an even more vicious history of colonization and political violence. Thousands of settlers overran their territory in the middle of the twentieth century. Later, their lands became key points of struggle between coca growers, narcotraffickers, left-wing revolutionaries, and right-wing paramilitaries. They lost almost all their territory, and their way of life suffered profound transformations. Today, most Colombian Cofán people do not speak A'ingae. Just a few practice the forest-based lifestyle of the Ecuadorian Cofán. Their subjection

FIGURE 2.2. *Roberto and Lucia fishing on the Aguarico River*

to political violence and organized criminal activity has led some to become violent themselves. The Ecuadorian Cofán declare that a large portion of their Colombian kin are "thieves" and "killers." Few of my Dureno collaborators trust their northern neighbors.

All Cofán communities lie close to the border. Cofán lands stretch from the imposing peaks and valleys of the Andean foothills to the flat, low rainforest of western Amazonia proper. The Cofán homeland is one of the most biologically diverse places on the planet. It is also incredibly beautiful. The Andean landscape along the western portion of Cofán territory is characterized by steep, forest-covered mountains and deep ravines pulsing with crystal-clear, boulder-strewn rivers. As you head east, the hills become smaller and the rivers become wide, sandy, and filled with sediment. The community of Zábalo sits at the eastern edge of Cofán territory, on the border with Peru. Its territory is filled with black-water lagoons populated by manatees, giant river otters, and freshwater dolphins.

Cofán people once lived even higher into the Andes, but a series of wars pushed them down and reduced their numbers. They first fought off the Inca Empire. Shortly thereafter, the Spanish arrived. In the sixteenth century, the colonizers battled Cofán warriors and captured many as slaves. Jesuit missionaries attempted to round up the remaining Cofán into concentrated communities with the intent to "civilize" and convert them. Epidemics soon decimated the Cofán population. Thousands died as introduced diseases took their toll. Still, the Cofán never gave up. They fought off the colonial forces who descended into their territory in search of gold. They laid siege to colonial outposts and burned colonial towns. Much of their past is unrecorded. Few people, Cofán or otherwise, know it.[3] We do know that toward the end of the nineteenth century, rubber workers battled for Cofán labor and Capuchin priests struggled for Cofán souls.[4] In new mission settlements, hundreds more died. The Cofán population hit a low point of little more than three hundred individuals after a 1923 measles epidemic struck a large mission on the San Miguel River. From a precolonial population of as many as thirty thousand people, the Cofán were on the edge of disappearance. The survivors of the epidemic scattered into remote stretches along the

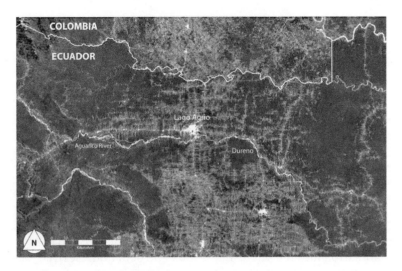

MAP 2.1. *Satellite image of deforestation from roads, pastures, farms, and towns in northeastern Ecuador. Adapted from Google Earth by Leah McCurdy.*

San Miguel and Aguarico. They were the parents, grandparents, and great-grandparents of the people I work with in Dureno.

Along the Aguarico River's east-west axis, Dureno is the midpoint of Ecuadorian Cofán territory. In 1978, the community received title to 9,571 hectares of land from the Ecuadorian government. It was a small fragment of the millions of hectares its residents used prior to the colonists' arrival. In 2007, the Field Museum of Natural History in Chicago did a rapid biological inventory of Dureno's territory. The scientists explored its hilltops, floodplains, lakes, and streams. Based on a week of research, they estimated that even in the small forest island, there are 2,000 species of vascular plants, 80 species of fish, 62 species of amphibians, 54 species of reptiles, 40 species of large mammals, and as many as 420 species of birds. Although a number of once-important game animals are no longer present, museum officials still describe Dureno's territory as "one of the few remnants of the richest lowlands on the planet."[5]

In satellite images, Dureno's territory is a rounded block of green surrounded by a scarred landscape of roads, pastures, plantation-style

25

farms, and colonist towns. At night, the urbanizing region's electric lights mix with glowing orange oil-well flares that stretch toward the sky. On clear evenings and from high ground, you can see natural-gas fires on all sides of Dureno. During the day, you can sometimes see their smoke, too. Most of the time, though, what you notice as you stand in the community are the homes of Cofán families and the forest that looms behind them. The Aguarico acts as a buffer between the world of the colonists and the world of the Cofán. On one side, cars, trucks, and buses rush through towns where the language is Spanish. On the other, the nasalized vowels, aspirated consonants, and glottal stops of A'ingae are the dominant sounds of human speech. Most Cofán people now live in zinc-roofed, hand-hewn, stilted houses that do not look very different from the abodes of the newcomers who have surrounded the village. But as you walk south from the river, you pass Cofán gardens filled with plantains, bananas, and manioc. Soon, you find yourself in the lush, green, moist, cool, and silent forest that the Cofán have called home for centuries.

People in Dureno used to live in one central settlement. Over the past three decades, families split off to form new population centers within the community's territory. People still call the oldest and largest settlement Dureno, the name of a small river on the other side of the Aguarico, but the other clusters now have their own names and government-funded schools. In the late 1980s, Pisorié Canqque (Village on the Pisorié River) was born along a road that Texaco built through the community to drill a new oil well. After the Cofán forced Texaco out, a group of families decided to make gardens and homes along the road to guard against invaders. Totoa Nai'qui (White Stream) formed next. People disagree about why Aurelio Quenamá, the son of Dureno's founding chief, left the central settlement to create the new site with his son and daughters. Some say it was because the boy was stealing too many goods from neighboring families. Others say Aurelio could no longer stand the young men who kept pestering his daughters for romantic attention. An old man named Luciano Lucitante then settled Bavoroé (River of the Bavoro Catfish) to plant bigger gardens on less crowded land. The last settlement was Opirito, named after a plant that is added to a drink made from the hallucinogenic vine *Banisteriopsis caapi* to increase the users' vision-ary powers. Cofán people call the shamanically essential brew *yaje*, but most outsiders know it by its more common name, *ayahuasca*, a word that derives from the Kichwa language. Opirito was a natural extension of the original Dureno settlement. By the first decade of the millennium, the new homes that stretched downriver were a bit too far for children to walk to the old center's school. With a new settlement, their lives became a little less difficult.

Dureno's stubborn indigeneity clashes with the world of colonist culture and oil-related infrastructure that surrounds it. It is tempting to view the community as a timeless holdout of Ecuador's precolonial past. To do so, however, would be naive. In addition to the social, economic, and political changes Cofán people have been experienc-ing for centuries, the landscape itself was shifting long before the petroleum companies arrived. It is fascinating to hear Alejandro and Lucia describe the Aguarico River as a powerful, agentive being. The land on which Dureno sits is *vueyi'su* (of the recent past). As it swells and subsides with the rains in the Andean foothills, the Aguarico *añe* (eats) and *angaye* (carries) land, through which it *tsin'coñe* (behaves) by *tsai'quiañe* (forming paths). What was once a giant island is reduced to nothing. What was the main branch of the river becomes a side branch, then a sandy beach, then a tall forest perfect for building a settlement. The changes can occur over many years, or they can be quite rapid. During one period of particularly high waters, Alejandro and I watched as the Aguarico consumed meters of Dureno each day. It took Alejandro's plantain field and the earth on which his neighbor's home stood. Throughout the night, we heard loud booms as the river dragged huge chunks of sand, stone, and soil into itself. A few days later, Valerio Mendua, one of Alejandro's best friends, put it poetically: "Da'ñomba tsu toeningatsse ñoñan canse" (The river lives by destroying and building anew). The Cofán have been living at Dureno for more than seventy years, but the central settlement has moved multiple times. It was originally on an island. Then it was downriver. Now it sits on a stretch of riverbank that was once the middle of the forest. Someday, thanks to the capricious ways of the Aguarico, it will move again.

—

FIGURE 2.3. *The Aguarico River*

The western Amazonian environment can be a frightening and tumultuous place, even for the Cofán. But in the decades before the oil companies arrived, the Aguarico River ran through a lightly populated landscape that offered plentiful resources to the Cofán people who called it home. There were periodic visits from priests and mestizo traders, but the only other permanent residents were the few families of indigenous Siona and Secoya people who lived far downstream from Dureno. They were also forest people whose way of living was fairly similar to the Cofán's, although their Western Tukanoan language was completely different; A'ingae is a linguistic isolate, unrelated to any known language family. The Cofán visited and drank *yaje* with the Siona and Secoya. The only other regular inhabitants along the Aguarico were the roving groups of Tetete people who passed Dureno on the north side of the river. Like the Siona and Secoya, the Tetete spoke a Western Tukanoan language, but they were forest recluses who wore no clothes and refused to maintain peaceful relations with anyone. They sometimes attacked Cofán households and stole their steel tools. Eventually, introduced diseases and Siona vengeance raids led to the Tetete's disappearance. The last time anyone saw them was in the 1970s.[6]

With millions of hectares of pristine rainforest at their disposal and few enemies to fear, the Dureno Cofán lived a life of plenty from the 1940s through the 1960s. If you ask any Cofán person over fifty what it was like "in the old times," they will smile and speak longingly of how much meat they ate before the settlers came and laid waste to their homeland. First with spears and blowguns and then with shotguns and rifles, the Cofán amassed huge quantities of game with relative ease. People reminisce about how full their smoking racks were in the old days. They had so much meat it would sometimes rot before they could eat it—a nearly unthinkable thought in today's world of scarcity. In the forest behind their Dureno homes, they hunted their favorite species: white-lipped peccaries, tapirs, woolly monkeys, and piping guans. Parrots and macaws were everywhere. People ate their flesh and turned their feathers into beautiful ornaments. The Aguarico was so clean that people drank straight from it. The river and its tributaries were filled with fish that could be had with the aid of hook, net, or *señamba*, a vine that people mashed into slow-moving river stretches to disrupt fishes' ability to process oxygen. The fish became "drunk" and floated to the surface. People grabbed them and killed them with a bite to the head before placing them in palm-fiber bags.

Although precolonization Dureno was a place of abundance, its residents spent less time in it than they do now. The whole Aguarico River belonged to the Cofán, and they made good use of it. Westerners often imagine foraging peoples as bare-bones survivors constantly moving from place to place in an exhausting search for food. As the anthropologist Marshall Sahlins argued long ago, the image is founded on a mistaken assumption. People who lived largely by hunting and gathering typically had much more leisure time than people do now. It would be better to think of their constant movement, Sahlins writes, as like a "picnic outing on the Thames" rather than a desperate flight from starvation.[7] Before the settlers took over their territory, Cofán families were often away from home. They stayed all over the Aguarico and its tributaries, making simple houses and gardens to enjoy for months at a time. They often traveled to a particular salt lick laden with game or a river stretch with beaches full of turtle eggs. Deji Criollo—a middle-aged Dureno resident, distant nephew of Alejandro, and one of my main research assistants—described the past subsistence style with clear nostalgia:

> It was really nice before the roads came. People didn't live right here. They traveled all over. They didn't know dates. They would tell people they would come back on a full moon or a new moon. They didn't worry about anything. They didn't long for motorized canoes. They poled their canoes, or they used paddles. They wandered without fear. They traveled according to their desires. If they got tired somewhere, they would just stop and sleep. Wherever they went, game was never lacking. They ate what they wanted. They were fearful of no one. They made little houses and slept in them. They slept on islands, on the riverbank, wherever. They had no troubling thoughts.

—

FIGURE 2.4. *Deji Criollo in his corn garden*

Before Texaco arrived, Cofán people were already buying and trading for outside goods, including blowgun poison, shotguns, ammunition, and fishhooks. The commodities were necessary elements of their wandering, forest-based lifestyle. Today, their way of living is radically different, depending on a much greater engagement with the market. People use a key term to describe it: *chavapa añe* (buying and eating). Some Dureno residents claim that one can still subsist in the community with little to no money. With just their labor, people can make gardens filled with plantain, banana, manioc, and corn. The produce can satisfy a person's basic calorie requirements with *cui'ccu* and manioc beer. With a net, it is possible to harvest fish from the Aguarico. With a machete and a pack of dogs, a skilled hunter can bag an armadillo, paca, or agouti, all of which are prized game species. But living without money is a trying proposition often accompanied by hunger. Most Dureno families prefer to engage in periodic wage labor so as to buy more reliable foodstuffs: tuna, sardines, chicken, noodles, rice, and salt. A number of nonfood items are also now necessities, including clothing, school materials, medicine, gasoline, metal tools, guns and ammunition, and soap. Today, it is difficult if not impossible to find the right trees to make canoes and houses. Consequently, fiberglass canoes and zinc roofing sheets have also become necessities. Game, too, is in short supply. Hunting cannot provide enough meat for everyone. "Living without buying" is no longer worth the effort for most people. Needs have changed; available resources have, too.

Although Dureno residents spend a good portion of their time earning money to buy things, the great majority still value a forest-based lifestyle. According to the economic diary I did with fourteen Dureno households, people eat game on nearly a quarter of their days. The same goes for fish. Hardly a day goes by that people do not use garden produce for *cui'ccu* and stews. Alejandro's household is a telling example. Lucia appreciates Alejandro for many reasons, but it would be hard to overestimate how much she loves the meat he brings back from the forest. For Cofán women, to be *ppu'chotssi* (fat) is to be beautiful and happy. A few years ago, Lucia suffered an undiagnosed medical problem that caused her to become "skinny," which made her miserable. She felt she was on the brink of death. With many trips to shamans and doctors, she got better. Currently, she looks overweight to most Westerners. Lucia, however, longs for the days when she was much bigger. Like so many Cofán people, she believes eating forest meat is the one thing guaranteed to bring on such an attractive and healthy state.

Lucia does not hesitate to let Alejandro know how hungry she is for meat. Alejandro also desires it, but as a man versed in shamanism, he also takes tremendous pride in his discipline and pickiness. To acquire supernatural powers is to abstain from many of the foods that others enjoy. One thing shamanism does not require, however, is giving up hunting. Old people claim the youth of today are too lazy to hunt much. My own observations suggest that nearly every Dureno male appreciates the chance to go out and amass meat. Still, individuals like Alejandro are exceptional in their dedication. Many Cofán people are so frustrated by Dureno's lack of game that they do most of their hunting by traveling far up the Pisorié River in a motorized canoe, which allows access to more lightly used lands. A few others canoe down to the Eno River, far outside Dureno but with stretches still available for shoreline hunting. A tireless hunter, Alejandro regularly walks straight behind his Dureno home for overnight treks, often crossing the Pisorié on thin log bridges. Cofán people appreciate all the resources the forest provides, but many fear the *cocoya* (malevolent supernatural agents) and "invisible people" who inhabit its inner reaches. As a shaman, Alejandro fears none of the beings. He can describe the different "shouts" of various *cocoya* and supernatural *a'i* (humans). They are the same creatures he contacts while drinking *yaje*. Most other people are terrified of encounters with the beings. By brushing against them in the forest, a person can lose their life force and quickly die unless a shaman intervenes to save them.

Alejandro had several jobs while I did research for this book, as a park ranger, employee in a Cofán fiberglass-canoe workshop, oil-camp guard, and paid provider of shamanic curing to Cofán and non-Cofán people. The labor exhausted him, and it cut into his hunting time and meat consumption. He and Lucia purchased a freezer in 2000 to store hunted meat with the aid of Dureno's newly installed electricity system. The freezer allows Lucia to have a supply of game on hand while Alejandro is away. Still, Alejandro's drive to hunt is about more than filling his stomach. One day, we were prepared to eat a meal of tuna and noodles when a neighbor came by and gave us a large chunk of smoked howler monkey. Alejandro pushed away the dinner Lucia had made and went to work on the monkey. We ate it all right then. The same night, he picked up his gun, headed into the forest, and did not come back until the following afternoon. On another occasion, Alejandro returned from a twenty-two-day work stint at the oil camp. Rather than rest, he walked over the hill behind his Dureno home for another day and night of hunting.

On many trips, Alejandro had no success. On more than a few occasions during my stay, he returned soaking wet from a night in the forest with absolutely nothing to show for it. The frequent failures were balanced by unexpected successes. One late afternoon, Alejandro said he was going to take a brief walk beyond his gardens to see if he could shoot a toucan for the night's dinner. Less than an hour later, he came back with a gigantic collared-peccary carcass slung over his shoulders. After one overnight trip, he returned early in the morning with an enormous load of Spix's guan, kinkajou, and paca. Even with his supreme skill, impressive physical condition, and deep knowledge of Dureno's territory, though, the unlucky days outnumbered the lucky ones. Unlike many Dureno men, Alejandro never let declining yields compromise his commitment to hunting. He and Lucia enjoyed the meat, but Alejandro also relished the act itself.

Cofán people have an amazing ability to go two or three days with nothing but *cui'ccu*, yet they would much rather eat meat—either bought or foraged—every day. Hunger is a periodic problem for a few Dureno families, but no one mentioned it to me as an urgent issue. Many older people, though, agree with Lucia that people in Dureno now are much thinner and smaller than villagers used to be. The image of yesteryear's plump, shining, and beautifully adorned Cofán people is one elders bring up often. They talk about the old-time people's huge muscles and astonishing acts of strength and endurance. They attribute those earlier conditions not only to life in a contamination-free environment but to a plentiful and satisfying diet

FIGURE 2.5. *Alejandro hunting in the forest behind his home*

of meat, fish, *cui'ccu*, and manioc beer. They talk about all the *yaje* the old people drank in their quest for shamanic power. Elders also drank *yoco* every morning and boiled an assortment of plants to induce vomiting. The act cleansed their bodies and strengthened their diaphragms for blowgun hunting. According to most of my more mature collaborators, such were the old-time Cofán: big, strong, beautiful, energetic, clean, and happy.

Hunger may not afflict many contemporary Dureno families, but plenty of other health problems do. A tuberculosis epidemic hit the community in the 1950s. Many adults still suffer with the illness. Lucia spent a year at a missionary health center in her youth while recuperating from the disease. Colds, flu, and diarrhea sweep through and affect many households at once, especially the children. Periodically, people suffer from malaria and dengue fever. Certain ailments seem to linger in particular segments of the population. Women struggle constantly with urinary-tract infections. Quite a few young and middle-age adults suffer with ulcers and gastritis. Headaches, dizziness, gastrointestinal distress, and skin fungi and infections plague many people, who often attribute them to contamination from oil production and sewage runoff from colonist towns. Some children have been born with congenital defects. Cancer has afflicted more adults than one would expect.[8]

The people of Dureno die for many reasons. In nearly every family with whom I worked, at least one child perished at a young age. One was born with intestines that could not properly digest food. Another died from snakebite. One more died from a strange combination of vomiting, diarrhea, and mouth sores. One adult died from an accident while hunting with his friend at night. Another died of drowning after he fell into the river, drunk and alone. A significant number of adults have died of cancer, typically of the stomach or liver. Many Cofán deaths go unanalyzed by doctors; few make it into official records. Cofán people often attribute a person's demise to the supernatural action of an enemy shaman, usually from a neighboring indigenous group. Shamans send *cocoya* to afflict both children and adults. The invisible creatures steal people's life force. Shamans also command snakes to bite people. The supernaturally empowered

—

38

aggressors know of many, many ways to end people's lives, which they do to avenge deaths in their own communities or simply to show off their power.

Dureno residents treat their health problems through a combination of plant medicine, shamanism, and Western biomedicine. To the surprise of many outsiders, curing through plants and curing through shamanism are completely separate practices. Visitors see a traditional-looking older man like Alejandro and assume he is a master of western Amazonia's natural pharmacopeia. He is fairly good, but I have seen a woman thirty years his junior tell him he misidentified an important medicine. When symptoms first present themselves, men and women get together to decide if the ill person has "become a medicine." Each ailment has its own plant *na'su* (master), which has the same name as the condition it is supposed to treat. A person must remove the plant from the forest, swallow it, rub it over a part of their body, or steam it into their nose for a cure.[9] If plants do not work, people suspect the illness is a "disease of the outsiders" or the effect of attack from an *aya* (spectral shade of a dead person) or *cocoya* that might be acting alone or under the command of a hostile shaman.

If the illness is a historically introduced disease, Cofán people are more than willing to utilize pills, injections, and treatments at clinics and hospitals. Western medical care used to be far too expensive for most Dureno residents until the Ecuadorian government created a much more extensive system of open-access care for the country's poor through numerous clinics and hospitals. The service is free for almost anyone, even a gringo anthropologist. I have used it myself. There is a clinic open to the Cofán directly across the river from Dureno in a colonist town also called Dureno. Cofán people can access other services at a larger clinic in the provincial capital Lago Agrio. They can undergo surgery in the town of Chaco or even in Quito, which is 285 kilometers away by road. Specialist care and certain drugs are sometimes unavailable in the free system, though. Despite the advances of recent times, many Cofán people are left without the treatment they need.

Government services and a still-undepleted forest make many Cofán individuals slightly less dependent on a steady income than

---

nonindigenous newcomers, but poverty is a pressing issue in Dureno. It is inconceivable to imagine living with no salt and no soap. Even hunting, fishing, and gardening demand access to commodities. Shotguns and shells became very expensive after the government criminalized their sale to anyone without a permit. Cofán people have no permits, which require money and political connections to acquire. Just a few years ago, it was possible to buy a shotgun shell for forty cents. Now they are sold on the black market for more than three dollars. Bought foodstuffs, too, are surprisingly expensive. Even with Alejandro's fairly productive hunting and Lucia's constant supply of *cui'ccu*, it was easy for me to spend $200 a month on food for our family of four. Many families eat just one meal a day. It is common to eat none. Too many days with just *cui'ccu* inevitably bring on sadness. Parents find it extremely difficult when they do not have enough money to buy clothing or school materials for their children. The inability to pay for medicines or specialist health care is even more painful. Even if a loved one is receiving free long-term care in a publicly subsidized Quito hospital, his or her family must find enough money to pay for their own food and lodging while attending to their sick relative.

Alejandro is one of a few shamanically competent Dureno men whom people pay to cure them. A much larger number of residents share his off-and-on occupations of park guard, fiberglass canoe maker, and oil company employee. Hardly anyone has stable employment, and many individuals have none. Other jobs sometimes held include elementary schoolteacher, worker in the municipal or provincial government, assistant on scientific research projects, member of a musical or dance group, worker with environmental and human rights organizations, child care supervisor in the community's infant care center, security guard for businesses in Lago Agrio, and occasional paid help aiding other Dureno residents to weed a garden or construct a house. Some people also sell goods including medicinal plants, woven handicrafts, garden produce (corn, cacao, plantains), and game, although community rules allow game to be sold only between Cofán people so as to avoid overexploitation. Typical monthly incomes range from less than $100 to more than $700.

The few Cofán men who own fiberglass canoe workshops can easily make thousands of dollars a month when business is good. The Cofán specialize in the craft. People from all over Amazonian Ecuador and even Colombia buy the canoes. No other ethnic groups have figured out how to make them with any degree of reliability. More than fifteen years ago, the Foundation for the Survival of the Cofán People brought fiberglass craftsmen from coastal Ecuador to teach the Cofán. After years of apprenticeship and designing their own models, Cofán people created at least five independent fiberglass canoe businesses that employ dozens of Cofán individuals.

The community has collective sources of income, too. Seven thousand hectares of Dureno's territory are part of the Ecuadorian government's Socio Bosque program, which pays landowners to protect standing forest. During my research, Dureno received $54,000 a year through the program. The community also received $35,000 a year for letting a company dredge rocks from the bottom of the Aguarico River to build roads. Recent agreements with two oil companies created additional sources of income. The contract with a Chinese company doing seismic exploration netted more than $500,000 for the community, distributed to families in the form of cash payments and outboard motors. An agreement with Petroamazonas to allow work on the western edge of Dureno stipulated that the company would buy eight trucks for the community and then rent them back for three years. Cofán leaders decided to disburse the income to each Dureno household in the form of a $100 monthly food allotment at a newly created, Cofán-owned grocery store in Lago Agrio. The service is an important aid for all Dureno families, especially the poorest ones. Other uses for community income include paying for park guards, the travel expenses of elected leaders, medical emergencies, parties and festivals, accounting services, and various other items, including a Cofán-staffed child care center for women who choose to work.

With the necessary move toward buying and living, money is more important than ever. The cash, as well as its absence, are shifting important interhousehold relations. For generations, the social glue that tied families together was a constant give and take of meat and labor. In the old times, whenever someone killed a significant amount

—

41

of game, the hunter gave a portion to other families in the form of raw, smoked, or cooked meat. When someone needed help to build a house or clear a garden, a large group of people got together to work on the task, share manioc beer, and eat a meal. People describe the sharing and reciprocity as *fuiteccopa cánseye* (living by helping together). The way of life is not completely dead. Alejandro still shares meat with a few households close to his home. People still call friends and neighbors to help on domestic tasks. But the absence of game, the hard work and economic expense of acquiring it, and the need for cash mean that living by helping together does not join people as it used to. It is increasingly common to share one's game or labor with another only when paid to do so.

More atomistic social relations have contributed to increasing levels of tension. The most intense conflicts usually involve a combination of alcohol, marital discord, theft, and political schisms. Take, for example, the case of Angel, whose real name I do not use in order to protect his privacy. One afternoon, Angel returned drunk from Lago Agrio with his wife and children. Before he crossed the river to Dureno, he drank more beer at a small stand along the road. By then, he was enraged. Reportedly, he had a dream the night before in which he saw his wife making love to another man in the community. When he got to his home, he picked up the community's weed whacker, turned it on, and waved it at his wife and children in a threatening manner. He then grabbed one of his small sons by his feet and ran with him into the forest. He brought a machete, too. People were terrified. Word spread that something horrible was about to happen. Two men followed Angel's footprints and found the child lying on the ground, unharmed.

Angel eventually calmed down, but the thought of him killing one of his own children was too much to bear. Community leaders called a meeting to discuss the matter even though Angel had already fled. He knew he was in trouble with other Cofán people and, possibly, outside authorities. His mother said that a *cocoya* had entered him. His father said that he was thinking of taking him to a church to see if it would help. Everyone else discussed what community rules against drinking exist and whether they should be strengthened. Dureno's elected president said that it is not permitted to drink in the community on a weekday, and it is prohibited to get drunk somewhere else and return to the community. He also said that physical fighting is prohibited, including between spouses. All present voted to sanction Angel. The decision meant he would not be able to receive community work or benefits for six months or more: no $100 monthly food distributions, no cash or outboard motors from an oil company, and no income for cutting the community's soccer field with the weed whacker.

The tension spread when one of Angel's nephews was caught stealing another Dureno man's gasoline. The community's elected leadership wanted to sanction the thief's entire family, even though the boy was already seventeen and impossible to control. At another meeting, accusations shot back and forth. The boy's family asked for leniency, claiming they had done all they could. His grandfather said that persistent poverty was the real problem. The boy's mother then launched counteraccusations at a community leader. She claimed the man was harassing her daughter for sexual favors and said the desire for punishment reflected an underlying interfamilial hostility, not the theft itself. People sympathized with different sides, but the sanction stuck. The boy's family would get no monthly food allotments. The rationale was that the boy would eat whatever his parents received, which would make any other punishment ineffective.

Without alcohol, many conflicts would not occur. Several Dureno households sell beer, the currently favored drink. The excessive consumption by young men led the community to prohibit its sale except on weekends. Young men sometimes fight when drunk. Husbands get angry at wives, and wives get angry at husbands. Men are more typically the aggressors, but some Dureno women have reputations for beating their husbands with sticks. I have never seen acts of violence, but I know they happen. Often, people forget about them when they sober up. The Cofán still pride themselves on their relative peacefulness. Although fighting occurs in the community, people do their best to stop it.

For both Cofán and non-Cofán people, the conflict, poverty, and environmental problems are defining elements of Dureno's image. The community's visible "Cofán-ness" is not as discernible as it once

—

FIGURE 2.6. *Dureno's main port on the Aguarico River*

was, which is why Alejandro's colorful difference is a heavily utilized symbol of a threatened way of life. Dureno residents acknowledge that others find it hard to distinguish them from most Ecuadorians. On most days, the great majority of community members wear bought shirts, pants, shorts, and dresses. They cut their hair in common regional styles. When they don their *ondiccu'je* and home-sewn skirts and blouses and when people listen closely to their language, their Cofán-ness is clear. In most contexts, though, the cultural specificity Dureno has lost is more apparent than the ways of speaking, thinking, and being it maintains.

The people of Dureno miss the healthy, calm, and abundant lifestyle they and their forebears once had. Most are proud of being Cofán; few seek to merge into Ecuador's nonindigenous population. Outsiders' interest in the survival of Cofán culture, however, is something they do not quite understand. For decades, anthropologists, journalists, tourists, and representatives of environmental and human rights organizations have visited Dureno. Cofán people ask themselves and each other if it is because they are different or because they are poor and suffering. Sometimes as individuals and sometimes as groups, North Americans, Europeans, and urban Ecuadorians come to Dureno to take pictures, see the forest, watch a dance performance, or hear tales of Texaco's atrocities. Sometimes they stay for weeks or months to do studies, workshops, and projects, and sometimes they arrive and depart on the same day.[10] Sometimes they pay people for their aid and give the community concrete goods, and sometimes they leave nothing.

One day Lucia laughingly asked me, "Why do tourists want to see our customs? Why do they take pictures of us as if we're woolly monkeys? Do they somehow make money doing that?" She has seen Alejandro's picture in books, which she knows are not free. Alejandro, too, suspects that outsiders come because they make money by doing it. He has heard that there is a picture of him in a Quito museum and that people pay to enter and look at it. He is partially right—there is a photograph of him in a museum near the Mitad del Mundo, "the middle of the world," where the first measurements for the equator were taken, and entrance is not free. Some outsiders have told him they use the pictures to help the Cofán. He thinks they are probably lying, although he can imagine that a few outsiders might see the people of Dureno as worthy objects of charity. He guesses that people might want to help the Cofán because their needs are so great. They live "poorly," Alejandro once told me, and their houses look dirty and old.

Outsiders are far more obsessed with the idea of Cofán cultural purity than Cofán people are. They prefer to take pictures of children who are wearing no clothes. They talk to the oldest, most traditional-looking people, even though elders are usually incapable of speaking Spanish, let alone English. They lecture the Cofán on the importance of their Cofán-ness. I heard one urban Ecuadorian tell my young research assistant that "nature" is more important than money and that he must continue to live "in his habitat," where he has "everything." An older Dureno resident described the common counsel of outsiders in the following terms: "Do not lose your customs, your language, and your way of doing things. Everything you have, everything your grandparents had, continue to have it." Cofán reports of other people's obsession with their cultural purity show how strange it can be. Alejandro's friend Valerio told me what North Americans said to him during a trip to the United States:

> The mestizo and gringo people in the United States really prohibited me from getting rid of our old-time houses, our houses with thatched roofs. That's what the gringos said when I went to the United States. They said that if we begin to think like mestizos, if we start making cement houses with two floors, they'll really dislike us. I heard them say that when I went to the United States. I went there to talk about oil, and that's what they told me.

Valerio had a hard time understanding why anyone would care what kind of houses Cofán people live in. Based on his conversations in the United States, he guessed that outsiders might want to help the Cofán attract visitors who can give them aid, including money. He learned that outsiders do not want to see new-style homes. They want to see something different. Echoing an oft-repeated Dureno

—

FIGURE 2.7. *A Dureno home*

sentiment, Valerio argued that people should make "nice" houses but keep a few old-style homes in the village. In the old houses, they would be able to put their handicrafts, spears, flutes, and drums. That way, outsiders would be able to witness the kind of cultural difference they expect the Cofán to value and exhibit. Simultaneously, the Cofán would be able to make the more practical choices that take into account their economic and ecological situation.

Outside expectations of appropriate Cofán-ness—and Cofán people's inability and/or unwillingness to practice it—are central themes of journalistic accounts of Dureno. In *Savages* (1995), a book that chronicles relations between oil and indigenous Waorani people, Joe Kane writes that the Dureno Cofán do not have their "dignity and spirit intact." He proclaims, "What is left of the Cofán nation are a listless and defeated bunch," most of whom "continue to live around Dureno, in what can be described only as abject poverty."[11] In *Amazon Stranger* (1996), Mike Tidwell tells the story of the Cofán community of Zábalo, which lies far downriver from Dureno in more pristine territory. He uses Dureno, "with its dearth of food and abundance of force-fed foreign ways," to describe just how dire the situation of the Zábalo Cofán could become. He reports that, given the "glut of cultural change all around," he was "half-surprised to see . . . [a] hut with the traditional palm-thatch roofing." Tidwell's tour of the village is extraordinarily depressing:

> Through the ghettoized center of the village, José [Tidwell's Cofán companion] led me, as if through a gauntlet. We passed the group of sullen two-year-olds dressed in charity diapers around a water well that didn't work. We passed the boisterous "drinking party" where more men in bell bottoms sat around a hovel stoop making *Cristal* [local rum] disappear. We passed the hut next to it with the boom box blasting bad and scratchy disco music up to a sky long since bereft of macaws.[12]

Chesa Boudin's account of his "coming-of-age in Latin America," *Gringo* (2009), is even more disheartening. Boudin spent five days in Dureno to learn about a people who "had the great misfortune to live on top of an oilfield during the petrol era." On a blistering day, he crossed the Aguarico in a canoe and was covered in sweat, but the "water was too polluted from oil operations for me to even consider cooling off with a swim." When he finally made it to the village center, "it was overrun with small children and emaciated dogs." People wore the "kinds of casual, threadbare clothes my family donated to the Salvation Army ten years ago." Even a small group of kids practicing a dance routine was depressing. The non-Cofán music they listened to was a "sure sign of a people whose culture was being infiltrated." Boudin wondered whether he was even in a native community: "Aside from the tunics and the Cofán language, A'ingae, spoken as a first and primary language throughout the town, there wasn't much to suggest that this was an indigenous community at all. Rather, Dureno had the air of a desperately poor rural settle-ment on the fringe of modern civilization." What "appalled" Boudin most, though, was the "rampant alcoholism in the small village." He arrived the day after a party and recounts, "[Most of the] men and adolescent boys I had run into around town were either busy drinking in groups or already in a drunken stupor." Boudin observes, "Cultures were clashing every day in this little patch of jungle, and it was painfully obvious who was losing. The Cofán in Dureno were too few to resist the onslaught of the West as it arrived across the airwaves and highways." After witnessing the "enormous" problem of alcohol and the "destroyed" environment in which people lived, Boudin says Cofán culture "seemed to be eroding in front of my eyes in a way that they had little control over." The Dureno Cofán's "way of life hadn't just changed with the times; it was on the verge of extinction."[13]

Documentary films reproduce the dismal imagery. In *Trinkets and Beads* (1996),[14] life in Dureno serves as a terrifying warning to other indigenous peoples considering oil operations on their land. The film follows two *ondiccu'je*-clad Dureno residents as they walk next to an oil-well waste pit in bare feet. It shows the crude-covered roads and filthy-looking company workers who populate Cofán territory. In *Crude* (2009),[15] plaintiffs' lawyers in the Chevron case bring the celebrity activist Trudie Styler (wife of Sting) to Dureno to learn about

—

oil's destructive powers. Before they arrive in the community, head lawyer Steven Donziger renders Dureno's lesson in extreme terms:

> We are going to a town called Dureno, which is a town where the Cofán people live. The Cofán are an indigenous group that, 30 years ago before Texaco came, had about 15,000 people who lived in this whole area. When the oil was found around here they got displaced. And out of 15,000 there's now only a few hundred who live in this town. They're the only Cofán left on their ancestral territory. . . . [W]e can't quite figure out how to compensate indigenous groups for something that probably can never be recovered, which is their culture and their land.

Donziger's dates and population figures are incorrect, but the Dureno Cofán's utility as a framing device is too good to ignore. *Crude* begins with an image of an old Cofán woman in traditional dress. In A'ingae, she sings a lament about her people's health problems, which she attributes to oil. Long segments feature Cofán leader and Dureno resident Emeregildo Criollo. Before a Chevron shareholders' meeting in Houston, Donziger helps Criollo craft a public statement, which ends with an ominous message: "[I]t is possible that in a few years, the Cofán nation will no longer exist." The film concludes with more footage of the Dureno Cofán. A large group crosses the Aguarico River in a crowded, unsteady canoe. They are all wearing *ondiccu'je* and home-sewn skirts and blouses. The A'ingae lament that began *Crude* plays in the background once again.

I could provide dozens more examples from websites, blog posts, and newspaper and magazine articles, many of which focus on the Chevron case. They are filled with the same words: "sickness," "extinction," "acculturation," and "loss." Few casual observers note anything of value or meaning in Dureno—aside from the potent symbolic yield of a people whose lands and lives have been decimated by oil. The images are not entirely inaccurate. They are, however, entirely one-sided. They depict the Cofán's cultural difference only in order to note its adulteration or bemoan its disappearance. In the popular press, the people of Dureno are tragic, past-tense figures. Their

—

suffering and assimilation are chalked up to oil. Sometimes, a hint of Western judgmentalism also shows itself: Why do the Cofán drink so much alcohol? Why are they so fixated on money? Why are they too ashamed of themselves to wear their traditional dress, live in their traditional homes, and eat their traditional foods? Why did they give up on their culture so quickly?

The indigenous peoples of the Americas have long had to negotiate the consequences of nonindigenous perspectives on how they should think, act, and look. In one chapter of his book *The Predicament of Culture* (1988), James Clifford examines the case of the Mashpee people of Massachusetts. Like many Native Americans, the Mashpee have struggled to meet externally imposed criteria in order to be recognized as a "native tribe." In a court case in which the judge ended up rejecting the Mashpee claim, lawyers, witnesses, and onlookers watched skeptically as Mashpee individuals took the stand. To many outsiders, the Mashpee no longer seemed distinct enough to qualify as indigenous. Although Cofán people have not experienced government rejection of their indigeneity, they, too, have watched a parade of outsiders look at them and see little more than a tragic story of decline and disappearance.

Despite reports to the contrary, the people of Dureno have not surrendered their culture or their identity. They are struggling to make their difficult lives better. Their lives also offer meaningful forms of satisfaction right now. In their fixation on the signs of difference Dureno lacks, outsiders miss most of what gives joy and purpose to its residents. After spending so much time in the community, I often find myself reflecting on the fundamental strangeness of Western fascinations with superficial markers of indigenous cultural difference. It is an obsession that I sometimes share. After all, anthropology was born as a discipline committed to analyzing—and ruling—non-Western peoples. Historically, it positioned its objects in the "timeless ethnographic present"; it was unable to acknowledge or understand the ways they were changing. Anthropology's colonial origins and contemporary politics are hard to ignore when you find yourself in the middle of a marginalized indigenous community whose inhabitants are not quite sure why you are there.[16]

FIGURE 2.8. *Two girls playing on a fruit tree in front of Alejandro's house*

I have had many, many conversations with Cofán people about
how I came to anthropology and why I am interested in their lives.
I tell them how disaffected I was as a youth in my own culture and
why I wanted to learn about something different. I tell them that as
a citizen of the United States—which uses most of the oil that comes
from their land—I feel responsible for many of the problems they
face. I explain that after my first conversations with Cofán people
in 1994, I developed a sense of obligation to them. I came to see my
collaborators as friends whose lives I wanted to understand so I could
help them—partially by letting the world know about their struggles
and partially by bringing in more direct forms of aid, whether work,
money, or projects that might be politically or economically beneficial. I also decided to serve on the board of an organization that funds
Cofán political and environmental efforts.[17]

My return to Cofán territory every year and the happiness and
laughter I exhibit there convince many Cofán people that I truly do

enjoy their company and that I view my time with them as an end in itself rather than as a means to make money. Yet they also know I earn a living by doing research with them. I give all my book royalties to Cofán communities and organizations, and the great majority of each grant I get goes to paying Cofán people for their help. But without the articles and books I write, I would have no job as a university professor. I would lack the time and money that allow me to return to Ecuador each year. The very fact that I am the one who can travel to see Cofán people rather than the other way around shows the deep inequality at the heart of our relationship.

No matter what intervention this book might make, outsiders will continue to arrive in Dureno. They will search for remnants of digestible cultural difference, which they will photograph for their books, websites, and Facebook pages. They will use the community to tell a story they already know: oil is a nearly unstoppable force that lays waste to humans and the environment. Cofán people are little more than props in the story, and their parts are scripted before any research begins. Alejandro's image will accompany the texts to show the world that a unique culture is becoming extinct. The writers and filmmakers will not take the time to listen closely to the people of Dureno and to learn something new from them. Few will understand what oil has done to the Cofán and how they have managed to survive in its midst.

—

FIGURE 3.1. *Alejandro's* yajé *pot*

CHAPTER 3

THE DEATH OF YORI'YE

To one side of me, Lucia and Roberto spread banana leaves and a cotton sheet over the earth, above which they hung their mosquito net. To the other side, Alejandro reclined in a hammock. His older brother Fernando sat in his own hammock to Alejandro's left, and Valerio strung a hammock to Alejandro's right. My hammock was in the middle of the *yaje* house, a starkly beautiful structure twenty feet wide and thirty feet long that Alejandro had built on the edge of the forest. Ten stout trunks of *bo'mbo*, a hard palm tree, supported its arched, thatched roof. The house was a perfect rectangle. It had no walls and a floor of compacted soil. The side closest to the village was for women and young children. The other half was for grown men and the few youths who came to drink *yaje*, which Alejandro kept in a metal pot at the far end of the house, near the forest. People of any age or gender crossed to the men's side to sit on the ground, where the curers looked into their bodies and

—

rubbed and blew tobacco smoke over their skin. Some placed their lips on the sick people's flesh to suck out the invisible objects that were harming them.

Long after the others drank, Alejandro gave me a gourd full of *yaje*. It was sometime before midnight. The bitterness of the thick, brown liquid lingered in my mouth, gradually receding with each cigarette I smoked. It was not my first time. I was expecting the nausea and the mild, unnerving hallucinations an amateur like me would experience. I knew that fasting would help me avoid vomiting and defecating on myself. I also knew that the less I moved, the better my stomach would feel. When I closed my eyes and listened to Alejandro's chanting and the shaking of the men's leaf bundles, imagined and remembered images appeared with vibrant clarity. When I opened my eyes, faint lines and shapes arose from the darkness. Although they did not cohere into recognizable forms, their colors were dazzling. Hours later, I sat up when I mistook a mosquito net for an old man in an *ondiccu'je*. The figure was standing over Lucia and Roberto. For a moment, it looked like it was urinating on them. I giggled. My guts were churning, but I was happy I saw something, even if it was a meaningless bit of *te'va'cho* (painting).

For a person like me who hates to lose control, drinking *yaje* is never fun. It is always interesting, though, and there is no way an anthropologist can understand much about Cofán culture without learning about shamanism. On the few occasions I have consumed *yaje*, it was easy to forget how much Dureno and the world outside it were changing. Before they drink, many men still ornament themselves with crowns, necklaces, and face paint. In the *yaje* house, the stereos and passing trucks on the far side of the Aguarico are impossible to hear. Forest sounds blend with the esoteric chants, the rustling leaf bundles, the flute notes, the bursts of laughter, and the exaggerated retching, sucking, and tongue-clicking noises. The only light comes from the men's glowing-orange cigar tips. On *yaje* nights, it is hard not to think about the great shamans of the past who left such a lasting impression on people like Alejandro.

In Dureno, the most admired and missed *atesu'cho* (knowledgeable one) is Yori'ye, whose legal name was Guillermo Quenamá. In

1941, he founded Dureno and became its chief. People called him Yori when he was alive and Yori'ye after he died in 1966, as the A'ingae suffix -*ye* is attached to a person's name after they pass.[1] Yori'ye's sister was married to one of Alejandro's brothers. Yori'ye was also the cousin of Eusebio Quenamá, who was Lucia's father and Alejandro's primary shamanic teacher. When Alejandro was an unmarried youth, he drank *yaje* with Yori'ye. His eyes light up when he recounts the man's exploits. Yori'ye, Alejandro said, could swallow whole pots of *va'u* (*Brugmansia suaveolens*), a hallucinogen even more powerful than *yaje*. He transformed into jaguars, anacondas, white-lipped peccaries, and tapirs. He called game to the village center. He engaged in vicious battles with shamans from neighboring peoples. He was a devious and funny man, proud of the fear he inspired. One of his favorite tricks was to wake in the morning and pull a blowgun dart from his mouth. With a smile, he claimed he had transformed into a jaguar during the night and attacked neighboring Napo Runa people. After Yori'ye devoured a few of their women, Napo Runa men repelled him with blowguns. The dart was proof of the assaults.

By Cofán standards, Yori'ye's life was not short, but he definitely died before he should have. He was about sixty when he perished near Texaco's base camp, which would later become the city of Lago Agrio. He was fat, healthy, and at the height of his powers. Although four Cofán people were present at his death, no one knows exactly what happened—except that three Texaco workers were there, too.

The story of Yori'ye's life and death offers important insights into the role of shamanism in Cofán culture and the tumultuous course of Dureno's history. Yori'ye was a strong leader with unmatched abilities. He used his powers to found Dureno and protect its people. For many reasons, living with Yori'ye could be difficult, but living without him was a terrifying prospect. Unfortunately, the people of Dureno had to survive his death much earlier than they had hoped. Without his care, life in the age of oil sometimes seemed like too much to bear.

No one knows what year Yori'ye was born. While visiting a graduate student who was writing his master's thesis on Capuchin missionaries at a Quito university, I happened across a scanned copy of Yori'ye's baptism record, which came from a Colombian archive. The baptism

—

occurred in 1908 on the Aguarico River, probably when Yori'ye was still a small child. His father was recorded as Santos Quenamá and his mother as Pascuala Mashacori.[2] An apparently non-Cofán man named Angelino Ortega was listed as his godfather. The officiating priest was "Jacinta Maria del Quito, Capuchino."

Yori'ye's father, Santos, was an important leader on the Aguarico for many years. During most of his life, Cofán people did not live in large, permanent settlements. Communities were often little more than the houses and gardens of an extended family or two. During my dissertation research, Alejandro's brother Atanacio, who was born in the mid-1920s, told me about the old-time settlements. He said family groups lived together in one large house, which they built on the ground rather than on stilts as is the custom today. To guard against attacks from wild animals and Tetete people, the Cofán used palm wood and bamboo to fence in their homes. They slept on mats or in hammocks. They held up their cooking pots with stones or ceramic stands. The only people who slept outside were menstruating women, who had their own small houses on the edge of the forest. Two groups of people stayed in the seclusion huts for longer periods: girls at menarche and postpartum women, who kept their babies with them.

Periodically, extended family groups consolidated at larger settlements, the biggest of which was Cuvoé, near the contemporary town of Cascales. I once visited the Cuvoé site with a Cofán team to compose a map of their ancestral territory. Cofán people's fruit trees are still there. Huge chunks of ceramic pots jut out of the ground. It is clear that many people lived at Cuvoé for centuries, if not millennia. Cofán oral history describes periods when hundreds or thousands of people lived in large communities on the Aguarico and San Miguel. Close to Cuvoé, there were villages named Bifeno and Sevoé. According to my informants, they extended far into the forest. There were so many Cofán people, elders laughingly told me, that the Aguarico was covered with human feces. People had to push away the shit to collect water. The stories are strangely similar to the more recent accounts of clearing spilled oil off the river to reach water.

By the time Yori'ye was born, the huge settlements were myths and memories. Over the previous three and a half centuries, epidemics

FIGURE 3.2. *Yori'ye (*center*) in the 1960s. Photo by Bub Borman.*

had emptied the region of most of its inhabitants. Men of Yori'ye's generation sometimes stumbled onto a Tetete house in the forest. They also found footprints on the beach across from Dureno where Tetete bands came to watch and listen as the Cofán drank manioc beer, played drums, and danced through the night. Small groups of Siona and Secoya people, whom the Cofán called Ai'pa, also lived nearby. Yori'ye and the rest of Santos's family sometimes stayed with them in multiethnic settlements. After all, Santos spoke their Western Tukanoan language. Santos's father was either Ai'pa or Tetete, categories that overlap for the Cofán—basically, an Ai'pa was a Tetete who wore clothes, lived on the river rather than in the forest interior, and was expected to act in a friendly manner. Yori'ye and his brothers spoke Ai'pa, too, and many Ai'pa people spoke A'ingae. The Cofán and the Ai'pa sometimes intermarried.

Santos was a renowned shaman, but no one remembers how he acquired his skills. He definitely associated shamanic power with the

---

61

Ai'pa. Aniseto Quenamá, Yori'ye's half-brother who was still alive during my dissertation research, told me that Santos brought him far downriver to an Ai'pa settlement near Angoteros, Peru, to learn shamanism. Santos brought Yori'ye to live with two Ai'pa shamans—Antonio and Mateo—on the Eno River. Santos could have trained Yori'ye, but shamanic powers do not pass easily from father to son. More than anything, shamanic learning requires privation and suffering. Most fathers cannot stand watching their children in such pain, which is why it is better for other people to do the job.

Yori'ye apprenticed under Antonio for years. After Yori'ye learned to transform into a jaguar, he returned to Cofán society. He rejoined his father at a settlement near the mouth of the Pacayacu River. With his new powers, Yori'ye had become arrogant. He was no longer afraid of his father. He began an affair with Santos's second wife, whom he got pregnant. When Santos discovered the betrayal, he viciously beat Yori'ye with a whip fashioned from tapir hide. He told his son that his shamanic power was equivalent to what Santos kept "in his little finger," that is, hardly anything. In a miraculous show of supernatural skill, Santos figured out a way to "eat" the fetus from inside his wife's womb. The pregnancy ended shortly after it began.

Despite his powers, Santos died in the 1920s, probably due to an extended battle with tuberculosis. Cofán families moved around for the next few decades. Some followed Yori'ye, who was already becoming a na'su (chief, leader, master, or owner). Yori'ye's main shamanic competitor was Gregorio, the son of Santos's younger brother. At an upriver settlement, the aspiring leaders lived together. Gregorio had an impressive biography. As a child, he and his family lived near the Cuvoé site until a measles epidemic decimated their group. His family fled downstream to the Cuyabeno River. There, another measles outbreak hit. Gregorio and his father were two of the few survivors. They fled up the Cuyabeno River, where they lived in close proximity to Tetete groups. Gregorio worked briefly for a mestizo man who traveled through the region collecting rubber. Later, Ecuadorian soldiers passed through and decided to take him as a porter and boatman. Gregorio stayed with the soldiers for years, which is how he learned Spanish. Later, he acquired shamanic powers from Ai'pa people on the Putumayo River. The skills intensified the violent demeanor the soldiers taught him, such as when Gregorio watched the soldiers destroy a Tetete settlement and massacre its inhabitants. He developed a reputation for getting in fistfights with all sorts of people: fellow Cofán villagers, nonindigenous traders and settlers, and even his own father.

Yori'ye was older than Gregorio and addressed him as "younger brother." He was also Gregorio's shamanic superior. Living in the same community, the cousins interacted in tense, unpredictable ways. Gregorio would cure a person and identify Yori'ye as the attacker, and Yori'ye would cure the same person and blame Gregorio for the affliction. Their relationship devolved into outright conflict. In the words of my assistant Deji,

> It became a huge fight. It was shaman against shaman, knowledgeable one against knowledgeable one. They would get together and drink manioc beer or *yaje*. When they became inebriated, one would say to the other, "I'm more than you. I know more than you. I know everything, everything." And then the other one would say, "No, I know more than you. I have everything, everything." And that's how they began to fight. They even got into a fistfight. The people had to pull them apart from each other. Yori'ye really hated it when that started to happen.

They did not stay together for long. Gregorio left with a small group of families and formed an upriver community that became the present-day village of Duvuno. For a few years, Yori'ye and his followers lived at a site called Santa Cecilia, where Capuchin priests once resided. It was close to the portage trail that connected the Aguarico River to the San Miguel River. Santa Cecilia was a meeting point for the entire Cofán population, but it was not the best natural setting. The swarms of mosquitos there were a continuous nuisance, it was nearly impossible to walk through the dense thickets of thorny bamboo that covered the area, and there were none of the *inayova* trees that were essential for making blowgun darts.

Cofán people were already familiar with the site that became Dureno before Yori'ye made a community there. There was even a small school staffed by Capuchin priests in the 1910s and 1920s. The hills close to the river are still covered with pottery shards, and people continue to find old stone axes in their gardens. In the late 1930s, while Yori'ye's group was in Santa Cecilia, a few people were already traveling to Dureno to make gardens and gather forest products. The game was plentiful. The rocks in the river were perfect for attracting *avu*, an important fish species. One day, when Alejandro's father was getting ready to leave Santa Cecilia for a visit to Dureno, Yori'ye packed up his canoe and told everyone to follow him. It was time to make a new village. Alejandro's friend Valerio explained,

> Yori'ye told everyone to live here. "This is good land. It's sandy here. The other places where we've been living, well, that land really isn't any good." Yori'ye had already been drinking *yaje* and looking at this land. He knew it was a good place to live. He said, "Come on, let's live here. Other places are too hilly or too muddy. Why would we want to live on that? It's easier to live on this sandy land, where we can be clean and comfortable."

Yori'ye was right. Dureno was a great place to live. Cofán people have been residing on the land continuously for more than seventy years. Even with a growing population and an increasingly depleted forest, it provides much of what they need. Yori'ye must have known something no one else did. According to my informants, he took the strange step of telling people never to leave Dureno, even after his death. Before, the death of a great *na'su*—almost always a great shaman—was an especially urgent reason to abandon a settlement. Shamans do not just die and disappear; they transform into *cocoya*. The *cocoya* afflict all whom they encounter, including friends and family members of the dead shaman. Yori'ye, though, promised not to kill the people who stayed in Dureno. In a reversal of the typical scenario, he vowed to attack them only if they left. According to Alejandro, Yori'ye said, "Do not throw away this land. Even after I die, stay here. If I die and you become afraid and go to the Coca River, or to Colombia, or to anywhere else, you will not survive. I will kill you. But if you stay here, I will become a *cocoya* and watch over you."

—

FIGURE 3.3. *Valerio Mendua smoking a cigar made with homegrown tobacco*

Respecting Yori'ye's wisdom and fearing his wrath, people decided to make Dureno their permanent home.

From its founding in 1941 until his death in 1966—and even after his death, according to some—Yori'ye ensured a happy life in Dureno. He feared nothing and no one. If people were sick, he cured them. If they were hungry, he called fish and game. In his dreams and *yaje* visions, he guarded his people from approaching enemies, supernatural or otherwise. He used the fear he inspired to maintain internal order, too. Wary of his anger and violence, people did their best to avoid fighting with each other. Yori'ye prevented tensions between families by deciding who could marry whom. In order to make Dureno a village where people did not have to marry *antianaccu* (incestuously), he recruited other people to the community. Their last names multiplied. He invited Imbiquito, an indigenous Shuar man who worked for Royal Dutch Shell, to marry a Cofán woman—and bring the last name Vargas. He told a Colombian Cofán woman with sons by two non-Cofán men to marry a Dureno man—and bring the last names Ortiz and Chapal. Yori'ye laughingly called the newcomers his "planted ones" and "pets." With more options for marriage in Dureno, people did not have to look elsewhere for spouses. Accordingly, Yori'ye's followers grew in number.

Yori'ye also allowed the Borman missionary family, who were affiliated with the Summer Institute of Linguistics/Wycliffe Bible Translators (SIL), to live in Dureno. When Bub Borman arrived from the United States in 1954, Yori'ye saw his amphibious airplane and steady access to manufactured goods. He wanted Bobbie, Bub's wife, to bring medicines to combat the diseases that were harming his people, including tuberculosis and whooping cough. The Bormans proved to be an asset. Their main mission was to create a writing system for A'ingae so they could translate the Bible into it. They never convinced Yori'ye or anyone else to give up many of their ways. According to people in Dureno, they hardly even tried. Although both Alejandro and Lucia grew up while the Bormans were in Dureno, neither was baptized. They both maintained their faith in shamanic healing, about which the Bormans said little. The Bormans' children spoke A'ingae, wore Cofán clothes, and played with Cofán friends.

In 2002, I interviewed Bub and Bobbie. They told me their view was that an A'ingae Bible would speak for itself; they saw little need to speak for it, although they did hold weekly meetings to sing hymns in A'ingae and talk about religion. They also created an A'ingae-language school, and they helped the community acquire its land title. Their oldest son, Randy, "went native," married a Dureno woman, and became an important Cofán leader and environmental activist.[3] Although other indigenous organizations forced the SIL out of Ecuador in 1982, the Cofán were not involved in the process. For the most part, they liked the Bormans. Few Cofán people have anything bad to say about them.[4]

Despite the Bormans' arrival, the following years continued as they had, and the logic of shamanism continued to organize Cofán lives. The community as a whole structured its activities to contain the supposedly contaminating power of menstruating women and expectant parents, male as well as female. Breaking the associated prohibitions could cause hardship in many ways. Under Yori'ye's leadership, everyone worked together to maintain Dureno's collective strength and health.

Cosmological concerns remain central to Cofán people's lives. The spiritual figures with whom Dureno residents interact are grouped loosely into *a'i* (humans) and *cocoya* (demons), although some entities pertain to both categories. All of the beings dislike the blood associated with menstruation, pregnancy, and childbirth. If they find someone tainted by it, they attack the person. Anyone can encounter a hostile being in the river or forest, but people involved in shamanism are at special risk. When they begin to drink *yaje*, supernatural people give them a clean, white, spirit *ondiccu'je* and invisible feathered ornaments. If the drinkers become contaminated, the garments become covered with ugly, red, horrible-smelling splotches. The beings who gave the objects become enraged.

To protect themselves and others from supernatural attack, contaminating women restrict their daily activities. In the old times, they secluded themselves in separate houses for months at a time after their first period and all births. Every month during their menses, they stayed in the houses for up to five days. Only after a ritual bath

—

FIGURE 3.4. *Etavina Quenamá, Valerio's wife, rolling palm fiber into thread*

did they return to their routines. Some Cofán communities still have special houses for contaminating women. Perhaps forty or fifty years ago, the houses in Dureno became simple attachments to normal houses. Later, they disappeared entirely.

Many Cofán women continue to follow the remaining prohibitions. During their periods, they touch no food or dishes; others feed them with a special set of plates. They sleep apart from their husbands. They bathe on land rather than in streams or rivers. They do not venture into the forest for fear of angering a *cocoya*. The same rules apply to expectant and postpartum parents, including fathers, whose bodies contain the reproductive blood of their wives. People who are *ega'pa* (in possession of "badness"), do very little. Husbands or daughters take over the cooking, cleaning, and feeding. *Ega'pa* people also avoid stepping over pots, cups, plates, and gourds. They try not to walk behind the backs of men involved in shamanism. By crossing the men's paths, contaminating people cut the invisible threads that trail behind *yaje* drinkers, putting their health and skills at risk.

Despite people's efforts to avoid contamination from reproductive blood, Cofán gender norms are surprisingly weak. Historically, many Cofán girls drank *yaje* before they began to menstruate. Reportedly, a few even underwent shamanic healing to prevent menstruation entirely to allow them to become shamans themselves. A few Cofán women hunt, and all men are prepared to cook, serve food, and clean dishes when their wives cannot. Some Cofán women say that they have *vacaciónme sombo* (taken a vacation) when they begin to menstruate. A few men jokingly told me that women's periods seem to get longer and longer each year, so men end up doing most of the domestic work. Alejandro, Lucia, and I often talked about the prohibitions. They both laughed in astonishment when I told them that I sleep in the same bed as my wife while she is menstruating. They laughed even harder when I told them that we sleep with our dogs. The prohibitions do not seem to cause hostility or disgust toward women or their bodies. They are simply the consequence of the preferences of supernatural beings, who have their own, often unknowable reasons for doing what they do.

People in search of shamanic power are especially careful about

—

the prohibitions. Historically, they avoided bathing with soap because supernatural *a'i* do not like it. Every morning, prospective shamans boiled, ingested, and vomited dozens of plant species to rid their bodies of contamination. Like girls at menarche, they did not eat the meat of most game animals, as those were considered too bloody. They engaged in no sexual activities. They drank *cui'ccu* or manioc beer only if it was prepared by themselves or postmenopausal women.[5]

On the mornings that the young men of Dureno boiled *yaje*, once or twice a week, Yori'ye gave the community special instructions. He told everyone to stay in their homes. No one was to go down to the river to bathe or wash dishes. Children were not supposed to play. No one was to shout or take hard steps on the ground. As the men consumed and vomited plants to cleanse their bodies and slowly ornamented themselves, most women gathered to sleep in one house. If everyone followed Yori'ye's counsel, the *yaje* would *ccúsiañe* (inebriate) them well. People's visions would be colorful and clear. They would suffer no nausea, diarrhea, or dizziness. The supernatural beings would be more likely to arrive.

The people who prepared *yaje* started early in the morning. Once they arrived at the house, they could not go back to their homes until people had finished drinking, which occurred the next morning. Chopping firewood and tending to the brew were hard work. The young men had to dig a deep hole from which to retrieve groundwater to boil the *yaje* vine with plant admixtures; flowing water from streams and rivers was far too contaminated with the traces of reproductive blood.

In the early evening, the drinkers began to arrive. The majority were men, but some women partook as well. Fasted and rested, they came with their headdresses, beaded necklaces, nose and ear feathers, face paint, and fragrant plants tied to their arms. The most accomplished men prepared leaf bundles and hung up an assortment of everyday objects—sticks, spears, tobacco, and sugarcane—that they supernaturally transformed and played as if they were flutes or drums. Someone usually burned incense. The scent repelled some supernatural creatures while attracting the beings the most powerful drinkers hoped to see.

—

Although nonshamans were in awe of Yori'ye and in fear of the beings he called, the atmosphere of a Dureno *yaje* night was often friendly and light. People smoked cigars, told jokes, and shared hunting stories. After sundown, Yori'ye was the first to drink. He blew and shook his leaf bundle over the *yaje* to cleanse it and took a gourdful for himself. Then, he sat back and returned to socializing with the others. Slowly, people approached him and asked for *yaje*. Some drank once, and others drank four or five times. Sometimes, a pot of *va'u*, the other main hallucinogen, was also present. It was much harder to handle. Yori'ye could down it as if it were water, but it caused everyone else to become unconscious. Hours later, its drinkers woke and became "crazy." The river, the forest, and the ground spoke to them. The effect could last for days. As Aniseto, Yori'ye's half-brother, proclaimed to me, "*Va'u* is a *cocoya*! When you drink it, you see with a *cocoya*'s eyes." Someone had to accompany *va'u* drinkers during the entirety of their experience so they did not injure themselves.

As the hours passed and the *yaje* took effect, the men began to shake their leaf bundles and chant. Yori'ye was first. His half-sung words were in the esoteric languages he learned from *cocoya* and supernatural *a'i*. Sometimes they sounded like senseless noises, and sometimes they sounded like repetitions of distorted A'ingae, Spanish, and Ai'pa words. As he chanted, the beings heard and approached. Then, the objects he brought to the *yaje* house became the objects of the spirits. They turned into musical instruments he could play. Often, Yori'ye and other *atesu'cho* left the *yaje* house and walked into the forest while hallucinating. From behind the trees, the sounds of their chants and instruments echoed through the night. As the *atesu'cho* came and went, they brought the supernatural beings with them.[6]

Talking to people who drank *yaje* with Yori'ye, I was amazed at how many kinds of supernatural *a'i* exist. There are star people, toucan people, sky people, tree people, and many others. Although great in number, they are difficult to encounter. The first things a *yaje* drinker sees are geometric designs, flashes of color, and bright animals, especially parrots and macaws. With their initial sense of confusion, helplessness, and terror, drinkers see jaguars, anacondas, and pit vipers that threaten to kill and eat them. If they push past their fear and drink more, they see the most helpful class of beings, *yaje a'i*.

Even before drinkers can see, the *yaje* people give them invisible clothes and ornaments that add to their visionary powers. Many of my informants said that their desire to witness the *yaje* people's beauty was their primary motivation to drink. The *yaje* people's faces and legs are intricately painted; their teeth and lips are dyed black; their feather crowns, beaded necklaces, and strings of jaguar and peccary teeth shine brightly. They are men, women, and children. But they do not menstruate, get pregnant, or give birth—and they do not die. If the *yaje* house and brew are clean, the *yaje* people come to imbibe alongside the humans. *Yaje* is their *cui'ccu* or their manioc beer. Their initial counsel is always the same: "Without fear, drink more." They become the advisers of people who continue to drink and maintain the prohibitions. They help their friends to diagnose and cure the ill. In dreams, they come to their allies to warn of approaching enemies. Some shamans even marry *yaje a'i* women and form supernatural families with them.[7]

As with other great shamans, Yori'ye helped people see and accumulate powers. People from Dureno and elsewhere approached him and asked, "Will you give me *yaje* to drink? I want to drink with you. I want to see what you see." If he agreed, he replied, "All right. If you have no fear, drink." Yori'ye knew how to speak to and transform into all the *a'i* and *cocoya* who came to the *yaje* house to see and converse with him. With sufficient practice and training, others could see the beings Yori'ye brought, learn their language, become their allies, and transform into them.

Both directly and through his supernatural helpers, Yori'ye offered seekers his spirit weapons, including invisible machetes, spears, and shotguns. The prototypical Cofán shamanic weapon is *davu*. As with so many Cofán cosmological concepts, *davu* is hard to explain. The word refers to a variety of objects a shaman displays in his practice. They look like small stones, glass shards, and bone fragments. While curing, an *atesu'cho* spits them out of his mouth and shows them to patients and onlookers. He puts them in a gourd of *yaje* when teaching others to acquire them. The apprentices must drink the *yaje* while

FIGURE 3.5. Va'u *flowers*

the *davu* is in it. The small objects, though, are merely vessels and representations of more powerful, invisible instruments. The masters of *davu* are *cocoya*.

After drinking *yaje* into which *davu* was put, a person must maintain strict prohibitions for months. He must sit in his home, eat little, drink *cui'ccu* made with unripe plantains, and smoke tobacco. In the aspirant's dreams and *yaje* visions, he sees the *cocoya* who own the *davu*. Later, the person enters the *cocoya*'s house. There, the *cocoya* give the person shining plates covered with weapons; they might look like the *davu* objects, or they might look like guns and bullets. After the person takes the weapons from the *cocoya*, the *davu* enter his body. When he drinks *yaje*, the objects look like glowing caterpillars, harpoon points, and machetes, kept inside his arms. When he falls asleep, he emerges in the house of the *davu* master who has become his protector.

Having *davu* allows one to see and extract the *davu* that other shamans have sent into the bodies of the ill. Inversely, having *davu* enables a shaman to shoot, blow, or throw the weapons into the bodies of his own enemies and kill them. If a possessor of *davu* breaks any of the prohibitions, the *davu* rip themselves from his flesh, causing illness and possibly death.

As people sometimes say, *davu* itself is a *cocoya*. Although Yori'ye possessed *davu*, his real specialty was the ability to transform directly into *cocoya* and kill in their guise. The word *cocoya* is difficult to define. I typically translate it as "malevolent supernatural agent" or "demon." Some *cocoya* naturally exist, and others are either dead shamans or living shamans who have transformed into *cocoya* to cure or kill. *Cocoya* also have weapons: *davu*, darts, spears, machetes, and guns. By becoming a *cocoya*, a shaman can use its weapons to attack his enemies. Shamans can also command allied *cocoya* to do their bidding.

Although supernatural *a'i* look like Cofán people, *cocoya* often appear as black, white, or mestizo beings—or as monstrous creatures that look nothing like humans. One has no head and spins through the forest as if pushed by wind. One is a white woman with white hair who lives underwater. Another river-dwelling *cocoya* looks like a giant

—

74

dog and shoots darts into people. An old man told me about a dream in which he found a *cocoya* village in a swamp. It was enveloped in mist and smoke. Its inhabitants appeared to be Afro-Ecuadorians with modern clothes. Their teeth, though, were long and sharp. They invited him into their homes. He knew they were trying to trap him, and he feared the illness and death that would result. He declined their invitation.

Cocoya are not the only creatures shamans control. Many Dureno residents told me that snakes and jaguars do not naturally kill people; they do so only if they are under the direction of a shaman who views them as his pets. Shamans can take the shape of animals as well. Yori'ye was a master at *ttesive di'shaye* (emerging as a jaguar). He acquired the power by drinking *yaje* and *va'u* with his Ai'pa teacher, who helped him see jaguars in human form. Yori'ye encountered them as people occupying a beautiful house. The structure was filled with different kinds of gloves, shirts, and *ondiccu'je* that corresponded to the varieties of jaguar.[8] After repeated visits to the house, Yori'ye was able to see the clothing, touch it, and put it on. When he covered his body with it, he became a jaguar in the waking world.

The jaguar people showed Yori'ye aboveground and underground paths to distant sites on the Aguarico, San Miguel, and Napo Rivers. In jaguar form, he raced across the land at superhuman speeds. He attacked and ate the people he encountered, who appeared to him as ripe, sweet pineapples. While transforming into a jaguar in the *yaje* house, he growled and scraped his claws into the earth. His half-brother Aniseto swore to me that long nails actually emerged from Yori'ye's knuckles.

Yori'ye's ability to engage in violent action—with *davu*, as *cocoya*, and in jaguar form—was the foundation of his power to ensure order in Dureno. People appreciated him, but they also feared him. Cofán shamans associate themselves so deeply with malevolent beings and forces that people view them as capricious, terrifying, quasihuman creatures. People showed their appreciation for Yori'ye by giving him meat and helping to weed his garden and maintain his house. Behind his back, though, they called him *cocoya*, *sumbi* (crazy person), or *injamambi* (fool). When he got mad at other *yaje* drinkers for

—

one reason or another, he stripped them of their powers, rendering them impotent.

Valerio told me a story about Yori'ye and Valerio's father, Polinario. The two men were drinking manioc beer with others and got drunk. Inebriated, Yori'ye pushed Calixto, Alejandro's father. Polinario was friends with Calixto, so he punched Yori'ye and knocked him down. Yori'ye then said to him, "A forest woman will teach you." A few days later, Polinario went hunting with his prized dog. He shot a curassow with his blowgun. When the bird fell from a branch, he went to retrieve it. Suddenly, a jaguar attacked him. He tried to beat it off with his blowgun. Using an old Cofán trick, he stood behind a small tree, around which the jaguar chased and lunged at him without being able to reach him. After a long struggle, Polinario saved himself, but the jaguar killed his dog. When he returned to the village, he saw Yori'ye. Polinario shared his tale and told Yori'ye how sad he was about his dog. With a menacing grin, Yori'ye replied, "Well, I told you to be careful in the forest." With the tone and delivery of the comment, Polinario and everyone else knew that Yori'ye sent the jaguar.[9]

For every story of Yori'ye's violence, there are tales of his miraculous feats as a game caller. When people had bad luck hunting or fishing, they turned to Yori'ye for help. He could call various animals, but white-lipped peccaries were his specialty. The na'su of white-lipped peccaries is a type of cocoya called vajo. Vajo are tall, human-like creatures that sometimes wear the robes of Capuchin priests. They are bloodthirsty killers. Yori'ye would drink yaje, chant to the peccaries, and transform into the animals. He filled the yaje house with the grunts and squeals of their newborns, juveniles, and adults. In his transformed shape, he saw and approached the vajo, who sat on a chair. Yori'ye told the vajo, "I have come for what you have, for your domesticated pigs, for your a'i. I want to take them back with me." The vajo kept the peccaries in a structure that looked like a corral. If Yori'ye spoke well to the vajo, it freed the peccaries and allowed Yori'ye to take them. The day after he drank yaje, Yori'ye would tell people where to look for the peccaries, which travel in herds of hundreds of individuals. He created paths to direct them to hunting sites. Once, Yori'ye even built a path to the village center.

—

The peccaries ran straight under people's homes. Men, women, and children killed dozens of them.

Even more beneficial than Yori'ye's capacity to maintain order and call game was his power to protect people from sickness and death. His ability to communicate with, transform into, and control the beings that do Cofán people harm made him a perfect caretaker. In the old times, elders say, people did not simply die—they were always killed, usually at the hands of enemy shamans. Shamans were constantly at war with one another, and they took out their rage on their enemies' followers. Shamans themselves were often too strong to be killed. *Cocoya, davu,* jaguars, anacondas, and pit vipers could be anywhere at any time. In his dreams and *yaje* visions, Yori'ye kept the threats at bay, often by locking up malevolent beings in spirit houses. In the words of Alejandro's brother Fernando,

> Before, in the time when we still drank a lot of *yaje*, Yori'ye would drink and say to us, "It's all right. Bathe without fear. What would you be afraid of? If something in the river gets angry at you, you will not die. The black jaguar that lives in the river is not here now. The anaconda is not here now. I've kept them away. In the forest, there are no *cocoya*. I've closed them up in the trunk of a kapok tree. They won't be able to get out and bother you. The only way they would be able to attack you is if another shaman sees them, opens the house into which I have put them, and takes them out. That way they would be able to snap your necks and kill you. But I won't let that happen."

Even in the company of Yori'ye, people did get sick. It was up to Yori'ye and Dureno's lesser shamans to cure them. The first step was diagnosis. For almost any symptom, a person would first try a plant medicine. The illness could be fever, headache, dizziness, stomach distress, general malaise, a mouth sore, or pain in one's arm or leg—anything. If the plant medicine did not work, the afflicted would go to Yori'ye. Sometimes with *yaje* and sometimes without it, Yori'ye rubbed the person's flesh and looked into their body. If he saw a lit white candle, he knew there was a chance to save them. He called his

—

allied supernatural *a'i* to help him examine the patient. His helpers showed him where *davu* was lodged in the person's flesh, or they helped him discover if a *cocoya* had captured the person's *canse'pa* (life force).

If a *cocoya* was at fault—or if an enemy shaman had stolen the person's *canse'pa* and lodged it in a *cocoya*'s house—Yori'ye had to find the being. When he discovered its abode, he entered. The *cocoya* sat cradling the sick person's *canse'pa*, which appeared as a pet bird, usually a macaw or parrot. Using the *cocoya*'s language, Yori'ye began to scold and counsel the being. Typically, the *cocoya* relented and gave the *canse'pa* to Yori'ye, who returned it to the afflicted, thus effecting the cure. Often, though, the *cocoya* would be uncooperative. Weaker shamans would give up and fail to retrieve the *canse'pa*, and the sick person would die. Yori'ye was usually too aggressive and powerful to fail. He sometimes fought the *cocoya*. As with all supernatural beings, however, *cocoya* are immortal. In the words of Alejandro's nephew Lorenzo, "*Cocoya* are unkillable. You cannot do it. You have to fight them. You scold them, hit them, and beat them. And then you carry them to their house, or wherever they stay. You put them in there, and you lock the door. That way, they won't be able to get out and bother anyone."

Enemy *davu* was a frequent cause of illness. Yori'ye began a *davu* cure by asking where the pain was most intense. If he had drunk *yaje*, his spirit allies helped him locate the offending object. He smoked cigar after cigar. He blew the smoke onto the patient's skin, which he rubbed slowly and deeply while peering into the flesh. Intermittently, he spat onto his palms and clasped them together before touching the person again. Eventually, he located the *davu* inside the patient's body. If it was small, he could remove it with his hands. If it was big, he had to place his lips onto the person's flesh. He made long, loud sucking sounds as he extracted the object. Periodically, he lifted his hands and mouth from the person's body, turned away from them, and blew over his palms to send the object far away. He chanted and shook his leaf bundle over the patient's body to cleanse it.

Yori'ye sometimes concluded a *davu* cure by spitting his own *davu* objects—his stones and glass shards—out of his mouth. He held them

---

in his hands and "read them as if they were books," as Alejandro explained to me. The examination allowed him to tell the patient who had attacked them. Often, he said he would kill the offending shaman. He sent the enemy *davu* to his own *davu* house, where the *cocoya* master of his *davu* stayed. The *cocoya* then ate the enemy *davu*, causing the death of the shaman who sent it.

For much of Dureno's history, Yori'ye protected the community from outside threats, whether natural or supernatural in kind. Royal Dutch Shell explored for oil in Cofán territory during Yori'ye's reign, but the exploration had little impact on the community or its land. The Borman family changed Dureno in more profound ways, but many of the transformations they initiated were appreciated. When a seismic company contracted by Texaco arrived in 1964, its operations were greater in scale than Shell's work. Cofán people, however, did not think there would be lasting consequences. Yori'ye befriended some of the mestizo workers. They spent nights in Dureno, where they drank and danced with people. Most Dureno residents feared the workers but also found them intriguing. The outsiders often brought cheap cane liquor. Yori'ye liked it, just as he liked many mind-altering substances.

In April 1966, Yori'ye went on a trip to Duvuno—his cousin Gregorio's community—with his daughter Margarita, her husband, Elias, Yori'ye's young wife, Marta, and Valerio, Marta's half-brother through their mother. (Marta is still alive; I changed her name to protect her privacy.) Marta was Yori'ye's fourth and final wife; the other three died in succession. She was in her twenties at the time of the trip to Duvuno. Marta and Yori'ye's only daughter had died nearly five years earlier.

On the way back from Duvuno, the group decided to spend the night at Amisacho, an old Cofán village site on which Texaco had decided to construct its base camp. A few Cofán people from Colombia had recently built houses there. At the riverside, Yori'ye saw a mestizo man named Elias Cortez in his canoe. Elias and his brother worked for the seismic company that Texaco had contracted. His brother's name was Ermilo, but Cofán people called him Shipicco (Cockroach). There are two stories of how he got the name. In the

—

first and most common, people say he sprayed insecticide to prevent malaria outbreaks. He entered Cofán houses and treated their
thatched roofs, which caused hundreds of cockroaches to fall to the
floor. The other story, which Lucia told me, is that Cofán women
named him Shipicco because when he got drunk, he crawled on the
floor to approach and attempt to seduce them. Lucia laughed and
said he reminded them of a cockroach.

The Cofán were on friendly terms with Elias. On that day at Amisacho, Yori'ye waved him over and asked if he had any cane liquor.
Elias said he did. He returned with a few bottles as well as his brother
and one of their coworkers. In the early evening, everyone started to
drink. As was his custom, Yori'ye began to chant when he became
inebriated. Eventually, according to the reports, everyone got drunk
and fell asleep. In the early morning, they heard Marta yell. She told
them to come and look at Yori'ye. He was cold and still. His face
was blue, and his neck looked bruised. As they soon determined, he
was dead.[10]

They brought Yori'ye's corpse to Dureno. People were terrified
and enraged. They immediately assumed Elias was responsible.
A number of Dureno men wanted to avenge Yori'ye by killing Elias.
They grabbed their spears, but others calmed them down. No one
thought that killing a nonindigenous person would put them in good
stead with Ecuadorian authorities, including soldiers, whom they had
always feared. They decided to let Elias go. With much sadness, they
turned to Yori'ye's body. As per custom, they placed him in a rolled-
up section of palm bark. They put his shamanic decorations with
him: his feather crown, his strings of animal teeth, and his beaded
necklaces. Then, they carried him downriver in a canoe. On the side
opposite from Dureno, they buried him without marker or memorial.

Soon, word spread that even though Elias had killed Yori'ye, Marta
was at fault. Before she married Yori'ye, she had a reputation for
promiscuity. She did not appear satisfied in the marriage. People
said that when the group was drunk at Amisacho, Marta told Elias
she wanted to marry him. He was excited at the prospect, but Marta
said he had to kill Yori'ye first. Allegedly, Elias then crawled over to
the inebriated, sleeping Yori'ye and strangled him. Some people say

he did it by pulling hard on Yori'ye's red bandana—a particularly significant method given that the bandanas were ethnic markers for Cofán men.

No matter how it happened, Yori'ye was gone. Despite his earlier command to stay in the community, some people wanted to flee Dureno and move east, west, or north, to Colombia. They were terrified of the *cocoya* Yori'ye would become. After much discussion, people decided to stay. They began to witness troubling things. Some people said Yori'ye had proclaimed he would die and emerge as a "spear eagle." A few weeks later, they saw an eagle with a call unlike anything they had heard. It sat in a tree on the hill close to the *yaje* house. It continued to call, and people became scared; they thought it would eat their eyes when they fell asleep. It flew into the house of Atanacio, Alejandro's brother. There, people killed it with a stick. In the upriver Cofán community of Sinangoé, a shaman said he captured Yori'ye's *cocoya* in the forest and put it in a palm-wood container. When he brought the container back to the village, it was empty. Another man from Sinangoé said that Yori'ye had transformed into a "giant river otter *cocoya*" and swam to the community. He saw it in the Aguarico and cut it up with a machete. In Dureno, people killed a jaguar that came close to the village. Its left front paw was injured. It reminded them of Yori'ye's left wrist, which he had hurt in an earlier accident. One of Yori'ye's daughters approached the dead jaguar and cried, "Father, they have killed you again!"

Today, no one knows the details of how or why Yori'ye died. Some people simply say, "The oil company came and killed him with alcohol." Others claim, "Marta said to the company, 'Kill my husband, and I will go away with you,'" after which Elias did her bidding. Lucia told me that Valerio, who was present at the death, continues to tell people that Marta was the one who asked Elias to strangle Yori'ye. After Yori'ye died, Marta spent many days and nights in the camps of Texaco workers. Some say she worked as a prostitute, and others say she slept with Texaco employees simply because she desired them. On more than one occasion, the company's helicopter came to Dureno and picked her up. Months later, it returned her. She had two children by two mestizo men, neither of whom married her.

—

81

FIGURE 3.6. *Yori'ye's oldest granddaughter, Laura Mendua, with one of her own granddaughters*

To me, Marta is a tremendously tragic figure. I have a hard time believing she told anyone to kill Yori'ye. While listening to the stories, I began to suspect that her time in the company of Texaco workers was deeply traumatizing. I cannot imagine what it was like for a young, monolingual Cofán woman to have sex with dozens if not hundreds of men she did not know, in a cultural world that was completely alien to her, away from a community that had become hostile to her. Were it not for the accusations of her participation in the death of her husband, I doubt she would have gone to the Texaco camps. She now walks with a limp—the probable result of syphilis. Children approach her at parties and ask if she killed Yori'ye. She sits silently, saying nothing in response.

I am friends with Marta, and I have interviewed her multiple times. During one session, my young Cofán assistant asked her how Yori'ye died. "He got drunk and died," she replied tersely. She did admit that people allege she was the one who killed him. She looked away as she said it, laughing softly. Then, she claimed that a Colombian Cofán shaman named Tiberio gave her a different explanation. He reported that Marta's now-dead uncle, whom people called Iyo A'i (Snake Person), was the one who killed Yori'ye. Iyo A'i was a powerful shaman who lived in Colombia. If there is one thing shamans strive to do, it is attack and kill other *atesu'cho*, whom they view as their enemies. Tiberio claimed Iyo A'i was successful in his battle with Yori'ye. Marta said that when she told Tiberio that Dureno residents believed she was responsible for Yori'ye's death, he burst out laughing.

Yori'ye still appears in Dureno. Recently, a story circulated that someone saw him walking in human form on the other side of the Aguarico. There, he met a mestizo settler and asked how to get to Quito. Shortly after that, the mestizo died. People sometimes see Yori'ye in dreams or *yaje* visions. If he is angry, people believe they will soon encounter a jaguar. Alejandro told me he once saw Yori'ye in a dream after attempting to cure a child. Yori'ye was a *cocoya*. He held the girl's *canse'pa* in his arms. Alejandro convinced Yori'ye to let go of the *canse'pa* and allow the girl to live. Alejandro said that even as a *cocoya*, Yori'ye knew it was Alejandro who was trying to save the child. Because of their friendship, Yori'ye's *cocoya* cooperated and let Alejandro have his way.

People in Dureno do not drink *yaje* as much as they used to, but several Dureno men continue to cure people. Alejandro is foremost among them. His specialty is curing attacks from *aya*, *cocoya*-like beings that emerge from everyone after they die. In dreams, they look like skeletons covered with rotting flesh. In waking life, they appear as small clouds of mist or smoke. When people, and especially children, walk through them, the *aya* steal their *canse'pa*. Alejandro rubs, blows smoke on, and sucks the flesh of people afflicted by *aya*. He sees small, thornlike objects under their skin. When he falls asleep and dreams after a curing session, he confronts the *aya* and scolds and berates it. Then, he retrieves the *canse'pa*. When his attempts are successful and the children recover, their parents bring him meat and other food. Sometimes, they also pay him.

Alejandro has drunk more *yaje* than almost anyone else in Dureno. He has an ability to consume huge amounts of it, chant, stand up, and walk into the forest, where he plays his flute. He also has supernatural allies and weapons. Nonetheless, he cannot heal the attacks of many *cocoya*, and he does not have *davu*. He has tried to acquire *davu* from other shamans, but the weapons drop straight out of his body after he swallows them, no matter how well he maintains the prohibitions. Behind his back, people say that *atesu'cho* refuse to give him their *davu* even though they act like they want to teach him. Although they know Alejandro's desires are good, they believe his body is bad. No matter how crazy the idea seems to me, the shamans reportedly suspect Alejandro would go on a killing spree if he had *davu*—an outcome they hope to avoid.

Alejandro continues to cure the residents of Dureno. In his own home, he smokes, rubs, sucks, and blows over the skin of the afflicted who come to him. In the *yaje* house, he sees into people's flesh and shakes his leaf bundle over them. On most nights, he shifts and speaks in his sleep. His dreams are filled with violent encounters. He uses his spirit weapons to threaten the beings that attempt to do him, Lucia, and Roberto harm. Sometimes, he cannot defeat the aggressors himself. In dreams, he periodically encounters his now-dead teacher—Eusebio, Lucia's father—who helps him do his supernatural work. If he cannot cure a person, the patient goes to someone else, often to Alejandro's brother Fernando, who has *davu*.

Alejandro does not like to travel to Lago Agrio. He knows that Napo Runa shamans are waiting there to blow their spirit darts into him. In Dureno, he feels safer. But no one in the community maintains the prohibitions as they used to. It is hard for Alejandro to sustain his powers or acquire new ones. A few Dureno youths, including Roberto, drink *yaje*, but people doubt they will achieve much skill. Everyone is afraid of what will happen when Alejandro and Dureno's four or five other shamans die. Even though people sometimes suspect that Dureno's curers harm, they are the only ones who can save the community's children from supernatural attack.

Many Ecuadorian and foreign tourists come to Dureno to drink *yaje* with Alejandro. Most are college students, backpackers, and older people interested in New Age religion. Stories of Alejandro's abilities circulate by word of mouth and through Facebook posts.

With the aid of young bilingual Cofán men, Alejandro also travels to other parts of Ecuador, where people pay him to preside over *yaje* nights. The outsiders know little about the logic and structure of Cofán shamanism. Instead, they view Alejandro as a wise, kind, all-knowing man who will help them "commune with the universe" and "connect with the healing powers of nature." They talk about *yaje* as a "spiritual mother" and a "sacred medicine." They think drinking it is an entirely benign practice.

The visitors do not know about the prohibitions, the supernatural *a'i*, the *cocoya*, the *davu*, the game calling, the shape shifting, and the overriding sense of violence and moral ambivalence that are central aspects of Cofán shamanism. The Amazonianist ethnographer Michael Brown has described how New Age spiritualists pick and choose some aspects of shamanic practice while ignoring its "dark side."[11] Outside appropriations of Cofán shamanism are even more one-sided, as the Cofán recognize no division between evil sorcerers and wise healers. For Cofán shamans, curing and killing are deeply intertwined; to combat violence is to enact it. Westerners have a hard time acknowledging the complexity of any Cofán practice, super-natural or otherwise. They see Cofán people as symbols of either total cultural destruction, timeless cosmological benevolence, or both. Real Cofán struggles to withstand old and new forms of violence exceed most outsiders' understandings. Western stereotypes are just too powerful, and they portray people like Alejandro in superficial, problematic ways.

Alejandro, however, does not mind the ignorance of the people who travel from so far away to drink *yaje* with him. He needs their money. He also appreciates the attention and respect they give him. For so much of their history, Cofán people have been insulted, ignored, and oppressed. They find it refreshing when outsiders view them in a favorable way, even if that way is mistaken. Between tourist visits, Alejandro continues to cure and drink *yaje* with the Cofán people who know a little bit more about his skills. He is eager to do what they ask of him. Hearing that one of his curing sessions was successful makes him happier than anything else.

—

CHAPTER 4

•

THE *COCAMA* ARRIVE

O n June 8, 2013, I visited the work camp of the seismic company that had recently entered Dureno to complete a study
of the oil deposits beneath the community. Cofán people
called the company BGP, the acronym for its full name, Bureau of
Geophysical Prospecting. It is part of the China National Petroleum
Corporation, which had begun exploratory work for Ecuador's state
oil company, Petroamazonas. Alejandro had taken a job as a BGP
guard. For twenty-two days at a time, he stayed at the company's camp
and watched over its equipment while other workers cut trails and
laid cables, sensors, and explosives across Dureno's forest and rivers.

The camp sat far up the Pisorié River and away from the community's central settlement and was more or less what I expected. It
was a hectare-wide clearing in the forest with three dormitory tents,
a covered dining area, and surprisingly clean bathrooms and showers.
Huge piles of orange and yellow rubberized cables littered the ground

—

between the camp and the river. After walking around with Alejandro to take pictures, he and I returned to the dining hall as people were eating lunch. Lucia and Roberto were sitting with Cofán workers and a Cofán family from the nearby population center of Totoa Nai'qui, whose inhabitants often visited the camp for free meals.

As we chatted in A'ingae, a portly, pale-skinned worker approached us and introduced himself to me. He was a *cocama*, the word Cofán people use for nonindigenous Spanish speakers, that is, most Ecuadorian and Colombian citizens.[1] He asked how I knew A'ingae. After listening to a brief history of my involvements with the Cofán, he invited me to visit a forest plot he owned along the Colombian border. He gave a vague and confusing story about wanting me to help him figure out how to use the property for tourism or the Ecuadorian government's Socio Bosque program—two possibilities about which I knew little, as I told him. Alejandro, Lucia, and other Cofán people listened to our conversation. When he asked me to write down my name and phone number, Lucia whispered to me, "Comba, conda-jama" (Ritual brother, do not tell him). I asked him instead to write down his own information. He scrawled his name, Manuel Ochoa, and phone number in my notepad. I told him I would contact him at a later date.

Cofán people are often apprehensive around *cocama*, so Lucia's counsel did not come as a surprise. Before my visit to the camp, many Dureno residents had told me how much they feared *cocama*, especially in the past. In interviews, they shared stories of the priests and soldiers who came to their communities to steal from, capture, and kill them. Often, the *cocama* brought devastating illnesses, too. Later, the *cocama* who worked for Texaco raped Cofán women. And many Cofán people believe that the *cocama* oil worker Elias Cortez killed Yori'ye. During my first year of fieldwork on this project in 2012, four armed *cocama* men kidnapped Felipe Borman, son of Randy and grandson of Bub and Bobbie, the missionary-linguists who had worked in Dureno. Felipe, a Cofán-identifying man with a Cofán wife and child, had been serving as the coordinator of the Cofán Park Guard Program, an initiative begun by the Foundation for the Survival of the Cofán People. Some say his captors were motivated by

—

FIGURE 4.1. Cocama *life in Lago Agrio*

anger at his efforts to protect Cofán territory. Others say the primary motivation concerned his father's white skin—a sign of wealth and potentially a hefty ransom. Fortunately, Felipe escaped after forty days of captivity in Colombian forest camps. Many people thought he was already dead. He survived without a single cent going to the *cocama* who took him, but his kidnappers remain at large.

By 2013, I had heard most of the tales of *cocama* violence. Only thirteen days after I met Manuel Ochoa, however, did I begin to understand the emotional force the stories hold for Cofán people. On the morning of June 21, a young man came to Alejandro's house to talk to Lucia. I listened from my hammock. The man told Lucia that Manuel Ochoa had come to Dureno's main settlement looking for me. He asked if I was still there and in whose house I was staying. Later, at the BGP camp, he reportedly asked Cofán children where he could find me. Their mothers told them to stay quiet. One Cofán person said Manuel's voice was similar to that of a *cocama* family rumored to be involved in Felipe's kidnapping. "Maicoma indiye tsu in'jan qquen in'jan'fa," the young man concluded—"We think he wants to capture Mike."

Two other women joined the conversation. Quickly, we worked ourselves into a frenzy. Kidnapping had become a common problem in the border region. It was a reliable business for armed factions and criminal gangs, many of whom crossed into Ecuador from Colombia in search of targets. Some kidnappers sought millions of dollars in ransom; others seemed satisfied with as little as $10,000. Many who were captured survived the ordeal, but some did not. Everyone I spoke to in Dureno that morning agreed I should leave as soon as possible and return only when the seismic camp and Manuel Ochoa were gone. I called Randy, who was in Quito, and asked if we were being irrational. He said no. In times like these, he explained, you can never be too careful. I called the national airline office in Lago Agrio. All flights for that day and the next were booked. I then called a long-term contact in Lago Agrio who uses his pickup truck as a taxi. He agreed to come to Dureno and drive me to Quito. My young assistant Martin said he would join us so I did not have to travel alone. Within ten hours, we were in Ecuador's capital.

—

Over the next two weeks, I called Martin, who had returned to Dureno, and other Cofán people to inquire about the situation. We learned that the number Manuel gave me was made up. Martin took a picture of Manuel I had snapped at the camp to BGP's central offices. No one there recognized him. They looked in their database and said they had no record of anyone named Manuel Ochoa on their payroll. Clearly, the *cocama* had lied to me. A week later, Alejandro called and said a *cocama* stopped him on the street in Lago Agrio. According to Alejandro's rudimentary understanding of Spanish, the *cocama* said that the "man in the picture" was no longer a problem and that I had no reason to be afraid. Alejandro had no idea who the man was. He did not know how the man recognized him or how he knew I was staying in Alejandro's house.

Two weeks after I left Dureno, I returned. I was afraid, but I wanted to finish my research. When I arrived, BGP was gone; the seismic exploration in Dureno was done. Reportedly, Manuel had departed from the community and followed BGP to a different camp, far away. Still, I was afraid every time a non-Cofán person showed up in the community. Alejandro told me to stop sleeping alone in the old hut next to his home and to move my mosquito net to the second floor of his house. There, I could sleep next to him, Lucia, and Roberto. We installed a second latch on the house's main door. During the night, we began locking the door at the top of the stairs, too. Alejandro kept a shotgun next to him as he slept, and I placed another under my own mosquito net. A few days after I returned to Dureno, Alejandro described a dream he had. In my field notes, I wrote,

Alejandro told me about his dream last night. He said he saw a *cocama* woman sitting in Dureno. He tried to talk to her, but she would not speak to him. So he got mad and slashed her neck with his machete, killing her. Then, he knew that other *cocama* would come for him, possibly soldiers. He prepared himself in his house, where he sat with his shotgun ready, pointing at the river. He was waiting for the *cocama* to come so he could shoot them before they shot him. Eventually, they arrived. He killed them. That was the end of the dream. He smiled as he told me about it.

—

Gradually, I stopped thinking about Manuel. I convinced myself that we had overreacted and that the man had probably represented no danger. Perhaps he was more afraid of me than I was of him. The *cocama* seismic workers definitely feared Alejandro. They knew he was a shaman. When he slept next to them in the company tents, he tossed and shouted during the night, as he often does. The experience with Manuel, though, taught me something essential. Fearing the possibility of *cocama* capture helped me understand how deeply Cofán people associate the newcomers with violence and death.

The lesson reminded me of Renato Rosaldo's conclusion in his famous essay "Grief and a Headhunter's Rage."[2] Rosaldo writes that he could not understand his Ilongot collaborators' explanation of why they took their enemies' heads: that rage, born of grief, propelled them to kill. Only when his own wife fell off a cliff and died during fieldwork, Rosaldo explains, did he feel the connection between rage and grief. The visceral realization finally allowed him to comprehend the headhunters' words. Similarly, nothing prepared me to appreciate Cofán stances toward *cocama* until I felt the fear the outsiders brought to my own life. Cofán people were the ones who drew me into their anxiety and apprehension. It was them, not me, who decided that Manuel wanted to capture me. Given their history, their fear made sense.

Most outsiders assume that oil's environmental destruction is its most harmful consequence for the Cofán. Just as important as contamination and its effects, however, are the tens of thousands of *cocama* people whom the petroleum industry's roads and operations brought to Cofán territory. The settlers slashed and burned the forest, displacing the Cofán and destroying their land. They became an immediate and irremovable presence in Cofán life. The development of oil infrastructure made interactions with *cocama* an everyday, unavoidable, and permanent fact. As the *cocama* population in Cofán territory continues to swell, Cofán people try to maintain their lives alongside the newcomers. In their hearts, many Cofán individuals worry that their children will one day become *cocama*. More than anything or anyone else, the *cocama* cause the inhabitants of Dureno to question their survival as a people.

—

FIGURE 4.2. *A* cocama *working on Dureno's millennium community*

For hundreds of years, Cofán people have depended on the commodities the *cocama* introduced to them. Early on, metal tools replaced stone ones; the Cofán stopped being able to manage life without steel centuries ago. Victoria Quenamá, Lucia's aunt, was born in the 1930s. I interviewed her in 2012. Although she was hard of hearing, she was blessed with an extraordinarily vivid memory. Around the time she was born, she said, a *cocama* trader would come from Colombia to exchange goods for the gold her family panned in the Aguarico, upriver from Dureno. They stored the gold powder in the quills of curassow feathers. In exchange, the trader gave them cloth. They also gave the trader peccary hides, bundles of woven palm-fiber string, and baskets of the cottonlike substance that falls from kapok trees in the dry months. Another *cocama* trader came from the south via the Napo River. He offered the Cofán cloth and exceptionally strong blowgun poison made by downriver native people. Victoria's father gave him animal skins and large plugs of cured tobacco. Victoria also mentioned gathering the dried stems of certain palms that *cocama* craftsmen used to make brooms and baskets. For that material, she said, the traders gave them rings and beads.

In the nineteenth and twentieth centuries, a number of *cocama* traders periodically visited the Cofán. Yori'ye even had the people of Dureno construct a small sleeping hut for the itinerant merchants. In addition to cloth, beads, blowgun poison, and rings, they brought axes, machetes, knives, adzes, metal pots, plates, sewing needles, thread, clothing, matches, fishhooks, and salt. Along with the gold, palm fibers, kapok cotton, tobacco, and peccary skins, the Cofán gave the *cocama* hammocks, canoes, rubber, and skins from jaguars, ocelots, deer, and otters. Sometimes, the Cofán traveled and worked alongside *cocama* traders who oversaw their collection of forest and riverine goods.

According to my collaborators, Cofán people were relatively autonomous producers. Instead of having overseers, they mainly collected the products at their leisure and waited for *cocama* traders to come and exchange goods for them. As one of my interviewees explained, "Cofán people weren't really ordered around by *patrones*. Traders came and we gave them the gold and other goods we gathered." Whether a person was *patrón'pa* (in a *patrón's* company or possession) was a sign of ethnic difference: it was a key quality the Cofán used to distinguish the Napo Runa people who came to the Aguarico River in the first half of the twentieth century with their *cocama* bosses. In some cases, the Napo Runa ended up staying. A few learned A'ingae, married Cofán people, and became Cofán. Others maintained their separate ways; Cofán people viewed them as pseudoindigenous invaders.

Although a few *cocama* men resided for long periods on the Aguarico headwaters and employed Cofán people, the Dureno Cofán have clear memories of only one *cocama* who lived on land they regularly used. His name was Froilán Acosta. He originally came from Colombia. Alejandro said his oldest brother, Atanacio, met Froilán in the 1920s. Yori'ye knew him, too. Alejandro said Yori'ye may have even worked for him, as did a few other Cofán men. Yori'ye's Ai'pa shamanic teacher Antonio and his brother Mateo periodically lived with Froilán. The people who labored for Froilán gathered rubber and grew crops that Froilán sold downriver. People say the *cocama* married a Cofán woman and believed in the game-calling powers of the Ai'pa shamans who worked with him. His sons reportedly spoke A'ingae and wore *ondiccu'je*. Eventually, Froilán moved back to Colombia. His sons went with him and slipped back into *cocama* society.[3]

Sometimes alone and sometimes in the company of *cocama* merchants, young Cofán men traveled to *cocama* settlements to acquire commodities. Some of my Dureno collaborators visited the Colombian town of Puerto Asís. Others went to Rocafuerte, a small town where the Aguarico joins the Napo River at the Peruvian border. Some of their fathers and grandfathers traveled even farther down the Napo. A few reached the Peruvian city of Iquitos. The trips could last for months or even years. Valerio's father, Polinario, helped Froilán bring his products to market. In an interview that Bub Borman recorded long ago, Polinario, who was probably born in the 1910s, shared his story:

> I never actually reached Iquitos, but I have gone past the mouth of our [Aguarico] river five times. I wanted to get to Iquitos but

—

95

missed my chance when the steamboat never showed up. I traveled with Fabián [Froilán], a *cocama* who married a Cofán woman and lived at Benachoé. He had quite a homestead there. I'm a true Aguarico—from here, grown up here, figure on dying here—so I was living up at the Amisacho village when Fabián came to get me to go with him downriver. We were gone for at least two months. We didn't have motors then—it was all by poling. We got down into the Peruvian section, too. I got to see all of it. You should go into a store down there—wonderful guns all over!

Polinario's account reveals how comfortable Cofán people could feel in the company of the *cocama* they knew best. The *cocama* individuals who became closest to them, such as Froilán, half-entered the Cofán way of life. To consider a *cocama* a dependable and trustworthy friend, though, was rare. The arrival of any unknown *cocama* caused fear. As one Dureno woman put it, "In the old times, when a *cocama* arrived, there was no happiness. We truly hated them. We were afraid of them. We never approached them." Most Cofán people say they desired to remain distant from *cocama* for two reasons: *fi'tti'sane* (to avoid being killed) and *indi'sane* (to avoid being captured). For centuries, Cofán people had learned to fear *cocama* because of the epidemics they brought and the violent acts they committed.

In the mid-twentieth century, as soon as they heard a motorized canoe approaching, most Cofán people fled into the forest. When it was clear that the *cocama* were not hostile, people returned. But they counseled their children not to shake the outsiders' hands as their canoes came to shore; the Cofán feared that the *cocama* would grab the children, pull them into their boats, and steal them. Later, during Texaco's exploratory phase, the people of Dureno ran into the forest when helicopters approached. Rumors circulated that the giant nets the helicopters used to carry equipment and supplies were also meant to capture people. Even as the Cofán learned to be less apprehensive around *cocama*, the fact that they could not speak Spanish meant that Dureno's inhabitants felt deeply uneasy in the outsiders' presence.

When *cocama* visited Cofán communities or Cofán people traveled to *cocama* towns and missions, epidemics often broke out. The residents of Dureno tell vivid stories of the illnesses that ravaged their ancestors—smallpox, measles, tuberculosis, whooping cough, cholera, chicken pox, malaria, and influenza. They know they have always suffered from fevers, headaches, and diarrhea, which they consider their own illnesses. They say the familiar ailments usually respond to treatment with plants and shamanism. All other sicknesses, though, are "of the *cocama*." Historically, Cofán people had little immunity to them; the most virulent viruses and bacteria could empty a village of its inhabitants in a matter of weeks or months. Some of my collaborators survived bouts with the illnesses; all have relatives who died of them. Many if not most Dureno residents were suffering with tuberculosis when the Bormans arrived in the 1950s. During that time, many people fled the village when an individual appeared to be coming down with an illness.

Alejandro shared a story about a downriver community where measles broke out. Before people could escape, it struck and killed everyone. The dogs ate their former owners' corpses that littered the ground. A Capuchin priest arrived and was horrified at the sight. He shot the dogs out of rage. Although the Dureno Cofán no longer suffer from such epidemics, colds and flus still pass through with alarming frequency. People always guess at their origin as an individual who recently returned from a *cocama* town or an outsider who recently visited Dureno.

Priests have been coming to northeastern Ecuador to round up, convert, and ostensibly civilize the Cofán since the arrival of the Spanish in the 1500s. First came the Jesuits. Later, others arrived, Franciscans, Capuchins, Josephines, and Carmelites. The people of Dureno speak mostly of the Capuchins whom their parents and grandparents encountered. Coming mainly from Colombia, the Capuchins entered the area in the late 1800s. They tried to concentrate the Cofán at a mission on the San Miguel River in 1914. The effort fell apart nine years later due to a massive measles outbreak. The Capuchins also established residential sites at Santa Cecilia and the mouth of the Dureno River. At the latter, they built a school in the 1910s and, often accompanied by soldiers, tried to "enroll" as many Cofán students as they could find. Parents relented under the threat of force. Alejandro's

FIGURE 4.3. *A cocama homestead and pasture near Dureno*

mother entered the school, as did Yori'ye and a few other relatives of my collaborators. As recorded by Bub Borman, Valerio's father, Polinario, described the site:

> In the days when there was a school here at the mouth of the Dureno River, I was barely more than a toddler. At that age, the priest called me and sat me down and told me to recite. I just broke down and cried, but he laughed and gave me some candy to calm me down. The school was right across the river from here. They'd ring a bell at dawn to gather the students. Marino and all the older kids were in school. I was the only one too young to go. They say I was too scared; that's why I never really learned to speak Spanish. All that *cocama* activity here—completely gone without a trace. The priests came, complete with horses and all. Where they went, I don't know. I was expecting this area to become quite a town, but it all disappeared. I never went over the trail. The *cocama* used it all the time. My father used to go over it with the old Napo Runa people. The trail used to come out on the San Miguel at the place they call Tutuyé [a mission site].

Most Cofán people who entered the Dureno school or other Capuchin sites described them with hatred. The priests berated and beat the students and made them labor on the mission grounds. They were also the reason measles killed so many Cofán people. The Capuchins tried to bring the Aguarico Cofán from the Dureno site to the San Miguel mission. As Alejandro's brother Fernando told me, Cofán leaders refused. The Capuchins told them Ecuadorian *patrones* would arrive and make them work hard for little pay. A leader named Ccareshe said that if any *cocama* bosses tried to mistreat his people, especially the women, "he would spear them as if they were tapirs," Fernando recounted. Ccareshe, like Yori'ye, was a *na'su* known for his fearlessness and violent temperament. Only the aggression of sha-manically empowered leaders could counter the force of the priests and soldiers. A Dureno man told me that when a Capuchin grabbed Yori'ye's ear to make him listen to him, Yori'ye was enraged and did the same thing to the priest. Yori'ye's cousin Gregorio reportedly beat a priest who had angered him.

A quasimythical story I heard many times describes how a group of Capuchin priests came from Colombia and ordered the Cofán to build a giant church with strong walls. The priests then called the Cofán inside, supposedly for a mass. After the Cofán entered, the priests barred the door, took out their machetes, and slaughtered everyone. In some versions of the tale, one or two Cofán individuals escaped. In my first book, I provide a detailed translation of the story as told by Atanacio, Alejandro's oldest brother.[4] According to Atanacio's telling, the Capuchins and the soldiers who accompanied them massacred the Cofán multiple times and stole the Cofán's "little god," a shamanlike being that protected the Cofán from illness and *cocoya*. Atanacio said that because the *cocama* still have the Cofán's little god, their own population grows as the Cofán become sicker and weaker. A middle-age Dureno woman shared a similar version of the story. In her telling, the priests stole the Cofán's golden bell. The bell, like the little god, was a boon to the Cofán nation. When people rang it, pregnant women's babies dropped straight from their wombs, quickly and painlessly.

Cofán people hated the priests for their insults, beatings, and commands and the sicknesses they brought. The story of the priests who trapped and killed the Cofán condenses centuries of fear, hostility, and depredation into one narrative.[5] Although soldiers sometimes accompanied the priests, they arrived on their own as well. When they approached in their canoes, people fled. The soldiers were known as *indipa angaqque'su* (beings that capture and carry away). Historically, they forced Cofán people to come to their camps and work in their compounds. They coerced people into laboring as porters and boatmen, too. In many stories, they caught and raped Cofán women. Multiple people told me that after waves of *cocama* colonists began to arrive in the 1970s, the Cofán were too afraid to reside on land next to roads—even though they had legal rights to it—because soldiers would be able to harass and capture them so easily. Consequently, the Cofán lost the territory to *cocama* usurpers.

When Royal Dutch Shell arrived to explore the Aguarico region for oil in the 1940s, at least four Dureno men decided to work for them. Shell's employees were neither priests nor soldiers. Some were an unfamiliar kind of human: Euro-Americans, whom the Cofán, following local usage, called "gringo." The gringo seemed friendly, but people soon suspected them of cannibalism. The canned food they brought looked like nothing the Cofán had eaten. Their giant barrels of cooking oil raised concerns, too. "Might the unrecognizable meat and fat come from human bodies?" people asked each other. Despite their trepidation, the men's desire for commodities motivated some to accept jobs as boatmen and seismic-trail cutters.

Shell's main camp was far downriver. There, the company's amphibious Grumman Goose airplane landed on the Aguarico. It was the first plane the Cofán had seen. The people who worked for Shell returned with wondrous tales of the machine. It was also the first time they saw rubber boots. Deji's father, Enrique, who worked for Shell, came back to Dureno and tried to tie leaves and vines to his feet to copy the boots' function. It was a humorous failure that people repeatedly teased him about.

Shell was on the Aguarico for only a few years, and it left without extracting any oil. Cofán people have no bad memories of it; apparently, it paid its workers well. The Cofán had little idea what Shell was doing. People were still unfamiliar with the substance known as *petróleo*. Fernando said they thought Shell was blowing holes in the ground to find *Chiga ttevaen'jen*, "the writings of God"—an A'ingae phrase for the Bible, which was the only paper many of them had seen. Randy Borman told me that when his father arrived in the 1950s, a Cofán man showed him a few tattered pieces of Shell's seismic readouts printed on blue paper. Somehow the man acquired them from a Shell employee. The man told Bub that Shell found the papers underground, where company employees said they were looking for something else, too.

From the mid-1940s to the late 1960s, few *cocama* came to Dureno. There were occasional visits from river traders and priests. By the 1940s, the priests were Josephines. They seemed peaceful, and they made no attempts to build missions or schools. Everything started to change in 1964. That year, Texaco began its campaign of seismic exploration on Cofán land. It contracted a company named Geodetic Survey Incorporated (GSI) to do its testing. Texaco and GSI built a base camp at Santa Cecilia, the site Cofán people occupied before coming to Dureno. Santa Cecilia was near the center of Texaco's planned operations, and it allowed access to the Aguarico and San Miguel Rivers by a portage trail. In short order, the *cocama* workers carved a huge space out of the forest. They built a concrete runway big enough to handle DC-4s and DC-6s. The planes began a near-continuous round of flights between Santa Cecilia and Quito, where they loaded up with seismic equipment, supplies, and everything else Texaco needed in its search for oil. The planes even brought in tractors and trucks; they were the first automobiles most Cofán people had seen.

In a matter of months, teams of *cocama* workers, alongside some Napo Runa men, spread across Cofán territory to clear land for seismic trails. They moved by motorized canoe and helicopter. The first step was to build forest camps at which the workers could eat and sleep during each phase of trail cutting. Every day, they departed from the camps and used axes and compasses to cut three-meter-wide trails through the forest. They chopped down everything in their path. It was hard, sweaty, exhausting work. While the workers were out, a camp cook prepared meals for them. Sometimes, one or two non-Cofán people were hired to hunt game to feed the workers. After the teams cut a few kilometers of trails, they moved to the next camp, out of which they based the following leg of work, which might last weeks or months. At the end of it all, the workers had built a grid of compass-straight, intersecting trails across the forest.

During the next phase, another team came through with small drilling rigs they used to punch holes at regular intervals. On the initial round of seismic testing, the trails overlapped every 250 meters. On later rounds and in special locations, trails could cross as close as every 75 meters. After the drilling team dug holes, other workers came through to lay cables along the paths, put sensors in the ground, and drop packets of explosives into each hole, with the detonating wire attached. When the trails were cut, the cables were laid, and the sensors were arranged, GSI detonated the explosives in specific patterns and studied the ensuing seismic waves. The results told them where oil deposits might be located.

Within two years, Texaco was drilling exploratory wells at sites it detected during its seismic campaign. Its first exploratory well was at Lago Agrio in 1967. The exploratory wells closest to Dureno were at Parahuacu and Atacapi in 1968 and Dureno in 1969.[6] The Lago Agrio well was drilled about four kilometers inland from the Aguarico and the historical Cofán village of Amisacho. The Parahuacu well was drilled directly across the river from Dureno and a kilometer or two into the forest. The one at Atacapi was on a tributary of the Dureno River. The Dureno well was upriver from the Dureno village, just inside the community's current western boundary next to a tributary of the Pisorié River. Texaco constructed the wells next to streams into which it could dump the drilling muds used to pressurize, lubricate, and cool wells, along with other waste by-products of the exploration process. Cofán people used the streams for hunting, fishing, and drinking. All of the waterways emptied into the Aguarico.

Texaco used helicopters to haul the necessary materials and equipment from Santa Cecilia and later Lago Agrio. The workers bulldozed large clearings in the forest for drilling rigs. They constructed houses and landing strips for small airplanes that took over much of the transport work from the helicopters after the initial construction. The exploratory wells were often deep in the forest and away from human settlements. Cofán people did not immediately detect them. Only after they heard noise from helicopters, tractors, or drilling towers or saw spilled oil in nearby waterways did they walk to the wells to see what was happening. After the drillers hit a petroleum reserve—an event that could send thousands of barrels of oil spewing into the forest—workers capped the wells and waited for roads and pipelines to be built. For some wells, it was ten years or more before the oil made it offsite.

The exploratory wells that Texaco drilled near Dureno were productive. With the sites proven, Texaco began to construct roads, pipelines, and other processing facilities such as separation stations to remove water from crude. By 1972, Texaco completed construction

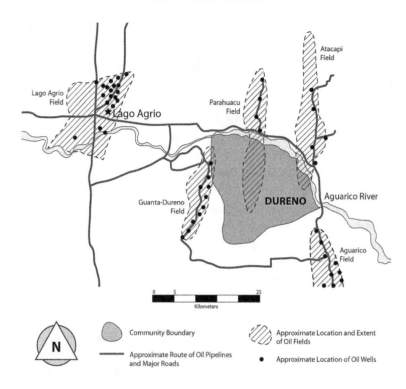

MAP 4.1. *Present-day petroleum infrastructure around Dureno.*
Map by Leah McCurdy.

of the trans-Ecuadorian pipeline, which brought Amazonian oil over the Andes to a refinery and export facility on the Pacific coast. Oil from Cofán territory began reaching world markets.

In 1972, Texaco finished the road from Quito to Lago Agrio. Over the next decade, the road system continued to expand through Cofán territory as Texaco built more wells and put them into production. By 1974, the road extended east from Lago Agrio and across the Aguarico from Dureno. By the end of the decade, Texaco had expanded roads, wells, and pipelines to the south and west of Dureno. The Guanta-Dureno field, including the Dureno exploratory well, did not go into production until the 1980s. At that point, the petroleum infrastructure had completely walled in the community.

——

By 1972, Lago Agrio had replaced Santa Cecilia as Texaco's base of operations. There were company buildings, equipment, workers, stores, and prostitutes. There was also a landing strip that could accommodate larger planes. Lago Agrio was quickly becoming a city. Initially, Lago Agrio's official name was Nueva Loja. Everyone called it Lago Agrio, though—"Sour Lake," the name of the Texas town where Texaco struck oil in 1903.

As the road system was constructed, Texaco built the majority of its production wells. When they began to produce, the exploratory wells were typically numbered "1" (e.g., Parahuacu 1). Every production well in the same field became a later number (Parahuacu 2, and so forth). Next to the wells, Texaco dug pits where, without lining them, it dumped drilling muds and chemicals, excess crude, and formation water, a brackish liquid that mixes with oil underground and is extracted with crude. All of the substances were toxic. When it rained, the pits overflowed and the wastes poured into streams and rivers. Slowly, the wastes sank into the groundwater as well. Texaco also spread sludge from the pits onto the region's gravel roads.[7] The roads became dusty under the tropical sun, and the tarlike waste material helped keep the dust down. Unfortunately, it also was a key form of contamination for local people who walked on the roads in bare feet.

Texaco built flares to burn off the natural gas that emerged with the crude. The flares burned twenty-four hours a day, sending smoke into the sky, killing insects and birds, and drying out nearby vegetation. Workers sometimes set fire to the waste pits to burn off waste oil and other flammable liquids. Huge plumes of thick smoke rose and mixed with the clouds. From miles away, people saw the ominous black pillars. Occasionally, workers also burned crude that spilled from broken pipelines, leaking tanks, or damaged valves. It was the cheapest and easiest way to dispose of it.

Initially, the underground pressure was enough to get the oil to the surface. By the mid-1980s, the pressure was decreasing, so Texaco built a pumping system to help move the crude out of the ground. By 1990, Texaco and other oil companies were injecting water into wells to help raise the oil.

Within months of their construction, the roads ushered in a stream of *cocama* settlers. Most were poor Ecuadorians from crowded Andean and coastal provinces. Some moved to Amazonian Ecuador spontaneously, and others were part of government colonization programs. They occupied any territory to which the roads provided access. They built houses and planted coffee crops and cattle pasture. Shortly after the road passed Dureno to the north, the Cofán abandoned their homes and fields on that side of the Aguarico. They were too afraid to live next to the *cocama*. The outsiders took Cofán land without warning or permission.

During each phase of oil's transformation of northeastern Ecuador—seismic testing, exploratory drilling, road building, pipeline construction, petroleum extraction, and *cocama* colonization—the Cofán watched and wondered about the consequences of it all. Sometimes the activities seemed distant from their everyday lives, and sometimes they reached the center of the community. At least four rounds of seismic testing passed through Dureno. During the first round, in the 1960s, Texaco's contractor GSI built a work camp in Dureno's central settlement. In a day or two, the helicopters came and the workers erected their sleeping tents and dining hall. Approximately thirty *cocama* lived in Dureno for a month. As far as anyone remembers, they paid the community nothing. Cofán people never told them to stop what they were doing. It was all so new, and the workers were much friendlier than many other *cocama*. They shared their food and liquor, played their music, and drank the manioc beer people offered them. Even after the workers moved to another camp, they regularly returned to Dureno for rest and relaxation.

Despite their lingering fears, Cofán people visited the *cocama* at camps and exploratory wells outside the community. The workers maintained their friendly ways. They gave people food, including cooked rice and meat as well as bags of dried rice, sugar, and other goods. Some Cofán people learned to exchange game, plantains, and manioc for *cocama* food. The workers gave one Cofán group metal rings from a drilling rig to use as bells. When a few Cofán individuals visited the Dureno exploratory well, the workers gave them four spoons; people joke that the spoons were Texaco's reciprocity for the

FIGURE 4.4. *A road into the Guanta-Dureno oil field west of Dureno*

millions of barrels of oil it would extract from Cofán territory. On that visit, the workers also gave the Cofán a bag of doughnuts. Even after the exploratory wells went into production and most of the workers left, some Cofán people continued to walk to the sites. The workers had spit watermelon and papaya seeds next to the wells. The fruits grew in abundance at the sites, and Cofán people collected and ate them. Given their proximity to the wells and waste pits, the fruits might have carried contamination in their flesh.

The most overtly violent story from Texaco's early years involves Yori'ye. Supposedly, a *cocama* worker asked Yori'ye if he could have one of his *yaje* or *yoco* gourds. Yori'ye said yes, but he wanted the *cocama* to pay him. The *cocama*, however, took the gourd without giving anything in return. Shortly thereafter, two canoes filled with *cocama* workers capsized in the Aguarico; almost all of them died. People say Yori'ye transformed into an anaconda and pushed the canoes over. The *cocama*'s theft enraged him, and the *atesu'cho* allegedly responded as *atesu'cho* do—with excessive, unrestrained violence.

As my conversations with Dureno residents progressed and we began to feel more comfortable with each other, my collaborators revealed another aspect of their early experiences with Texaco. People smiled as they talked about the workers' food, music, and entertaining ways. Throughout their stay, however, the *cocama*—who were nearly all men—did their best to have sex with Cofán women, whether single or married, and even girls as young as eleven or twelve. In most of the accounts, it is impossible to understand the balance of consent and force at play. Many of the women were drunk. A few men told me they heard women scream after *cocama* led them into the forest. They said such episodes were truly cases in which the workers *indipa da'ñon* (captured and damaged) or *violaron* (violated or raped, in Spanish) the women. Cofán men were angry when they learned of the events, but they were afraid, too. To the best of my knowledge, they never intervened. After Yori'ye died in 1966, few Cofán people possessed the aggressiveness and courage to confront the *cocama* directly. Old fears lingered.

There are stories of Texaco workers who tried to pull Cofán women into their canoes when they encountered them outside the central settlement. In the versions I heard, the women escaped. Surely, there are many more stories people have not told me. My female collaborators did not speak of the assaults during formal interviews; only men did, although Lucia and a few other female confidants provided confirmation during informal conversations. Although I knew that some women had children by *cocama* oil workers, I did not want them to feel obligated to discuss the matter when they spoke to me. For their part, most men acknowledged that *cocama* sometimes used force in their relations with women. The men said some women desired and possibly initiated sex with *cocama*—an explanation of the acts that might function as a coping mechanism for men who failed to prevent or stop the violence. Some *cocama* gave the women goods and money after they slept with them. It is possible that a few women wanted sex with *cocama* as an end in itself.

Although I can say with certainty that rapes occurred, I believe it is both improper and impossible for me to make an authoritative declaration on the true nature of most sexual encounters. Alejandro's nephew Rufino summarized the events with a simple comment on their generational legacy: "Now, there are few true Cofán here. These are children of *cocama*, black people, Napo Runa, and Shuar.[8] Cofán children haven't been reproducing here. The *cocama* came, and that's what these children are."

The arrival of the Texaco workers was a mystery and a novelty. People did not know what the outcomes of the company's operations would be. The seismic explosions terrified them. The ground shook, and people feared game animals would flee and never return. After exploration was over, people used the seismic trails for hunting. They collected the cables to make fishing leaders, clotheslines, and baskets. A few even pulled the explosives out of the ground before they were detonated. *Cocama* traders had taught them that dynamite could be used to catch fish. They affixed a wick to the dynamite, lit it, threw it in the river, and waited for it to go off, after which hundreds of dead and stunned fish floated to the surface. A few brave Cofán men figured out how to do the same thing with GSI's explosives.

The wells were loud and smelly, and they clearly polluted streams, rivers, soil, and air. But people did not know what the contamination

—

FIGURE 4.5. *A road and oil pipelines east of Dureno*

would do to fish, other animals, or themselves. People even saw the roads in a partially positive light. The *cocama* told the Cofán they would no longer have to work so hard to pole their canoes to Santa Cecilia and Lago Agrio to buy commodities; they could hop on buses and arrive in the towns in no time and even travel to Quito if they wanted. Also, the *cocama* said roads would make goods cheaper and more plentiful.

In hindsight, it is important to remember that the workers did not arrive en masse with a giant banner that read "TEXACO" over their heads. The Cofán did not understand the structure or power of multinational corporations. The workers were just individuals, many of whom acted in a friendly manner. They came and went. People did not know how long they would stay, what they would do to the environment, or that *cocama* settlers would follow the roads, take over Cofán land, and never leave. In the words of Emeregildo, my assistant Martin's father,

In the old times, we didn't know that the company would come, drill the holes, and take out the petroleum. We just thought, "Hmmm, are those some *cocama* workers who are passing through, making paths?" That's all we thought. And when Texaco came and actually made their wells, we didn't think they had come to damage our land. We did see the oil. It was all over the river. But we didn't think to try to stop it. We didn't know how. It didn't occur to us. We also didn't know that, later on, we would all get sick because of it. We even walked all over the contamination, on the roads.

Although they had suffered many incursions throughout their history, the Cofán had a hard time believing the oil workers would permanently transform their lands and lives. Could the company really build a road all the way from Quito to Dureno? Impossible, most people thought. Would *cocama* really arrive and build farms, pastures, and towns deep in the forest, away from the Aguarico? Not a chance, the Cofán told each other. Deji explained, "We Cofán said to each other, 'No way, they will never arrive and work in the middle of the forest. How could they?' Our *na'su*, Yori'ye, said that you can't go deep into the forest and live there. You'll die. There are too many *cocoya*. There are so many bad things there—how could anyone do it? That's what we thought."

During an interview in Quito in 2014, Randy Borman, who spent much of his early life in Dureno, explained Cofán people's passive acceptance of *cocama* colonization in two ways. First, he said, many outsiders had come to Cofán territory over five centuries, but they all eventually left. There were soldiers, gold miners, priests, rubber collectors, and many others. They worked on their projects, transformed the land, and moved on. A few years later, there was little trace of their activities. When the settlers arrived in the 1970s, no one believed they would stay forever.

Second, Randy explained that the Cofán concept of property is completely different from the *cocama* concept, although they seem superficially similar. Cofán people hold that if a person builds a house or garden on a piece of land, that land is theirs as long as they work it. After a person stops devoting labor to it, anyone can use it. The

—

113

idea of a person coming and claiming permanent ownership of the land itself as well as the ability to sell it was completely alien. How could anyone own land per se? No one made the land. It would be like owning air or rain. Added to the second point was the novelty of the idea that even if a person resided on and worked a piece of forest, others would not be able to use it for hunting, fishing, gathering, and temporary residence. The Ai'pa people who lived downriver from the Cofán always allowed Cofán families to subsist alongside them, and the Cofán reciprocated. It was simply what one did. Apart from the crops one planted or the house one constructed, the resources were for everyone. Prevent someone from using the rivers and forests, even if we use them, too? That was one more impossible thought.

Because the Cofán's understanding of the nature and conse- quences of colonization was so murky and because they continued to remain fearful of *cocama*, acquiring a land title was a challenge. Three Dureno residents were key to the effort: Yori'ye's son Aurelio, Deji, and Deji's half-brother Silvio Chapal. Although he spoke no Spanish, Aurelio had some leadership status, given his father's posi- tion. Deji and Silvio were naturally bright people who spoke some Spanish and had participated in an SIL teacher-training course. Most of my Dureno collaborators said that the first person to urge them to obtain a land title was Bub Borman. In the late 1960s and early 1970s, Bub repeatedly explained that the *cocama* would come, steal Cofán land, and never give it back. At Bub's urging, the Cofán cleared two small paths from the Aguarico River to the Pisorié River to claim their territory.

In 1974, just as Texaco was constructing the road on the other side of the Aguarico, Aurelio, Deji, and Silvio traveled to Quito with Bub and William Eddy, an SIL public relations officer. Bub and William arranged a meeting with a representative of Ecuadorian President Guillermo Rodríguez Lara to discuss the Cofán land claim. Amaz- ingly, Deji and Silvio told me, the *cocama* official looked at their hand-drawn map and said the land they wanted was far too small for their needs. With the authority of Rodríguez Lara, the representative extended Dureno's legal claim west to the Cujavoé River, south to the Eno River, east to the Tururu River, and north to the new road. Deji said the revised claim was approximately forty thousand hectares. The president's office promised it would immediately send employees from the Ecuadorian Institute of Agrarian Reform and Colonization to mark the community's limits.

With the president's authorization in hand, the Cofán returned to Dureno. Deji and Randy hung hand-painted signs along the road signaling the Cofán claim. By the time the boundary-marking team arrived, however, the majority of Dureno residents had decided that the land Rodríguez Lara ceded to them was too large; they thought they would never be able to use it all. Moreover, the idea of inhabiting forest so far inland from the Aguarico seemed impossible, even scary. They long believed the forest interior was the abode of *cocoya*. Also, protecting land on the north side of the Aguarico was a daunting prospect. The likely confrontations with *cocama* terrified the Cofán. Consequently, they decided to restrict their territory to the south side of the Aguarico. There are even rumors that a few Cofán people covertly tore down the signs Deji and Randy had hung for fear that they would anger *cocama*.

At the end of the process, the Cofán had cut and marked boundary trails from the mouth of the Tutuyé River on the west to the mouth of the Pisorié River on the east and south past the Pisorié's main branch. The resulting territory was less than ten thousand hectares—far smaller than the allotment the president had designated for them. The government officially recognized their reduced territory in 1978. In 1981, it granted the community full legal personhood as a *comuna*, with land held in common by its members.

By the end of the 1970s, the Dureno Cofán's mode of living had become what it is now; community members focused their subsistence activities on their small island of forest, bounded by roads, pipelines, and the Aguarico River. A few Cofán people continued to fish and hunt outside their demarcated territory. Their way of using the forest, however, was different. Even the most confident hunters learned to walk in a cautious, fearful manner. After repeated run-ins with irate *cocama* landowners, most men stopped hunting on their old lands altogether. When I asked Alejandro where he hunts now, he replied, "Now, I don't travel anywhere to hunt. I just hunt on our *comuna*, this little piece of land we have. That's it. I don't hunt on the other side of the Aguarico. I'm afraid, afraid that a *cocama* will kill me."

Many men and women told me about *cocama* settlers who threatened to kill them when they found the Cofán hunting on "their land." Alejandro shared three stories. The first was a secondhand report from Enrique, Deji's father. Enrique and Deji went past the community's downriver boundary to hunt. They passed two *cocama* settlers in the forest. The *cocama* asked what they were doing. Deji replied that they were hunting monkeys, which most *cocama* refuse to eat. After the encounter, they became careful as they searched for game. When they looped back toward their canoe, they saw the *cocama* sitting in trees, with their rifles pointed toward the ground. The *cocama* were waiting to kill them, Enrique said. He and his son turned back, took another route, and made it home without injury.

In the second story, Alejandro went hunting with his brother Fernando on the other side of the Aguarico, near the mouth of the Dureno River. Suddenly, they heard a *cocama* shout from his farm and send his dogs into the forest. Alejandro and Fernando hid behind trees and kept their shotguns ready. The *cocama* came crashing toward them, swinging his machete and telling the "thieves" to get off his land. One of his dogs found Alejandro. Alejandro grabbed a stone and threw it at the dog's head, killing it. Alejandro said he would have shot the *cocama* if the *cocama* had found him; luckily, he did not.

In the third story, Alejandro and his friend Arturo were hunting paca on the other side of the Aguarico. Once again, a *cocama* heard them and came screaming. Alejandro hid behind a tree. Arturo showed himself, smiled, and yelled "Hola, compadre!" in a friendly tone. Arturo's peaceful gesture only infuriated the *cocama*, who rushed at him with his machete raised. Then the *cocama* saw Alejandro behind the tree with his shotgun. The *cocama* lowered his machete and stopped, but he told Alejandro and Arturo to leave. He said too many people were stealing his chickens. Later, Alejandro and Arturo found a headless chicken on the land. It was clearly killed by an ocelot. Laughing, Alejandro told me they took it home and ate it.

There are dozens of similar stories. One or two Cofán people have

---

friendly relations with *cocama* landowners. A few of them allow the Cofán to hunt less-preferred species such as primates on the forest fragments next to their farms. Other Cofán people have learned the habits and movements of *cocama*. One Dureno family hunts on a certain *cocama*'s land only on Sunday mornings, when the *cocama* is in church. For the most part, the people of Dureno stick to their own territory. The risks of being killed are simply too great. Also, shooting an aggressive *cocama* in self-defense would probably lead to a prison sentence.

Although much of the forest in *cocama* hands is ecologically degraded, the environmental destruction is only part of the story. Just as important are the tense social relations that now restrict the Cofán's use of their homeland. To add insult to injury—or, to heap injury upon injury—some *cocama* now sneak into the south side of Dureno's demarcated territory to hunt. They have depleted the game near their farms, so they kill paca, peccary, and deer on Cofán land. They eat the meat or sell it in Lago Agrio. Cofán people who live near the community boundaries hear the *cocama*'s shots throughout the day and night.

The Cofán have long known that *cocama* men desire Cofán women. During the 1970s, they also learned that some *cocama* would like to marry Cofán women and move onto Dureno land to clear forest for farms and pastures. After all, not all *cocama* have their own lands; many are poor, and the second and third generations of the original settlers now populate northeastern Ecuador. *Cocama* men married some of Aurelio Quenamá's daughters and moved to Totoa Nai'qui. By 1980, however, the Cofán decided to stop *cocama* from entering their community and becoming *comuneros* (legal *comuna* members). They created a rule that prohibited Cofán people from remaining in Dureno if they married *cocama*.

Any Cofán individual from any Cofán community is free to marry a Dureno resident and live in the community. Siona and Secoya people can marry in, too, as long as they undergo an observation period without disrupting community norms. There is much greater reluctance to allow in Napo Runa people, who continue to arrive from their overcrowded homeland south of the Aguarico. According to my

—

collaborators, the Napo Runa are too similar to *cocama* to make good neighbors or family members.

The people of Dureno do not want *cocama* marrying their children or living in their community for many reasons. First and foremost, they consider *cocama* to be thieves and killers. When I asked Lucia whether she was more content in the old times or contemporary times, she replied, "The way we live now is really bad. We're fearful, and there is no calmness. We worry that the *cocama*, all of those thieves, will come here. If you walk around in Lago Agrio, they'll grab you and kill you. They want your money. That's what we're afraid of now. In the old times, it wasn't like that." When I asked a young man the same question, he said, "I think our old-time lifestyle was much more calm and satisfying. We just lived among ourselves. There were no *cocama* near us. We didn't worry about them coming, harming us, and stealing from us. When it was just us Cofán, we lived well." For most Dureno residents, living with *cocama* means more fear, more theft, more fighting, and more killing—things no one wants.

The Dureno Cofán have also decided to prohibit *cocama* from marrying into their community because of how the outsiders use the forest. No matter how much Cofán subsistence has changed—with more wage labor, more market engagement, and less hunting, fishing, and gardening—Dureno residents continue to view themselves as people who depend upon the forest rather than destroy it. *Cocama*, in contrast, are people who radically transform the environment and eat purchased food three times a day every day. They live with and for money. They criticize the Cofán for being poor and lazy. If *cocama* men were to marry Cofán women and move to Dureno, people believe they would cut down too much forest. The few *cocama* who married Aurelio's daughters planted huge fields of corn, coffee, and cacao.[9]

When I asked whether the Cofán and the *cocama* are the same, Silvio, one of the three Cofán men who worked to secure Dureno's land title, responded,

> *Cocama* want to finish off all the forest. They do that so they can plant their pasture, put cattle on it, and sell the cattle. Doing that, they make money so they can buy food and live. We Cofán are not

like that. We want the forest to exist. It's where we have our meat, our medicine, and our fruit. We don't cut it down. But the *cocama* insult us and call us *vago* [lazy, in Spanish]. "Why don't you work? You have good land, but you don't do anything with it." That's how they speak badly about us. But that's just the way we are. We don't cut down the forest and raise all sorts of animals on it. That's not who we are. We just plant a little banana, plantain, manioc, and corn. We don't do *negocio* [business, in Spanish] with it. We just live with it. We eat with it.

There are other reasons Cofán people do not want to live with *cocama*. For decades, *cocama* openly insulted the people of Dureno. They called the men "women" when they saw them in their long *ondiccu'je*. They told both men and women that their nose feathers made them look like elephants. They said the Cofán were nothing more than poor, dirty, uneducated *indios* (Indians, in Spanish), a term the Cofán hate. The *cocama* have a reputation for infidelity and "throwing women away," even after they get them pregnant and marry them. Many people think the outsiders are far more selfish than the Cofán. In the upriver community of Sinangoé, where there is more intermarriage, the *cocama* reportedly do not go to community meetings, help on community work projects, or share their meat and labor with neighbors. They are not *ñotssi a'i* (good people), most Dureno residents say. Finally, some Cofán people claim that they simply do not want the community to become "less Cofán." If outsiders were to marry in, the markedly Cofán last names—Quenamá, Mendua, Criollo, Lucitante, Queta, and Omenda—would become less common.[10] And even though they already have fairly mixed genealogies, many individuals do not want Cofán faces and bodies to look even more like *cocama* faces and bodies. Some of them have a hard time differentiating each other from the other people of eastern Ecuador. The changing appearances make many elders, including Alejandro, sad.

When I wrote this chapter in 2016, Roberto was fourteen, just a few years before he would begin to think about marriage. He already claimed to have an *a'mbian'cho* ("possessed one," girlfriend).

Alejandro, Lucia, and I have continued to talk about whom Roberto might marry and what he might do in the future. As his ritual father, I am expected to offer him advice and support. Alejandro and Lucia want Roberto to marry a Cofán girl. If he were to marry a *cocama*, they say, he would have to leave Dureno. Also, they remember Yori'ye's counsel. Alejandro explained, "Yori'ye said it's bad to give your child to a *cocama* to marry. Their blood is bad. Yori'ye said that if you marry a *cocama*, Chiga [God, also an old word for the sun] will burn you. You won't go to Chiga when you die. Instead, you'll become a mule. That's what the old-time people said."

Apart from the quasi-Christian eschatological fears, most Dureno parents share Alejandro's and Lucia's sentiments. They want their kids to marry other Cofán people and stay in Dureno. Given their lack of fluency in Spanish, many Dureno residents would not feel comfortable speaking to *cocama* in-laws. In addition, they would not know what to feed them or how to interact with them. Finally, they would not want to be the object of constant *cocama* observation and judgment. Many Cofán people do not enjoy spending long periods of time with the settlers.

I have no idea what Roberto will become. A few years ago, he seemed especially rebellious. He constantly used A'ingae's command suffix (*-ja*) to give orders to Lucia. It seemed disrespectful, and it annoyed and worried me. Now, he appears to have calmed down. He loves to hunt and fish, and he has begun to experiment with *yaje*. Like many Dureno youths, he also plays soccer, watches martial arts movies, listens to *cocama* music, and wears *cocama* clothes. His favorite songs are in the bachata style that originated in the Dominican Republic but is now popular across Latin America. He also listens to the Andean-influenced music that many Amazonian peoples, including the Cofán, produce in their own languages. A few years ago, I gave him an iPod. My earlier gifts included a BB gun, a tent, binoculars, a fishing pole, and a portable, battery-powered DVD player. Like all Dureno youths, Roberto continues to use A'ingae as his primary language, although his Spanish is improving. Unlike a few young people in the community, he shows no hesitation to speak A'ingae or wear his *ondiccu'je* in Lago Agrio.

FIGURE 4.6. *Roberto harvesting plantains*

When Roberto finished primary school in Dureno, there was a chance he would enter high school in the *cocama* town on the other side of the Aguarico, as Dureno has no high school. Some people told me that the Cofán students there are starting to drink alcohol, get in fights, steal things, and become obsessed with easy money. The fears are probably exaggerated, but they reflect Cofán anxieties about *cocama* ways rubbing off on their children. I told Alejandro and Lucia I would pay for Roberto to attend a private school near Lago Agrio named Abya Yala. Well-educated volunteers from Ecuador, Colombia, Chile, and Spain teach there alongside paid indigenous instructors. The school is only for indigenous Amazonian students. Although most instruction is in Spanish, teachers encourage students to speak in their own languages. Administrators also require students to wear their traditional dress a set number of days each week. Most importantly, the school has a reputation for rigorous, high-quality instruction. I want Roberto to have options in life. Although I hope he remains proud of his Cofán-ness, I want him to be able to support himself, his family, his community, and his people. To access the resources and deal with the challenges of the non-Cofán world, Roberto must be proficient in the ways of that world. Avoiding it is impossible.

Along with Dureno's parents, grandparents, and great-grandparents, I worry about the future of the community's children. Their environmental, economic, and political situations already present many challenges that will likely get worse. Yet there are individuals who give me hope. I think of Felipe Borman, who speaks English, Spanish, and A'ingae, has a college degree, and continues to identify with and support the Cofán nation. I think of Nancy Chapal, who teaches elementary school in Dureno, leads the women's Asociación Socu (Toucan Association), and is managing a partnership with a North American artist to design and market Cofán handicrafts through the Internet. I think of Toribio Aguinda, a Cofán high school teacher whose past involvements include leading Cofán protests against the oil industry and whose present commitments involve the acquisition of shamanic power. I think of Emeregildo Criollo, a Cofán man who lived in Lago Agrio and worked on the case against Chevron. He now works for the Ceibo Alliance, an environmental and indigenous rights effort funded largely by Leonardo DiCaprio.

Recently, Emeregildo returned to Dureno and built a house there. While he was still living in Lago Agrio, I interviewed him. I asked whether he thought Cofán people would eventually become *cocama*. He replied by speaking about himself:

> Well, I think about myself. I will never become a *cocama*. I already speak Spanish fairly well, but I will never stop speaking A'ingae. And the things I eat and drink, I will never give them up. . . . I live in Lago Agrio now. But some days I still eat forest meat. I can't sleep without drinking *cui'ccu* before going to bed. I can't live by drinking what *cocama* drink. I will never change. My flesh hasn't changed. I haven't become white. My customs have stayed the same. I wear *cocama* clothes, but my face, my color, is the same. How could anyone say I'm becoming a *cocama*?

Emeregildo's pride and confidence could remain the rule, or they could become an exception. Cofán people are struggling to adjust their way of life to trying times. The land within and outside their community is changing. The desires, fears, and hopes of their children are changing, too. When I began working with Cofán people more than two decades ago, I was primarily worried about "the Cofán" as a people. Over time, I learned to care much more about them as a group of individuals. They are my collaborators, friends, and family. I have known them for decades; some have died, and others have become parents and grandparents. No matter what happens to their culture or ethnic identity, my main concern is their health and happiness. Oil has done much to threaten the future of their way of life, as they define it. To a great degree, their joys still depend on the existence of that way of life. As it changes—and as the world of the *cocama* pushes further and further into their thoughts, bodies, relationships, and lands—the people of Dureno will do all they can to make sure their own lives, as well as the lives of their children, remain meaningful and satisfying. It will be a struggle, however—one that will likely never end.

CHAPTER 5

DAMAGED WORLD

lsira and Enrique are an endearing older couple. Elsira always wears her traditional skirt and blouse, and Enrique always wears his *ondiccu'je*. Both are well into their seventies. A baseball hat usually covers Enrique's head, which I suspect is bald. Elsira has light skin, blondish hair, and piercing blue eyes. Among Cofán women, she stands out. She came to Dureno from Colombia in the 1950s. Yori'ye told her to marry Enrique, and she complied. She jokes that she got her looks from her gringo father, who was a cannibal. She might be right, at least about the gringo part; a few North American ethnobotanists passed through the area from which she came before she was born. It is more likely that she owes her appearance to her grandfather, who was rumored to be a *cocama* rubber worker.

Before she came to Dureno, Elsira had two children, Silvio and Arturo, by two *cocama* men. Elsira's first child with Enrique was Deji, my research assistant. Deji's younger brother, Manuel, wears an

———

---

ondiccu'je like his father's; Deji gave up his tunic for shirts and pants long ago. Deji is also one of the few Cofán men who wear glasses, a fact that accounts for my joking nickname for him: Doctor. He is also very smart.

Enrique's name often comes up when I talk with the people of Dureno about oil spills. One afternoon in the late 1970s, he poled his canoe to the colonist town upstream from the mouth of the Dureno River, hoping to sell a blowgun to a settler. At first, no *cocama* wanted to buy it. With the little cash he had, Enrique bought a bottle of cheap rum and started to drink. As the hours passed, he got drunker and drunker. Eventually, night came and he decided to head home. He stumbled down the riverbank, got into his canoe, and began to paddle back. Soon, he hit some logs. He stepped out of his canoe to pull it past the obstacles. Immediately, he slipped and fell into the river, where a fresh oil spill had just come through. After he splashed around in the crude for a bit, Enrique righted himself. It was a struggle, but he made it home. At the shore, he tried to clean his clothes and body. No matter how hard he scrubbed, he could not remove the crude. He grabbed some manioc leaves from his garden and tried to scrape off the oil, but it did not help.

By the time Enrique walked up the hill to his house, he looked like a monster. Elsira was terrified when she saw him. He was entirely black; the only white spots on his body were his eyes. The leaves he used to try to clean himself were matted on his back and legs, making it look like he had a tail. Elsira thought he was a *cocoya*. When she realized it was just her husband, she was angry. He had trailed the oil all over their house. Even with soap, they could not remove it from him or anything else. Only the next day, when they got their hands on some gasoline—which is one of the few things that can cut through crude—were they able to clean him up.

The tone in which people talk about Enrique's story is representative of a general Cofán attitude. For the people of Dureno, the tale is exceptionally funny. Just like everyone else, Enrique and Elsira smile about Enrique's unlucky fall. It was just one of those crazy, comic, seemingly harmless things that happen to the Cofán. Why not laugh about it? After all, Enrique is still alive; his unfortunately timed swim did not lead immediately to loss of life or limb. Over the past fifty years, however, Cofán people have gradually learned that oil presents complicated risks to their well-being. Most have heard of *cáncer*, a deadly disease that lies latent until, years later, it kills you. When I interviewed Arturo about Enrique's fall, he also laughed. My young assistant Martin laughed, as well. But Martin concluded the conversation with a story he heard from a *cocama*. While he was working for an oil company, the *cocama* fell into multiple oil spills. He did not find humor in the story, but he thought he was fine. Fifteen years later, a doctor diagnosed him with cancer. In an anxious whisper, Arturo replied to Martin, "Tsa'caen ti?" (Is that how it is?). Clearly, he was worried about Enrique.

Most Cofán people are not sure what to make of oil contamination and its effects on human health. They tell many detailed stories about detecting the smell, sight, taste, and feel of oil in water, air, soil, and the flesh of fish and game animals. But they are not epidemiologists or chemists. They do not know the technicalities of how oil—and the wastes generated in its production—move through the environment and into their bodies. They also do not know what happens once it is inside their flesh and organs. Nonetheless, they are certain that their lands and rivers have been absorbing crude and other toxins since Texaco drilled its first exploratory well fifty years ago. After hearing their stories—told in their own language and clearly not scripted for public consumption—any impartial listener would find it hard to deny that the Cofán of Dureno have been living in an oil-saturated world for decades. It is difficult to prove the health effects of the contamination, but it is even more difficult to believe they do not exist.

The person who alerted the public to the environmental destruction done by petroleum in eastern Ecuador was Judith Kimerling, a lawyer, legal scholar, and professor at Queens College in New York City. In 1989 and 1990, she traveled through Amazonian Ecuador and interviewed everyone she could find about the nature and costs of oil extraction. Based on her own research and an extensive review of existing literature and archival sources, she published *Amazon Crude* in 1991. The slim book, filled with disturbing photographs, describes the ecological dynamics of each step of oil exploration and production.

———

FIGURE 5.1. *Hydrocarbon-filled runoff from an*
abandoned waste pit in Cofán territory

As Kimerling notes, for more than two decades Texaco dumped oil wastes directly into the Amazonian environment with no treatment. There was the crude itself, but many other substances were also involved: formation water, natural gas, water- and oil-based drilling muds, industrial solvents, chemical additives to enhance petroleum recovery, and produced water, created when formation water is removed from crude at separation stations. In horrifying detail, Kimerling lists the typical toxic components of the materials: "aluminum, antimony, arsenic, barium, cadmium, chromium, copper, lead, magnesium, mercury, nickel, zinc, benzene, naphthalene, phenanthrene, and other hydrocarbons, as well as toxic levels of sodium and chlorides" (in drilling wastes); "sulfates, bicarbonates, hydrogen sulfide, carbon dioxide, cyanide, and heavy metals such as arsenic, cadmium, chromium, lead, mercury, vanadium, and zinc" (in produced water); "oxides of nitrogen, sulfur, and carbon, as well as heavy metals, hydrocarbons, and soot, or carbon particulate" (in burned gas, oil, and oil waste); and crude itself, which is "very toxic."[1] Many of these substances are known carcinogens. Many also bio-accumulate in animals, including the tissue of fish and game. Most of them entered the water that Cofán people drank and used to wash their bodies, dishes, food, and clothes. And many entered the air that Cofán people breathed.

When Kimerling did her research in 1989 and 1990, the amount of oil wastes that were entering the Amazonian environment was astounding. When each well was drilled, approximately 42,000 gallons of waste oil and 4,165 cubic meters of muds and mud-coated drilling wastes were generated. At separation stations, 4.3 million gallons of produced water were released and 53 million cubic feet of natural gas were burned each day. Routine well maintenance involved the dumping of approximately 5 million gallons of wastes each year. Spills from secondary pipelines sent 17,000 to 20,000 gallons of oil into the environment every two weeks. From 1972 to 1990, the thirty major recorded spills of crude from the trans-Ecuadorian pipeline totaled 16.8 million gallons—much more than the 10.8 million gallons spilled during the *Exxon Valdez* disaster in Alaska. During the same period, approximately 19 billion gallons of produced water entered the environment.[2]

Kimerling wrote about the pollution's reported health effects, as well. The most cited information on oil's medical consequences in Amazonian Ecuador, however, comes from a series of peer-reviewed studies published in the early 2000s.[3] The studies' main authors are Anna-Karin Hurtig and Miguel San Sebastián of the Department of Public Health and Clinical Medicine at Umeå University in Sweden. Together, the findings they present are troubling: elevated levels of cancers of the stomach, liver, rectum, pancreas, throat, skin, blood, soft tissue, gynecological system, lymph nodes, and breast. Some of the high rates they detected occurred across demographic groups, and some were specific to men, women, or children. Rates were especially high among people who lived close to oil-producing facilities. The investigators also found high rates of miscarriage in women who lived near contaminated streams. A subsequent study by a different team shows that individuals who worked for oil companies in Amazonian Ecuador exhibited elevated damages at the DNA and chromosomal levels that are associated with increased rates of cancer and birth defects.[4]

A very different peer-reviewed study asserts that there were no detectable links between cancer mortality and residence near Ecuadorian oil-production facilities.[5] The first line of acknowledgments in the 2009 journal article by Kelsh, Morimoto, and Lau reads, "This research was funded by Chevron." Supporters of the plaintiffs in the Chevron lawsuit have criticized it on a number of grounds: the long-term association of its authors with Chevron, its reliance on cancer mortality rates measured by official death certificates rather than cancer rates themselves, its suggestion that many of the liver-cancer diagnoses that do exist are mistaken, and its comparison of cancer rates in oil-producing areas to cancer rates in urban Quito rather than cancer rates in rural areas distant from the oil industry.[6]

Perhaps the most serious obstacle to discovery of how oil harms humans in Amazonian Ecuador is a history of nonexistent or substandard care and minimal reporting of sicknesses and deaths, especially among indigenous populations. From the 1960s to the 1990s and even more recently, many Cofán people got sick and did not go to doctors. Many also died with no official cause of death investigated or reported. Even with the best medical care and reporting systems, it is extremely difficult to conclude with scientific certainty that a specific environmental contaminant caused a specific health problem.

In *Polluted Promises* (2005), the anthropologist Melissa Checker writes of the difficulties facing poor African Americans who live in an industrial contamination zone near Augusta, Georgia. Checker asserts that her subjects can expect minimal clarification of their medical problems from scientific studies of pollution's health effects for at least seven reasons. Most studies are statistical or probabilistic in nature, and they have little to say about the specific problems afflicting specific individuals or communities. Most information on the toxicity of contaminants comes from experimentation on populations of lab animals, whose extreme genetic similarity differentiates them from the variations found in human communities. Studies that are based on humans use populations composed largely of healthy, adult, Euro-Americans whose genes and bodies represent only a small proportion of human biological diversity. Laboratory studies assume "normal conditions" of chemical exposure rather than the complex and often chaotic ways in which toxins are released, distributed, and encountered in real-world situations. Most studies look at only immediate or short-term effects of toxin exposure rather than long-term consequences that may take years to emerge. Most studies examine only one toxin at a time rather than the synergistic effects of multiple toxins. And most studies attempt to isolate one cause of adverse health outcomes even though many if not most health problems have multiple causes; preexisting sicknesses or genetic profiles can trigger or exacerbate contamination-related illnesses.[7] The factors Checker highlights make it nearly impossible for scientists to link pollutants to illness or death with the degree of certainty courts demand in legal disputes in the United States or elsewhere. The difficulties are multiplied for poor, marginalized communities that often lack the money, social networks, formal education, and political power to press their claims.[8]

The Cofán of Dureno did encounter hydrocarbons before Texaco arrived. One man told me that the old-time people spoke of "an underground substance that lights as fire." The idea is probably related to two images: the Christian vision of the afterlife and underworld, where Chiga (God) burns people to punish them; and the fire-spewing volcanoes of the Andean foothills, which some old-time shamans visited in their quests for power. Historically, Cofán people started fires with flint and took burning embers from their neighbors when their own fires went out. They made candles with kapok cotton and beeswax. By the mid-twentieth century, *cocama* river traders had introduced them to matches and kerosene, which some Dureno residents used for lamps.

By the 1940s, Royal Dutch Shell and a *cocama* trader had brought motorized canoes to the Aguarico. Eventually, other machines with internal combustion engines came to Cofán territory: planes, helicopters, trucks, tractors, bulldozers, chainsaws, drilling rigs, cars, buses, and generators. To refer to the processes of starting, driving,

FIGURE 5.2. *The Parahuacu 2 oil well*

and managing the machines, Cofán people use the word *jeñañe* (to make sound). For them, the age of fossil fuel began as the age of noise. In the words of Rufino, Alejandro's sixty-four-year-old nephew, "In the old times, we Cofán people were just of the forest. There was nothing. No planes, no helicopters, no motors. There was no noise. No noise from cars, no noise from generators. Nothing. We didn't know about it. It was just the forest. We heard frogs, howler monkeys, white-lipped peccaries, and collared peccaries. We just heard the animals. It was silent. There was nothing, nothing."

Although kerosene, gasoline, and motor oil entered their world before the 1960s, the Cofán saw no crude until Texaco began dumping the substance onto their lands and into their rivers. They had no idea what the more familiar hydrocarbons looked like in their unrefined form. They did not even know the word *petróleo*. When they found the thick liquid in their environment, they called it *simpe'cha'a*. The word is morphologically complex. *Si-* clearly means "black" or "dark." My assistant Martin said that *-pe'cha* is a morpheme that means something like "thick" or "viscous." Neither of us is quite sure what the ending *-'a* means. Similar words, Martin said, include *cunape'cha* (fermented manioc beer mash) and *quiccupe'cha* (stew thickened with grated plantain). When you ask Cofán people what *petróleo* or *crudo* is like, they use a variety of words and expressions: *ámundetssi* (dirty), *tssu'jutssi* (stinky), *sintssi* (black or dark), *tu'atssi* (sticky), *sampe'chatssi* (thick), *chápetssi* (soft), *yaya'pa'caon* (like fat), *ccoqqui'can* (like the dark beeswax used to make blowguns), *tena'tssi* (like water covered with thin pools of grease or fat), *chhari'ccoe* (with an appearance like polished stone or pottery), and *qquítssatssatssi* (like syrupy liquid that slowly drips down one's throat). They also say that crude *ancañe* (attaches itself to objects) and is difficult to *battiye* (get rid of or remove). In addition, most people claim that crude is very *ega* (bad).

Like crude itself, the idea of toxic contamination or pollution was unfamiliar to the Cofán before Texaco arrived. Avoiding contamination by reproductive blood is a central principle of Cofán culture. I was surprised to learn that few if any individuals use blood pollution as a metaphor for petroleum pollution, even though both cause

---

harm from the Cofán perspective. Cofán people use the Spanish word *contaminación* when talking about oil; they never use it when discussing reproductive blood. When you ask them to explain the word in A'ingae, they typically say that it is *ámundian'cho* (something that has been made dirty) or *seje'paen'cho* (something into which poison has been put).

Dirtiness and poison, however, are complex ideas. People call the Aguarico River "dirty" when it becomes reddish brown because of all the sediment it is carrying. But, they explain, before Texaco came they always drank and cooked with such dirty water, and it never made them sick. The word *seje'pa* means both "poison" and "medicine." There is no other A'ingae term for the latter, whether the substance in question is a forest plant or a Western pill. People note that the two key forms of poison they use to get meat—blowgun poison and *señamba* fishing poison—allow them to kill animals. But they can eat the *seje'pa*-filled meat with no harmful health effects.

Taking the associations into account, *contaminación* is a strange kind of dirtiness and a strange form of poison. In short, it is "dirtiness that harms or kills," a relatively new concept that is difficult to express, at least in A'ingae. As Deji laughingly remarked during one of our many conversations about contamination, "We Cofán don't have a word that says 'a thing that becomes dirty and then damages or kills a person.' In our language, it's hard to convey that thought. It's not something we created, so it's difficult to talk about. It's like a hammer or a shoe. We don't have words for those, either, because they're things that came from other people." People still have a hard time getting their heads around the notion of toxic contamination. In recent years, they learned to use insecticides to kill cockroaches in their homes. They also use herbicides to kill weeds and grass along trails and in gardens. Over the past ten years, many men have spent their days fabricating canoes out of fiberglass and industrial resins. As far as I can tell, they worry little about what the materials are doing to them.

More than anywhere else, the people of Dureno encountered oil wastes in streams and rivers. To include all my collaborators' testimony on the matter would require hundreds of pages. Here,

I present just a few recollections from three individuals. The first is Emeregildo, the oldest son of Alejandro's brother Fernando and the father of my assistant Martin. Although Emeregildo eventually moved to Lago Agrio to work on the suit against Texaco (and then Chevron), he spent much of his early life hunting and fishing. He was born in 1959. During one trip when he was still a child, he went hunting with his father near Amisacho, the village site that eventually became Lago Agrio. Just downriver from Amisacho, they saw crude in the water. They did not know what it was. As they maneuvered through it, everything became black: their canoe, their poles, and their paddles. Quickly, navigating the river became difficult; their paddles were too slippery to grasp.

Emeregildo said that on that day and others, people learned to hate crude even though they had no idea it would harm them. If they touched it, it got on everything. If they stepped in it, it trailed behind them. It was nearly impossible to clean off their bodies and *ondiccu'je*. It mixed with sand to create a thick, messy, ugly substance. They were upset when they saw it coming down streams and the main body of the Aguarico. Emeregildo said the Dureno River was one of the most damaged waterways. For much of the time, all the sticks along its banks were black; you could not even touch them. "Ni ja'masiaven ja'cho," Emeregildo lamented—"It became impossible to travel on." Like most Cofán people, Emeregildo is not at all adept at estimating the dates on which events took place, but he guesses that the Dureno River became truly contaminated after 1973. His estimation makes sense; by 1974, Texaco was constructing roads, pipelines, and production wells near the river.

Arturo, son of Enrique and half-brother of Deji and Silvio, told me about a hunting trip that probably occurred in the late 1960s. Although he was still a teenager, Arturo was already an expert hunter. With an adult named Elias Lucitante, Arturo went in search of woolly monkeys and white-lipped peccaries on a small stream that drains into the Dureno River. It was a great trip; they killed five peccaries. Although Cofán people have trouble remembering how many oil spills they witnessed on a certain river, they can report with certainty how many animals they killed on a single hunting trip that occurred fifty years earlier. They can also remember the sexes and ages of the animals, their reproductive states, and the taste and thickness of their fat. It is a truly amazing ability.

The peccary carcasses were huge. On their first trip back to their canoe from the forest interior, Arturo carried one carcass on his back and Elias carried one and a half. Elias was something of a giant. He originally came to Dureno from the upriver community of Sinangoé, where the founding *na'su*, Soju'ye, was rumored to be well over six feet tall. When they reached their canoe, they were thirsty and hungry. At the time, the drilling tower was already in operation at the Atacapi exploratory well upriver. When Arturo reached into the river to mix water into the *cui'ccu* mash he had brought from his house, he saw that the stream was covered with a shiny substance that smelled like gasoline. Nonetheless, he thought the water itself was clean—there is no A'ingae word for "safe"—even though it reeked. In his words, "I pushed away the crude, gathered some water, mixed it with *cui'ccu*, and we drank it right there."

Traditionally, Cofán people never drank straight water; they always mixed it with *cui'ccu* pulp or manioc beer mash. Consequently, for Arturo and Elias, the taste of the crude was less pronounced than it would have been had they consumed the water alone. The alcohol in manioc beer might be especially good at masking the taste of oil wastes. Before Cofán people learned about oil contamination, they went on long hunting trips with plantain or fermented manioc mash folded into leaf pouches that they kept in palm-fiber bags. They stopped at any stream or river to mix water into the mash so they would have something to drink and, in effect, eat; *cui'ccu* and manioc beer are filling, nutritious, and high in calories. Carrying prepared *cui'ccu* or manioc beer on extended treks was a true chore. People learned to do it only grudgingly; it was not even an option before they acquired plastic buckets and bottles. On long trips, a few old men still mix their drinks with water taken straight from the Aguarico even though they know it is a bad idea.

Arturo said that neither he nor Elias suffered immediate health effects after they drank from the waste-covered stream. But nearly thirty years later, Elias died of stomach cancer. When he speculates

FIGURE 5.3. *The Lago Agrio 1 oil well*

about why Elias perished while others did not, Arturo says Elias hunted and fished constantly, sometimes at night. He probably drank from many contaminated streams, Arturo imagines, especially during the first two decades of oil extraction, when petroleum pollution was at its worst.

Even though he spent much of his youth in missionary schools, Randy Borman returned to Dureno to hunt whenever he could. He and Arturo are probably the two best hunters of their generation. Although fully proficient in the forest skills of his Cofán peers, Randy also has a Western knack for thinking in terms of dates and other numbers. After completing most of my fieldwork in Dureno, I interviewed Randy in Quito, where he was working on Cofán territorial campaigns as director of the Foundation for the Survival of the Cofán People. Having discovered how quantitatively vague most Cofán accounts of oil contamination are, I wondered whether Randy had any specific memories. Speaking in English, he had a lot to say:

I think the deal here is really the magnitudes. That's what sticks in people's minds. People don't remember the frequency. The thing is, from 1966 on, when the first oil came out of the ground, it was all just dumped into the rivers. We just had multiple, multiple, multiple small-scale spills going into the river. It was a daily occurrence. You'd go out fishing and say, "Oops, in this section of the river the fish are going to taste really bad because the Pisorié is full of oil right now." It eventually hit the Aguarico and was diluted, and then it was processed slowly through the biodegradation that is normal for an Amazonian ecosystem. But it was a constant thing.

I asked if the contaminants from oil production were in all the streams. Randy replied,

Yes. The Pisorié, Pocattonocho, Dureno, Tutuyé, Tururu—all the streams in the area, starting from the Posino River on down. As long as you couldn't see and smell the oil in the river, you weren't too worried about the fact that just upriver there was a stream coming in loaded with crude. It was pretty much like that until the year 2000, when the regulations got stiffer. . . . The low-grade constant contamination was just something that everybody was dealing with. When I'm on my political pedestal, I talk occasionally about having to cut my son Felipe's hair because of all the oil globules that were in it. That was just a spill that occurred on the Tutuyé and got into the Aguarico. By the time it got down to Zábalo, where we were living, it was getting stuck in people's hair. But it wasn't thick enough to make anything big and obvious on the river itself.

Randy said that until 2000 he told journalists he could guide them to an active oil spill within an hour. He said the Guanta-Dureno field was constantly leaking. Its wells and production facilities drained into the Pisorié River, which runs straight through the people of Dureno's territory. In late 2014, I traveled to rural Michigan to visit Randy, who was spending time with his parents at the home of Randy's brother Rick. Bub's energy was fading, but Bobbie was as sharp as ever. When I told her about my project on oil in Dureno, I half-expected her to be skeptical. Instead, she immediately began talking about how beautiful the Aguarico was before Texaco came. I explained that I had a hard time getting my collaborators to recall specific incidents with sufficient information to estimate their dates. I asked how many oil spills she remembered. With visible anger, she replied, "In which month of which year?" According to Bobbie, an evangelical Christian and anything but a left-wing rabble-rouser, spills were constantly occurring near Dureno. She shook her head as she lamented what oil did to the Cofán.[9]

There are many other stories. Some are remembered, and some are forgotten or soon will be. Over the past five decades, innumerable small spills and waste emissions have polluted the streams and rivers of Cofán territory. There have been several disastrously large ones, too. People definitely recall the giant 1974 spill that occurred when a flood broke the trans-Ecuadorian pipeline at a bridge near Lago Agrio. They also remember the thousands of barrels of crude that covered the Aguarico after a 1987 earthquake.[10] The biggest spills could take months to pass. As the rivers rose, crude covered the shoreline. The waters eventually receded. When they rose again, they washed high-water oil residues back into themselves, creating a series of contamination aftershocks.

Apart from the oil that covered the water and everything it touched, there were subtler forms of waste that passed with little detection. Cofán people have impressive abilities to sense the qualities, beings, and transformations of the Amazonian environment, but they do not see, smell, or taste everything. Often they did not realize the toxic substances were present. Pollution lingered in riverbeds, shorelines, and eddies for years; people used the spaces for bathing and washing. For decades, they drank the water, too. Slowly, they learned to obtain water from small forest streams that do not pass by oil wells. When they got metal roofing sheets for their homes, they began to collect rainwater for cooking and drinking.

The people of Dureno did more than drink and bathe in oil-filled water—they ate the fish that lived in it. The Cofán are river people. They hunt, but they do not like to go too far inland from rivers; the deep forest is a traditionally feared place because of the *cocoya* that reside there. In addition, the deeper they go, the harder it is to carry game back to their canoes. Fish are just as essential to their diet as forest animals. During the dry months when rivers are lowest, fish are especially important. Cofán people eat dozens of fish species, fish that stay toward the bottom of rivers and fish that roam the surface, fish that eat seeds and vegetation and fish that eat other fish, fish that swim alone and fish that travel in schools, fish that weigh as much as a person and live for many years and fish that are small with a short life cycle.

Every single Dureno resident I interviewed told me they have caught contaminated fish. Unlike hunting, fishing is a relatively gender-neutral pursuit, and it is something that both the very young and the very old do. The words that occur most frequently in people's accounts of damaged fish are *tssu'jutssi* (stinky) and *keroseneme'tssi* (like kerosene). The first term requires no explanation. The second makes sense given that kerosene was the hydrocarbon with which the Cofán were most familiar when Texaco arrived to their territory. People have countless stories of catching fish that smelled like kerosene and *jabón* (purchased soap, in Spanish). Some say the smell was

FIGURE 5.4. *Fish caught in the Aguarico River*

most common in long-lived and bottom-dwelling catfish. Others say it was more characteristic of fish that live toward the surface and suck on stones and sticks to eat, such as *avu*, a very common species known regionally as *bocachico* (small-mouth, in Spanish). Most of my collaborators, however, agree that after Texaco arrived, nearly all fish species in nearly all waterways began to smell like kerosene.

Often, people caught fish and did not notice anything strange about them. When they took them home and cooked them in stews, however, the distinctive smell emerged. A few people say the smell was strongest in the fishes' heads or gills, but most assert that the fishes' entire bodies reeked. The smelliest substance was the broth in which the fish were cooked. People say the scent made the typical Cofán stew—fish or meat mixed with salt and green plantains—seem like a pot of kerosene. After a hard day on the river, some people disposed of the liquid but ate the flesh, which smelled less. Others threw out everything or fed it to their dogs. A few people smoked the fish to try to get rid of the scent and taste.

On the day Randy told me about cutting globs of crude from his son's hair, he shared a tale about one of his first encounters with oil:

My first trip into a live oil well was when I was a young teenager. I went back in the forest to Dureno 1, the exploratory well. When we got back in there, they were dumping drilling mud in the river. It was all going into the stream. And there were a bunch of *natte* fish dead in the stream. And I was excited, because they were nice, big *natte*. I wanted to collect them. And Hector Quenamá, who was older than me, picked up a *natte* and hit it over the head with a machete to kill it. He picked it up, smelled it, and said, "This doesn't smell right. This mud has made it really bad. This is not good mud. Leave it alone, leave it alone." I wanted to take it with me, but he said, "Leave it alone." And so I reluctantly obeyed and threw it away. And then we just looked at the rest of the dead *natte* there in the stream. We were aware that it didn't smell right. It didn't look right. They were right at the bottom of the well.

Randy's story is striking, but it is an outlier. He and his companion noticed a strange, smelly, visible substance in the river—close to a known oil well—and they realized the fish were contaminated before they cooked them. Most polluted fish were not so obvious. Although dozens of people told me about discarding cooked fish that smelled like kerosene, I am certain that each of those individuals ate many fish whose tainted flesh was just below the threshold of what the Cofán could sense. Polluted fish were an essential part of their diet for decades. Even though oil production has become cleaner in recent years, people still catch fish that have the same distinctive odor, especially in certain streams near active wells and production facilities.

Water is the principle vehicle through which oil wastes travel, but near wells and waste pits, it is easy to see that land, too, has been damaged. The hard, blackened soil rarely covers more than a hectare. In the middle of the forest, contamination is difficult to detect at all. On a number of occasions, oil found its way out of the rivers and waste pits in and on the bodies of animals. Caimans, an important food species, often appeared covered in crude's black sheen. Their contamination makes sense; they spend most of their time in the water. The people of Dureno saw many other oil-covered animals: capybaras, pacas, agoutis, acouchis, deer, and armadillos. Many of the animals frequently pass through water. Others had the misfortune of being trapped on a river island during a crude-filled flood that covered them as it rose and then receded. In waste pits people saw the corpses of many birds of different species that tried to eat the insects attracted by the well flares. They got too close, were burned, and died.

It is important to remember that numerous species survive by drinking river water, just as the Cofán did. The animals also eat the fish and plants that live in or near the water.[11] The saline fluid found in waste pits attracts some species, just as salt licks do. Through all the vectors, animals' bodies gradually became filled with oil wastes. Consequently, the people of Dureno absorbed contamination directly and indirectly; they ingested pollution, but they also ingested the fish and forest animals that ingested pollution. The waste products accumulated in the flesh of the species that sat at the top of the food chain, many of which—such as caimans and large catfish—are cherished parts of the Cofán diet.

Even when they saw animals covered in crude, Cofán people killed and ate them. Arturo shared a typical story. He was hunting by a stream near the Parahuacu oil wells, across the Aguarico from Dureno. His dogs picked up the scent of a capybara and began to chase it. The pursuit lasted longer than Arturo expected. The capybara ran through a well site. Intentionally or unintentionally, it plunged into a waste pit and exited on the other side. At that point, tracking it became easier, as it left black footprints everywhere. Eventually, Arturo caught up with the capybara when it fell into the Aguarico. There, he killed it. He said, "It was all oil, covered in oil. It was entirely black. I killed it and butchered it. Even its flesh appeared to have oil on it. I smoked it and ate it. That's why I say to people that I have eaten all kinds of *egatssiama* [bad stuff]."

When I asked Deji about Arturo's story, he said the same thing happened to other people, including himself. In the typical Cofán way, he found humor in the encounters because they were so bizarre—and, he now knows, they were so foolish. He smiled and proclaimed, "We saw black capybaras, killed them, and ate them—and we laughed about it." Deji laughed especially hard when he recalled the time his younger brother asked their father "if black capybaras truly exist." The boy found one in the forest, but he did not realize it was covered with crude. He just thought it was a species he had never seen before.

When they killed animals covered in oil, people almost always ate them. They were pragmatists. After they scraped off the fur with knives—part of the regular butchering process—they examined the flesh and determined that it did not smell bad, at least not as bad as *keroseneme'tssi* fish. They assumed the meat was clean. No one I spoke with mentioned eating animals that contamination had already killed. Nonetheless, they may have done so without realizing it. In the past, the Cofán had a custom of eating dead animals they found in the forest as long as they were not visibly rotting. As one older woman explained to me, "In the old times, we used to pick up dead animals and eat them after we found them in the forest. The old people said they were given to us by the forest people, the invisible people. The beings had compassion for us, hunted the animals, and left them for us to eat." I have no idea when the people of Dureno gave up the practice. Some likely continued to eat the corpses of animals they found long after oil wastes began to saturate their environment and kill creatures that lived in it.

By the 1980s, many Cofán families had acquired tanks—sometimes nothing more than used oil barrels—to collect rainwater for drinking and cooking. The Bormans had taught them that untreated water from the Aguarico and most other rivers was far too contaminated for consumption. Oil wastes were one problem; the sewage and garbage that emptied into the river from Lago Agrio and smaller colonist settlements had also become impossible to ignore. When rain fell from zinc roofing sheets into barrels, people thought it was safer, and it probably was. But Texaco and other oil companies were still burning many of their waste products. Next to all production stations and many oil wells were flares that burned off the natural gas that emerged with the crude. And when waste pits grew too thick or high or an unexpected spill occurred, workers often set fire to them to get rid of the unwanted materials.

Randy has a video his father took of one fire in 1985 or 1986.

———

Even Randy sometimes has trouble remembering dates. It was near Christmas, and the Bormans were traveling up the Aguarico from Zábalo in a canoe. A holding tank in Lago Agrio had broken open, and thousands of barrels of oil spilled into a stream. A worker set fire to the water. The result was almost too overwhelming to describe: giant billows of pitch-black smoke appeared to stretch for miles into the sky, where they merged with increasingly dirty clouds. Images of BP's Deepwater Horizon disaster remind me of the video. Even with the fire, a significant portion of the crude made it into the Aguarico, past Dureno, and down to Peru.

Cofán people saw many such fires. Lucia's brother, Davíd, said the winding smoke pillars reminded him of anacondas. The fires mainly occurred at wells and production facilities, but wind blew their particulates across the land. Flares were not as spectacular, but what they lacked in grandeur they made up for in regularity. The natural gas from the wells and production stations burned twenty-four hours a day on all sides of the community—and it still does. In a field note, I recall one of the first times I saw the flares from Dureno's central settlement:

Tonight at about 8 or 9, I noticed an orange glow flickering through the low- to mid-sky to the northeast of Alejandro's house. At first I thought it was lightning, but the color was different. Then I thought it was lights from Lago Agrio or another town. But when I went up to Alejandro's second floor, I looked out the window and saw the glow emerging from a very condensed point to the slight northeast of the main settlement, across the Aguarico. (It was definitely much easier to see from the second story.) I'd seen something similar before, but I always thought it was the colonist town across the river. Tonight, it was clear that it was a flare—or multiple flares—from the Atacapi oil wells. Then, I looked to the northwest and noticed another orange light right over the roof of Timoteo's house. It must have been from the Parahuacu wells. For whatever reason—perhaps the way the clouds had formed and allowed the light to reflect up and out—the flares were especially visible tonight, although you couldn't see the flames themselves, just the glow that beat and burst from them.

FIGURE 5.5. *Well flares glowing behind a Dureno home*

When I asked Alejandro where the smoke from the fires and flares goes, he replied, "That smoke ends up in the tank over there, the one we use to drink. Sometimes when it rains, it seems like kerosene is in there." In the past, he said, they often drank the water even when it smelled bad. "We didn't know," Alejandro said with a laugh. After the fires began, the rain itself sometimes looked different as it fell from the sky; it had a black, red, or violet tinge the Cofán had never seen. It was especially noticeable during the first shower after a dry spell. The tanks intensified the experience of pollution. The collected water could look strangely dark. The smells that emerged from the barrels were much stronger than the scent of the rain. Sometimes, one woman reported, the water smelled like iron. Deji said it smelled like smoke or fire. When people placed cloth over the tops of the tanks to filter the rainwater, the cloth eventually became black, as if covered with soot. At times, people noticed nothing strange about the water, but when the levels got low during a dry period, they saw a thick layer of dark sludge at the bottom of the barrels. They cleaned them out and continued to use them.

When I asked Alejandro if he had ever seen the sludge in his own tank, he said he had. Then, he shared a thought: "Because we drank that black water, did our stomachs become black at the bottom just like the tanks did?" In recent years, a US nonprofit organization named ClearWater provided the people of Dureno with much better tanks to collect rainwater. They are made of special noncontaminating plastic, and they are fully enclosed. They also have filtration systems. People like Alejandro and Lucia, however, bypassed the filters because they became too burdensome to maintain. Now they are left with tanks that do not even allow them to see what is at the bottom, but at least they are not drinking from old oil barrels. Laura Mendua, Silvio's wife, seemed sad as she declared their current situation:

> With all of this, we finally understood that the oil wells are bad. We began to ask ourselves, "Are we really drinking all of that stuff that goes up into the sky? All of that smoke that drifts up there?" Yes, it gathers there in the clouds, and then we collect it in our tanks. We poor ones are drinking that. In the old times, we drank straight

from the Aguarico, and nothing bad happened to us. We had no diarrhea, no rashes. Early in the morning, my mother told me to bathe in the river. At four o'clock in the morning, I bathed and then came back and made *cui'ccu*. Like that we lived. None of us were sick. Now, we're all sick.

Even if the people of Dureno were to keep wells out of their community and stop future wells from polluting the streams and rivers they use, they would be unable to avoid the contamination that falls from the sky. In a discussion about whether the people of Dureno should oppose oil development on their land, my assistant Martin said there was no way to return to their former *quínsetssi* (strong or healthy) way of living. Flares burn on all sides of them. Even if the wells and production stations are far, Martin stated, wind blows the *paqque'su* (sickness—literally, "things with which one dies") into their community. "That's why we say that we already reside inside of that," he said. "We already live inside of oil contamination."

Everyone in Dureno agrees about the worst forms of contamination: polluted rivers and streams, polluted fish, polluted game, polluted skies, and polluted rain. The effects of other forms of contamination are less certain. Some people say that toxic rain has caused garden crops and forest fruits to become smaller and less plentiful. Some share vivid stories of the times they walked barefoot on roads that the company covered with pit wastes in order to keep down dust. Older people insist that contamination made their land smell so disgusting that many game animals fled and never returned, impoverishing the Cofán diet. These observations may be accurate, but they lack the systematic agreement and consistency that characterize Cofán accounts of oil's other destructive powers.

No one has studied oil's specific effects on the health of Cofán people. Most Dureno residents have suffered ailments they associate with petroleum pollution; all can tell stories of people who allegedly died because of it. A few of their accounts are supported by authoritative reports from Western doctors, but most are not. Oil was a new and confusing phenomenon for the Cofán, and so were the health problems it might have caused. For decades, the people of Dureno

———

lacked attention from medical experts who would have been able to diagnose, treat, record, and report their problems. As poor, marginalized, and suffering citizens, they still need better care. In addition, they maintain their own set of beliefs and practices for the diagnosis and treatment of illnesses, whether through plant medicines or shamanism. The latter practice has an especially wide scope, and the conditions it attempts to treat are difficult to distinguish from the illnesses that scientists and doctors believe to be caused by oil wastes. Gradually, through the lessons of direct observation and interactions with activists and health care workers, the people of Dureno developed a better sense of what oil might be doing to their bodies.

The Cofán know with certainty that they have been drinking, eating, and bathing in oil wastes for approximately fifty years. When they visit oil wells or production facilities, they say the fumes make them dizzy and give them headaches. In Dureno, the most common supposedly minor ailments they associate with contamination are skin and digestive problems. Especially in the first few decades of oil production, they developed rashes, itchiness, and ulcer- or pimple-like eruptions after bathing in the river. The problems were especially severe in children, who spent much of their days playing in the water. Arturo told me he has seen multiple doctors about a dandruff-like condition he cannot get rid of. The scaly flakes on his scalp are impossible to remove no matter how hard he scrubs and which shampoo he uses. He also says they feel "sticky." He is not quite sure what to make of them, but he definitely attributes them to pollution.

Digestive problems are equally common ailments associated with contamination. Nearly every Dureno resident suffers stomach pain and diarrhea on a regular basis. The problems linger even after people take medicine for intestinal parasites. Recently, many people told me that doctors diagnosed them with gastritis and ulcers and gave them medicines that only sometimes helped. A few people say that none of the children in the community are as big or as strong as Cofán kids used to be. They ascribe their stunted development not only to a lower-quality diet but to all the digestive ailments that go along with drinking contaminated water and eating contaminated meat.

Sometimes the problems are much more serious, resulting in

death or disability. They can take years to develop, or they can arise abruptly. Florinda is an older woman who always wears her traditional blouse and skirt. She told me she hates hospitals, does not trust doctors, and fears needles. In 1995, her husband, Vijirio, died. In his genealogical records, Bub recorded Vijirio's likely cause of death as tuberculosis. Florinda disagrees with Bub's conclusion, at least with regard to what pushed Vijirio over the edge. During an interview on the community's health problems, she said,

> My husband did not die well. He went to fish for *avu* on the Dureno River. There was an oil spill, and it covered everything. He fell into it and crude entered his nose. With that, he was truly damaged and died. He shouldn't have died then. He was still very strong. But he said that when the oil entered his nose, he couldn't stop smelling it. It made him dizzy. We brought him to shamans so he could be cured, but they couldn't do it.

No one will ever know exactly why Vijirio died. Perhaps his system was so weakened by tuberculosis that it could not withstand newer threats, including oil-related toxins. There is little doubt that petroleum wastes had entered his body for many years in multiple ways. Emeregildo has a similar story about the deaths of two of his sons. One died soon after an encounter with oil pollution, much as Vijirio did. The other was born with a birth defect that cut his life short. Birth defects are relatively common in Dureno. A congenital intestinal defect killed one of Deji's children, possibly two children were born more recently with deformed brains, and one neurologically impaired teenager remains locked in his father's house; he cannot speak, and if he gets out, he enters other families' homes, sticks his hands in their *cui'ccu* pots, and defecates on their floors. Emeregildo's account, which he has shared with a number of journalists, is a poignant description of what it is like to suffer such problems and to wonder if oil caused them:

> My children died soon after the contamination became bad. My first child was very young. My wife was pregnant, and we were still

drinking from the Aguarico, which was often contaminated with oil wastes. My child was born, but he couldn't grow. Before he was born, the contamination had already entered him. He was a tiny infant, and he never developed. I brought him to the SIL missionary clinic at Limoncocha. They tried to treat him but couldn't. So they sent me to Quito. It was during the time when I still couldn't speak Spanish well. I brought my child to the doctor there. He told me there was no medicine that would make my son better. Back then, I wasn't like I am now. I didn't know to ask what sickness was hurting my son. When people interview me, though, I tell them about that child and that I think he died because of contamination. Then there was my other son. That one definitely died because of contamination. He was born healthy. At the time, I was already learning how to be a health care promoter with the SIL. I knew we had to drink clean water. When my son was three years old, I brought him to the Aguarico to swim. He swam, but he also drank a lot of contaminated water as he played in the river. When I brought him back, he began to vomit. He kept on vomiting, and then he suddenly died. That's how my child died.

I asked Emeregildo how he knew it was contamination that killed his son. He replied, "Because it didn't happen to my other children. That child was the one who drank contaminated water on that day. The others didn't. That's when I had that realization, 'Did contamination kill my child?'"

The most pervasive oil-related health problem in Dureno is cancer. The illness, though, is as confusing and complex for the Cofán as it is for most people in the world. When I asked Alejandro if he knew what *cáncer* was, he replied that it is a *cocama* sickness. He heard that one gets it by eating something or that it grows in the lungs. He does not know how it develops, but he knows it is bad. A decade ago, Randy brought Alejandro to a Quito hospital to remove a troubling-looking mole from his face. The doctors cut if off, but Alejandro, who speaks little Spanish, did not recall whether the doctors said it was cancer. Listening to Alejandro's story, Martin reflected that Cofán people are not like gringos. They do not go to doctors as soon as they suspect a health problem. Instead, they let it linger for a long time.

Other Dureno residents have heard about cancer from doctors, environmental activists, and people involved in the Chevron lawsuit. A few have even read the cheap pamphlets on sicknesses and remedies that *cocama* vendors sell on buses. One young man told me he saw a booklet about cancer. According to his reading of it, cancer is a small yellow thing that emerges inside women's breasts, on one's gums, or in one's lungs. After a year, it kills you. During one of my stays, a medical team with a portable X-ray machine visited Dureno. They examined all consenting women for breast cancer. Most were fine, but in Arturo's wife, Laura told me, they detected a "small piece of hard meat." Many people say cancer is *seje'masia* (incurable). If it is in you, there is nothing that can be done, and you will soon die. The belief discourages many people from seeking medical treatment.

Some people say the quick process of dying from cancer is experienced as a loss of strength, energy, body weight, and hair. Emeregildo, who has had some health training and is familiar with much of the medical evidence in the Chevron case, has the clearest understanding of cancer: "Cancer begins as a hard spot inside your body. It usually emerges where there's pain. If you find it early, you can survive. Sometimes, though, even if they operate and cut it out, it will emerge again and again. It is then a sickness you cannot overcome. Many people say oil contamination causes cancer."

Unless some other cause of death is immediately identified, people now often assume that oil-related cancer is the culprit. Likewise, many believe cancer will be their own cause of death because of the contamination inside their bodies. Laura told me that in the old times, they just died from epidemics like measles. Or *cocoya* killed them. "But now it's not like that," she said. "Cancer is emerging in all of us and we're dying because of it. I think about how bad those oil wells are. It's getting close to the point where they're getting rid of us all." I asked her if that is why so many people hate the oil companies. She replied, "When we became sick we started to think like that. If it weren't for that, we wouldn't know. We didn't know anything, and

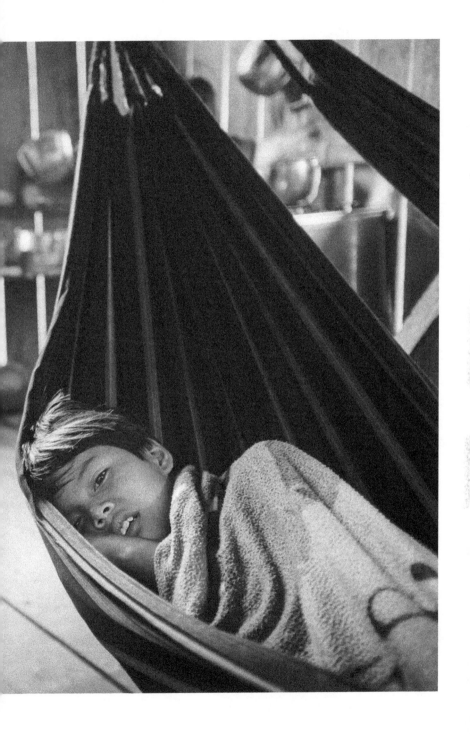

FIGURE 5.6. *A Cofán boy sick with fever*

then cancer emerged and killed so many of us. We thought, 'Oh, was it Texaco that damaged us? Did they contaminate the rivers, and did we bathe in those rivers, and did our children get sick?' That's when we knew." Even though his uncle Santiago was never treated by a doctor, Deji thinks that because he became weak and skinny so quickly, it was cancer that killed him. Arturo feels the same way about many people in the community:

> Bolivar's father, Elias, and Julia's father, Rubén, died before they even got old. They just drank the company's contaminated water and ate contaminated food and then they died. That's what I think. Elias died because cancer emerged in him. Rubén was so strong, and then he died so quickly. His son died first, and then Rubén died. Then, Rubén's wife died very quickly. Think about it: they were some of the ones who drank most from water the company had contaminated.

Elias's 1997 death from cancer is the one Dureno residents mention most frequently. There are two reasons for it: first, doctors actually diagnosed him with stomach cancer; and second, he was an exceptionally strong and rugged person whose brutal battle with cancer was shocking and visible. He lay for nearly a year in his Dureno home before he finally succumbed. While there, his skin started to flake off. Some say it made him look like an iguana. A *cocama* told Elias's family to wash his skin with oatmeal and water, and they did. Seeing that made Alejandro decide he would never eat oatmeal again. With a sullen look, Silvio told me that he believes he, too, will die of cancer. But he hoped it would not be drawn out like it was for Elias. He said he did not want his family to suffer through caring for him.

Because they are certain that cancer was the cause of Elias's death, people speculate about how he "caught" it. Arturo said Elias hunted constantly, often at night, and probably drank from many contaminated streams without knowing it. Emeregildo claimed Elias often fished for *avu* at night and likely fell into oil spills and drank water and ate fish from contaminated rivers. Randy said Elias's house was directly in the path of the Atacapi wells' smoke; consequently, the rainwater he drank was particularly polluted. Randy told me that Elias's wife, Margarita, also died from stomach cancer right after her husband. Because she died quickly, though, people do not remember her sickness in the same way. In Randy's words,

> With regard to the black smoke, the Atacapi wells were always heavy, heavy flarers. And the smoke would come right across to Dureno. The ones who were most affected, who had black rain all the time, were Elias and Margarita. And I'm 99 percent convinced that that was the cause of their death. Both of them died with what apparently was stomach cancer. Their symptoms were very similar, but Margarita died much faster than Elias. Elias lasted a long time. He fought the cancer for maybe a year before he succumbed. Margarita just lasted a few months. They were the ones who were drinking black rainwater all the time. They were constantly fighting it. I remember going over there and them giving me *cui'ccu*, and Margarita said, "Well, we just threw out all the water because it was all black." They were constantly fighting that. They were right at the target, right at the drop spot, where the weather would drop it. I've always felt they were cancer victims from oil, from smoke pollution.

There were other, doctor-certified cancer deaths. One woman, Antonia Quenamá, spent most of her early life in Dureno but moved to Duvuno to marry a man. She was Lucia's aunt. According to Emeregildo, Antonia began to experience severe mouth pain. Eventually, she went to Ecuador's major cancer hospital in Quito, the Society for the Fight against Cancer. There, she was quickly diagnosed with mouth cancer. After staying in the hospital for three months, the doctors told her to return to Duvuno so she could die at home. By then, the cancer treatments had made her lose her hair. Lucia visited her and said she looked horrible. Lucia assumed the cancer itself made Antonia go bald. Lucia also thought a Napo Runa shaman might have attacked Antonia. She used to be a big, fat woman, Lucia reported, but she became extremely skinny. She also had an awful-looking tumor hanging from her lip. Lucia said it was black and filled with liquid. Shortly after Lucia's visit, Antonia died.

There are other cancer deaths that have some corroboration from medical experts. My good friend Antonio Aguinda, who moved from Dureno to Zábalo in the early 1980s, died from liver cancer in 2014. Quito doctors diagnosed him but could do nothing for him. Yori'ye's daughter Gavina, who also moved to Zábalo in the 1980s, reportedly died of stomach cancer. Although Alejandro believes a *cocoya* was to blame, Randy told me that Alejandro's older sister Elvira died of stomach cancer. Another Duvuno woman allegedly died of bone cancer. In 2016, a young girl died from a problem her father reported as *tumor*, although it was clearly some form of cancer. Randy told me that two men from Sinangoé died of cancer, one from liver cancer and the other from stomach cancer. The latter two deaths confuse the Cofán, as Sinangoé seems too far upriver to be affected by oil pollution. But, some people assert, the men spent long periods in and around Dureno, and they ate fish that may have traveled upstream from the pollution zone.

During my 2014 interview with Randy, I asked him when people began to worry about the health effects of contamination. I remarked that so many Dureno residents appear to be fatalists; they assume the damage is already done, so they see no point in either thinking about it or avoiding further exposure. Randy said,

Like you say, I don't know how deeply ingrained the idea is even now. There is that fatalism, "Well, we've been doing it all this time. One more time isn't going to hurt us." The links are slow. People say, "Well, yeah it was probably cancer." But even I hesitate to place the blame too frontally on cancer from oil because there are all sorts of other things out there that are gonna get you, too. It's not as though the only culprit is oil. But the amount of exposure that all of us in that generation had to oil contamination was incredible. And the incredible thing is we've had as little effects as we have. A few people still make it to eighty-five years old in spite of that. Not everybody does. But certainly the incidence of cancer for the size of population that we have and for the dietary and physical attributes of the population is unusually high. There's no doubt about it. . . . The interesting thing to me in Dureno was that it was pretty much a particular age group that was heavily exposed and ate a lot of contaminated fish. And many of them wound up with stomach cancers. And they all died very quick, all in their forties and fifties. They didn't even really make it into their sixties, although Elvira was maybe sixty-five when she died.

Randy's comments show just how difficult it is for the people of Dureno to answer two questions: Do we really know how many have died because of cancer? And do we really know that oil contamination was the cause of that cancer? For many reasons, the questions are ultimately unanswerable. The necessary data, records, and studies are not there. Even with the best medical care and scientific research, it is exceedingly difficult to determine that a certain form of environmental pollution was the certain cause of an individual illness or death.

Another complicating factor is that the people of Dureno experience many health problems that could trigger or occlude cancers related to contamination. On my trip to Dureno in 2016, Roberto was taking antibiotics. His stomach hurt, so Alejandro and Lucia brought him to the health center on the other side of the Aguarico. The worker there told them Roberto had a bacterial infection from *Helicobacter pylori* that was causing gastritis. I do not know if the worker did lab tests or simply diagnosed Roberto based on his reported symptoms. Even a brief perusal of Internet sources reveals that infection with *Helicobacter pylori*, like residence near oil-producing areas, is a possible cause of stomach cancer.

During our discussions about cancer, my Dureno collaborators often asked what I knew about the disease. I told them that I myself was a cancer survivor. In March 2005, I was diagnosed with malignant melanoma, an aggressive form of skin cancer. A nurse noticed a strange mole on my back and sent me to a dermatologist, who did a biopsy. He made the diagnosis and excised the cancer before it spread. Luckily, it never returned. My diagnosis came after I spent

---

2001 and 2002 doing dissertation fieldwork with the Cofán. From 2003 to 2005, I returned to Cofán territory regularly to work on conservation projects as an employee of the Office of Environmental Conservation Programs at the Field Museum of Natural History. Chances are that a genetic predisposition and too many early childhood sunburns caused my cancer. Nonetheless, the thought that I had spent so many days bathing in the Aguarico River crossed my mind many, many times. I use my story to urge the people of Dureno to see a doctor as soon as they notice troubling pains, lumps, or marks in or on their bodies. If it were not for my early visit to a nurse, I tell them, I would probably be dead.

A few weeks after the July 2014 oil spill—just after I started bathing in the Aguarico again—I developed another serious health problem. While I was eating a bowl of Lucia's collared peccary stew, my throat seized up. A chunk of meat got caught in it, and I almost choked. Over the next few days, my throat never loosened. I was reduced to subsisting on water, juice, and *cui'ccu* that Lucia pureed in an electric blender. Nothing solid could pass through my esophagus. I went to the health center on the other side of the river, but the Cuban doctor there offered no help. Soon, other people in the community, including Lucia, reported that they, too, were having trouble swallowing. When I returned to Dureno in 2016, Alejandro attempted to cure a small, skinny, and poorly developing girl who could not eat because her throat had "closed up," according to her mother. Perhaps my swallowing problem was more general than I had imagined.

By the end of the month, I was back in Quito. I saw three doctors at the city's best hospital. They did not know what was wrong with me. A day after I returned to the United States, I saw my gastroenterologist. For years, I have had issues with acid reflux, and I regularly take prescription antacids. The doctor dilated my esophagus, which helped a little. A few months later, he did it again. In January 2015, a different doctor referred me to an ear, nose, and throat specialist, who diagnosed me with a cricopharyngeal bar and Zenker's diverticulum. Basically, a muscle in my esophagus had spasmed and would not loosen, causing part of it to protrude into my throat, which allowed only soft food and liquid to pass into my stomach. After another

---

FIGURE 5.7. *Alejandro curing a girl held by her mother*

dilation, I still had problems swallowing. Finally, the specialist used an endoscopic laser to cut the spasmed muscle, a procedure that was intended to resolve the issue permanently.[12]

Unfortunately, the doctor mistakenly perforated my esophagus without realizing it and sent me home. Over the next four days, the liquids I drank seeped into my chest cavity. I soon developed a serious infection known as descending necrotizing mediastinitis. Putrid fluids inside my chest did not leave my lungs sufficient room to expand, and my oxygen level became dangerously low. Luckily, my wife took me to the emergency room just in time. After forty days in and out of intensive care, three complicated surgeries, and massive amounts of antibiotics and painkillers, I pulled through. I returned to my house in San Antonio, where I spent the next four months recovering.

Through Facebook messages, emails, and phone calls, my collaborators in Dureno inquired constantly about my health after Randy, my wife, and other friends told them about the medical crisis. I did not know if they attributed my initial condition to oil contamination, shamanic attack, or some other cause. Although I was unable to travel to Dureno in 2015 because of my illness, I returned in February 2016. Alejandro, Lucia, and Roberto wanted to hear my story, as did everyone else. In A'ingae, I described it as best as I could. I showed Lucia a picture I asked a nurse to take of me in the hospital. I was gaunt, pale, and nearly naked, with my robe in my lap. Four drainage tubes stuck out of my chest, an open wound covered my neck, and heart sensors were taped to my rib cage. Lucia looked like she was going to cry. She said she would not be able to sleep after seeing the way I had suffered.

Like the kidnapping scare, my health problems gave me an immediate appreciation of the difficulties the Cofán have been facing over the past five decades. The people of Dureno feel profound pain and uncertainty. They watch as their young ones cry because of digestive aches and skin lesions. They cope with the deaths and difficult lives of children who were born with misshapen organs and inexplicable behaviors. They care for the cancer-filled bodies of their spouses and parents. Many fear that they, too, will succumb to the disease.

I survived my sicknesses only because I had access to reliable medical care. I also had insurance, which covered the nearly $1 million cost of my treatments. The Cofán of Dureno are not so lucky. When I think about the company that for more than two decades threw billions of gallons of oil wastes into their streams and rivers and burned billions of cubic feet of natural gas and thousands of gallons of toxic substances into their skies, it is hard not to become enraged. Since 1993, Texaco and Chevron have spent hundreds of millions of dollars arguing that they are not culpable for the problems of the Cofán and their neighbors. I do not know how their executives and lawyers manage to sleep at night. Perhaps they are truly ignorant of the companies' legacy in Amazonian Ecuador. Perhaps they have come to believe the narratives their expert witnesses have spun. Or they might console themselves with the conviction that scientists will never be able to prove a link between Texaco's operations and Cofán suffering. The idea probably assuages their guilt. It might also calm their fear that they will eventually have to pay for what the company has done. No matter what their beliefs and intentions, their words and actions amount to a "labor of confusion" that multiplies doubts about oil's assault on human health.[13] The people of Dureno are left to suffer the consequences and hope that the pain and sickness will one day go away.

FIGURE 6.1. *Lucia washing clothes in the Aguarico River*

•

CHAPTER 6

PROHIBITION AND PROTEST

L ucia spends most of her days near her house and the river. After she struggled for years with an undiagnosed illness, Alejandro told her to stay away from the forest because she would be too vulnerable to *cocoya* attacks. As an older woman, she does not have to obey menstrual or pregnancy taboos, so she cooks all her family's meals. She also sits for hours on the riverbank, where she washes clothes and dishes, butchers fish and game, and socializes with women who are similarly occupied. Although she is now an elder, she has never attracted much attention from tourists or scholars. Like most women, she cannot sing the A'ingae laments and lullabies that outsiders want to hear. Nor does she consider herself well versed in Cofán culture, history, or politics. She wears her traditional clothing only for organized community events.

I have probably spent more time talking to Lucia than to anyone else in Dureno. During one of my research trips, Alejandro was

---

working at the seismic camp and barely around. From early morning to late evening, Lucia and I chatted about anything and everything. Over the course of many such conversations, I learned so much about her, the way she thinks, what she fears and desires, and the contents of her dreams, both literal and figurative.

My closeness to Lucia is unique. She is the only Cofán woman I felt I truly knew during my time in Dureno. I talked with many women, informally and in interview contexts. But it usually seemed like they were holding something back. No matter how much they appeared to trust me, I had the feeling that they related to me as they related to most non-Cofán men. They seemed anxious. Their replies to my questions often took the form of one-word answers or claims of ignorance. The reticence was especially pronounced in younger women. Many of them preferred to do our interviews with their friends or husbands at their sides. Older women were different. I think the chance to speak A'ingae with an outsider was inherently interesting to them. They also may have felt they had more authority to discuss cultural and historical matters.

For centuries, nonindigenous men have perpetrated acts of violence against Cofán women. No matter how harmless, mild-mannered, and comically inept I appeared to myself, the women of Dureno probably saw me in a different light. Because I could never quite overcome the barrier, I relied mainly on conversations with men to develop my understanding of oil in Dureno. Consequently, I probably remain unaware of important parts of the story. Perhaps after another twenty years of collaboration, the gender-based wall between Cofán women and me will finally fall. I certainly hope so, because I know they have much to teach me.

Although Lucia is just as shy and self-effacing as many Cofán women, she eventually became comfortable enough with me to do interviews. I paid my collaborators $10 an hour when the recording started, which certainly motivated some of them to participate in my project. Lucia knows little about the history of the oil industry. Like so many Dureno residents, she does not even say the word *petróleo* very often. Instead, she talks about the *companía* (Cofán pronunciation of the Spanish *compañía*), a general term that can refer to Texaco,

Chevron, Petroecuador, Petroamazonas, or any other past or present oil company and even to companies, plural.[1] I discovered that the easiest way to get people to discuss the petroleum industry's impacts was to inquire about what life was like before and after the *compañía* came. In order to elicit more information, I asked why people "liked" or "disliked" the *compañía*. My strategy usually worked, although my interviews often became wide-ranging, open-ended affairs. The topics I pursued bled into everyday conversations. I was always trying to cross-check my data and learn which opinions were shared and which were unique.

With the help of my assistant Martin, I titled one set of questions "Iyicco'fa'cho Fuesundeccu Fuite'cho," which means something like "Our Fights and Struggles and the Ways Other Peoples Have Helped Us." They formed the interview in which I asked people to tell me how and why they took action against the *compañía*. Although the Cofán are widely known as victims of oil, they are also celebrated opponents of it. In 1987, the people of Dureno blockaded a road that Texaco attempted to build into their territory without warning or permission. In 1993 and 1994, the residents of Zábalo kidnapped oil workers, burned a Petroecuador heliport, and closed an exploratory well. In 1998, hundreds of individuals from multiple Cofán communities came together to shut down Dureno 1, the well that Texaco drilled inside Dureno's territory in 1969. Environmental and indigenous rights organizations heralded the Cofán for their bold and successful protests. For decades, they were known as one of the world's most anti-oil indigenous peoples.

Lucia participated in the 1987 and 1998 actions, but she knew little about them even while they were happening. Today, she often confuses the two events, and she cannot remember when they occurred. She was silent during the recent community meetings in which people debated whether to allow seismic exploration on their land. In 2013, they decided to do it—a choice that disappointed many of the Cofán's nonindigenous allies. For decades, environmental and human rights activists had lauded the Cofán's steadfast opposition to any collaboration with the petroleum industry. Some of the organizations enjoyed a reputation as supporters of the Cofán's anti-oil efforts.

By tarnishing the Cofán's image as defenders of the rainforest, the people of Dureno were complicating the fund-raising efforts of the groups who had aided them.

During our interview about protests against the oil industry, I asked Lucia why people hated the *companía* so much. "Because they behave in such a dirty manner," she replied. "Ritual brother, we truly *se'pi'fa* (prohibited) the *companía*. Even now, most of us want to prohibit them. But the leaders here have made us lose ourselves. They tell us to do things, and we become lost. But we still hate the *companía*." I asked her to explain people's antagonism. She responded, "It's because the *companía* makes everything so dirty. They do that, and our fish and game have disappeared. They have contaminated everything. The Aguarico, the Pisorié, everything. The rivers became black. The fish stank. I have seen that." When I asked Lucia what would happen if the community were to allow more oil wells on their land, she replied, "It would become bad. We would all get cancer and die." She laughed lightly as she looked me in the eyes and uttered the words.

After reading so many pages about the damaging changes the oil industry brought to the Cofán and their territory, opposition probably seems like a natural response to the companies' presence. That assumption, however, is based on a conceptualization of oil that clashes with Cofán perspectives and experiences. When I first became interested in studying oil in Dureno, my primary question was why Cofán people waited nearly thirty years to shut down the Dureno 1 well. The Cofán's hesitation seemed so strange. All of the activist literature I had read made oil's destruction of Amazonian Ecuador appear to be the most blatant and insufferable thing in the world. When I first visited Dureno in 1998, I expected to see oil and its effects everywhere. I expected to hear people constantly lamenting its presence. I expected Cofán sadness, rage, and pain to stare me in the face. Fortunately and unfortunately, I was disappointed.

Unlike the whirlwind tour of death and destruction I imagined, my initial trip to Dureno was much more subdued. People were clearly poor and some seemed sick, but their ever-present humor—all that smiling and laughing—was hard to ignore. People also appeared to wrest much of their life from the remaining forest, which I had assumed was far too damaged to be of much use to anyone. Perhaps A'ingae was the cause of the misrepresentations that had formed my expectations. Usually, it is the only language spoken in the village. Hardly any non-Cofán people understand it. The linguistic wall makes it particularly easy for outsiders to write their assumptions onto Cofán lives. Furthermore, because many Dureno residents do not feel comfortable speaking Spanish, they often resort to scripts when using the language to communicate with ethnic others. The scripts typically do a better job confirming outside stereotypes than expressing the nuances of Cofán perspectives. As I learned A'ingae and became close to people, I began to understand the oil-Cofán encounter in a different way. My first question gave way to two better ones: How did Cofán people begin to view oil as a threat that demanded a collective response? And how did Cofán history create a sense of fearful passivity that made that response difficult?

The questions are related. Ever since their initial encounter with Royal Dutch Shell in the 1940s, oil was never a simple matter for the Cofán. It was both *simpe'cha'a* and *companía*. It was a new collection of people, a new mix of substances, a new set of sicknesses, and a new cascade of damages. To assemble all the phenomena into a single thing called "oil"—and to come to know that thing as the reason for their suffering—was anything but a straightforward process. In addition, the people of Dureno had to view that thing as a force they could counter through a new form of action. Before the 1980s, the Cofán were not familiar with "protest." They now describe it as *se'piye* (prohibiting) and *iyiccoye* (fighting), but the terms are extremely broad. A term incorporating a borrowed word—*paroeñe* (to make a *paro*, a strike or protest, in Spanish)—is more specific, but the activity to which it refers was novel and strange. In large part, the Cofán had to learn to protest the *companía* from the non-Cofán people who claimed to be their allies.

The history of *cocama* encounters also troubled Cofán people's opposition to oil. Aside from such *na'su* as Yori'ye, few Cofán individuals were willing to engage in violent confrontations with *cocama*. After hundreds of years of coercion, capture, and epidemics, the

---

169

Cofán had developed two main responses to incursions: flee from the *cocama* or wait for them to leave. Centuries ago, Spanish chroniclers described the Cofán as a warlike people who fought the crown's soldiers, burned its towns, and martyred its priests. Today, Cofán people have a hard time believing they were ever so violent. They sometimes joke about their ancestors' alleged possession of a wooden club called a *shombe* (literally, "property of the vagina"). Supposedly, men used the instrument to bash unfaithful wives over their heads. The story is more about depopulation than violence, though. People remark that the Cofán were so populous in the ancient times that one could dispose of a spouse and grab a new one the next day. Most Dureno residents admit that their ancestors fought and killed Tetete people, but only if the Tetete attacked them first. Mainly, people associate Cofán violence with shamans. They never liked shamanic violence, but they depended on it for protection. Even shamans, however, killed *a'tutsse* (in hidden ways or invisibly). No Cofán people killed *a'tatsse* (visibly—literally, "during the day"). For the most part, the Cofán thought of themselves as shy, peaceful, and friendly. By the middle of the twentieth century, outsiders saw them the same way.

Many individuals were involved in developing the Cofán's ability to resist the oil industry, whether by helping them to understand it as a threat or by mobilizing them to oppose its presence. Perhaps the person most responsible for forming Cofán anti-oil activism was Toribio Aguinda. I met Toribio in 1998 during my initial trip to Dureno. I had just finished my first year of graduate school at the University of Chicago. I showed up in Lago Agrio with little idea how to get to Dureno or to whom I would speak when I arrived. In the city, I saw an old man in an *ondiccu'je*. I asked in simple Spanish if he was from Dureno, and he said yes. He told me I could take the bus with him back to the village. He got off at the road to the settlement of Pisorié Canqque. I continued a bit further to the point where a small stone track heads south to the Aguarico. Alone, I walked to the river and waited. Eventually, an old woman and her granddaughter paddled over in their canoe. I asked them to take me to the other side, and they agreed. When I inquired whether the *jefe* (chief, in Spanish) or *presidente* was there, they brought me to Toribio's house.

———

At the time, Toribio was not the president of Dureno, but he was the president of the Cofán ethnic federation, the Organización Indígena de la Nacionalidad Cofán del Ecuador.[2] When the young girl called to him in A'ingae, he appeared at his door and invited me in. I sat on the split-palm floor, and he sat crossways in his hammock, right above me. Before our conversation began, he put on his feather crown. He spoke simple but clear Spanish. As I began to explain my interests, his wife entered with a steaming plate of fish and rice, which she handed to me. Even though I was a vegan at the time, I ate the food. (Anthropological lesson no. 1: Always accept offered food when you are trying to establish relations with someone.) Toribio appeared to understand my interest in studying the relationship between the community and the oil industry. He invited me to stay with him for a few days so we could learn a bit more about each other. I happily accepted. I also returned the next year for a month of preliminary research and the opportunity to compose an agreement with the community concerning the terms of our potential collaboration.[3]

I have always liked Toribio. My appreciation for him is about much more than his willingness to work with me. He was in his mid-fifties when I began my research for this book. His half-brother was Antonio Aguinda, who was my host and best friend in the community of Zábalo until he passed away from liver cancer in 2014. Although they grew up in Duvuno, Toribio and Antonio came to Dureno to marry sisters Rebeca and Saura Mashacori, respectively. Toribio's Spanish is very good by Cofán standards. He spent years training to work as a teacher, his primary occupation. He has taught in many Cofán communities in both Spanish and A'ingae.

Toribio has a round, soft face and a thin moustache. He is short and slightly pudgy. Upon talking to him, most outsiders would not be able to detect his Cofán-ness. After knowing him for so many years, I have learned that there is something unique about his personality. He is a kind, calm, and smiling man, but he has a way of looking past you—when he is looking at you—that reminds me of the otherworldly thinking of shamans. Even though he is a careful and attentive listener, his mind often appears to be somewhere else. In a way, his mental distance grounds his personality, making it hard for him to be

—

FIGURE 6.2. *Toribio Aguinda. Photo by Michael Cepek.*

shaken by gut reactions or unforeseen circumstances. It is as though he has a shaman's strong sense of self without sharing their violent inclinations. That said, over two decades since we met, Toribio has become increasingly interested in shamanism. He began to drink *yaje* with Avelino Quenamá, Yori'ye's nephew who lives in Pisorié Canqque. He was also present when I drank *yaje* with Alejandro. People say Toribio has shamanic weapons, including *davu*. But he is one of the least aggressive and boastful people I know. He is an intriguing mix: a combination of shamanic discipline, otherworldly concerns, and a more altruistic, this-worldly commitment to bettering the lot of his people.

During my first stay in the village, Toribio took me to Dureno 1. After we crossed the river on our way to catch a bus and taxi to the well, we walked on the same stone road I used to get to the river two days earlier. Toribio was wearing dress shoes, a tucked-in shirt, and clean pants. When he saw a squirrel on the forest floor next to the

———

path, he immediately took off running to catch it. He seemed half-embarrassed by his instinctive (and failed) attempt, but I had already learned that meat was not as common as it once was in Dureno and that no chance to acquire it should be wasted. Slightly muddy, Toribio then led me to the main road, which we followed to Dureno 1.

I had never been that close to a functioning oil well. It was of the "old" variety, with a large, black, uncovered, and unlined waste pit next to it. The pit was probably more than a hundred square meters. It was filled with dead insects and stinking sludge. An overflow pipe spilled the pit's contents into a ravine that fed into a stream that connected to the Pisorié River. Two flares burned loudly and constantly. A couple of separation tanks were next to the wellhead, which at that point was the small amalgamation of gauges and valves that people refer to as a *muñeco* (doll, in Spanish). I took pictures of the scene. It was the one thing that met my dismal expectations—it was an ugly, smelly, depressing mess with absolutely no contamination controls. Toribio affirmed that it had done much damage to his people. That was why, he said, they were going to shut it down in one month, on October 12, 1998. I did not believe him. Later that year, I learned he was right.

By the time I began research for this book, Toribio was living and teaching in Zábalo, but he kept his home and gardens in Dureno, where he is a formal community member. I did not see him much, but he sometimes passed through during vacations and work trips to Lago Agrio. One day, Martin and I got the chance to do a three-hour interview with him about the history of Cofán anti-oil protests. Although he said he could not talk long because he had to work on his gardens, as soon as he began to speak it was clear he had a lot to say. His typical calmness transformed into animated pride when he told us about the 1987 and 1998 actions. He also excitedly recounted his decision to join the people of Zábalo in their 1994 occupation of the exploratory well. Toribio was present for the Cofán's most important acts of anti-oil resistance and a major player in each of them.

By the mid-1980s, a small group of Dureno men were becoming involved in Ecuador's national indigenous movement. Toribio was among them, as were Deji and Emeregildo. They were three of the best Spanish speakers in the community. Along with Randy, they are some of the few individuals who can recall the 1987 blockade with any degree of certainty. Randy was already living in Zábalo at the time, but he returned to Dureno frequently. According to Toribio, by 1987 the small group had begun to organize larger community discussions. Catholic priests, mainly Carmelites but also a few Capuchins, were critical in the politicization of Toribio and other Dureno leaders. By the 1970s, Latin America's Catholic Church had become radicalized. Many young priests held left-wing commitments to liberation theology, social justice, and environmental activism. Toribio said a Carmelite named José Luís Trueba was an important influence on him. The priest was young, trustworthy, and *putsa'su* (bold or fierce). He helped the Cofán leaders during community meetings. He also taught them how to compose reports, letters of protest, and requests for aid from state officials and nongovernmental organizations.

In the summer of 1987, Texaco began to build a road into the western edge of Dureno's territory. The company neither notified the Cofán nor asked their permission. The community had already cut and marked its boundary trails, but Texaco simply ignored them. The area was far from the central settlement, and no one noticed the work until a hunter heard the machines. By the time people went to see what was happening, Texaco had already made kilometers of road and a drilling platform. For years, rumors had circulated that during an earlier round of seismic testing, Texaco had detected eighteen or nineteen potential well sites in Dureno's territory. No one knew which field the new wells would belong to. Some said the Parahuacu field stretched south under the Aguarico River into Cofán territory. Others said the Guanta field extended east toward the village center. Still others said the new wells would belong to the Dureno field, a supposedly distinct geological formation. No one knew, and Texaco was not telling them. The only certainty was that the company intended to build at least one new well far inside the community's boundaries. The platform was already there, but drilling had yet to begin.

In conversation with the Carmelites and community members, the leaders decided, in Toribio's words, "to scare the *companía* and force it to leave." Although some people were afraid, everyone ultimately agreed to confront the Texaco workers. In October 1987, a group of Cofán men and women hiked to the platform in traditional dress. They spoke to the site supervisor, who was a *cocama*. Toribio told him the platform and road were on Cofán land. The supervisor replied, "No. This belongs to the state. You cannot prohibit us here. We are here to drill oil that belongs to the state." He was referring to a point of Ecuadorian law, that although indigenous groups may have title to land, the government claims ownership of all subsurface resources, including oil. Toribio then said, "But we have a land title for this property. You must listen to us and have compassion for us." The supervisor replied, "I don't know about that. You have to go speak to the chief of operations in Lago Agrio. We're all just workers here."

A few days later, Toribio and other leaders went to the Texaco office in Lago Agrio. They tried to begin a dialogue, but the company officials refused to engage with them. Upset, they returned to Dureno and discussed the matter with elders and other adults. They decided to go back to the site in larger numbers with freshly made spears. People were afraid of a confrontation with soldiers, but they were fed up with the company's arrogance. Dozens of people returned to the platform and confronted the workers. They announced they were there to remove the company from their territory. The supervisor said there was nothing he could do. Toribio then lied to him. He said a large group of Cofán men in black *ondiccu'je* were hiding in the forest. If they got angry, Toribio warned, they would attack the workers without mercy. Toribio laughed when he told that part of the story.

Alarmed, the supervisor said he needed his boss's permission to halt operations. Toribio replied that his boss's permission did not matter. At that point, the workers decided to comply with the Cofán's demand. Trucks came and removed the machinery from the platform site. The Cofán even asked them to use a tractor to drag logs onto the road to block further encroachment. The workers agreed to do it. They were not hostile; it is more likely that they were sympathetic or afraid. Most of them were simply unskilled *cocama*. A few might have been indigenous people from neighboring ethnic groups.

The Cofán knew the struggle was far from over. Immediately, almost all community members moved to the site. Some say they

—

were there for a month; others say their occupation lasted at least three months. The priests came to provide aid and supplies. Representatives from other indigenous organizations arrived, too. Native Amazonian allies stayed for a long time, but the Andean leaders who came to provide support remained for only a short while. They could not handle life in the forest, Toribio recalled with a laugh. People from the Cofán communities of Sinangoé, Duvuno, and Zábalo came, too. Allies put out a call for aid on a Lago Agrio radio station. Friendly *cocama* responded with visits to express solidarity. They also gave gifts of pots, dishes, and food to help the Cofán extend their occupation.

It was a festive, inspiring, politicizing moment for the Cofán. They set up a twenty-four-hour watch along the road. At different points, Cofán men hid in the forest and waited for soldiers to arrive. They devised a plan to send word of coming threats through a set of imitated birdcalls they would use to relay messages back to the platform site, where most people were camped. At the urging of the priests and more experienced indigenous leaders, the Cofán decided to plant gardens along the road to solidify their presence. After the occupation was over, a few families decided to build houses next to the gardens and create the population center of Pisorié Canqque; they still watch to make sure no outsiders enter Dureno from its western edge.

During the takeover, Toribio traveled back and forth between the platform encampment and Lago Agrio. He finally arranged a meeting with a Texaco chief of operations. He went with five other Dureno men as well as the priest José Luís, but the chief said he would speak to only one of them. Toribio agreed to do it. He entered the office and told the man that his people simply wanted to live well. The chief claimed to understand Toribio's position. In reciprocation for Texaco's entrance and planned drilling, he offered the community three cars, a schoolhouse, and 150 million *sucres* (the Ecuadorian currency at the time).[4] Toribio replied that he could not make the decision alone; he needed to return to the camp and speak to the rest of the people. When he got back, he told everyone about Texaco's offer. At that point, the priests and leaders of the pan-indigenous organization Confederación de las Nacionalidades Indígenas de la

FIGURE 6.3. *Deji Criollo and his wife, Gavina Aguinda, returning from their garden with manioc and plantains*

Amazonía Ecuatoriana (CONFENIAE) shared their perspectives. In Toribio's words,

> The priests and other indigenous leaders said to me, "Yes, you can take their money. But what about your land, your forest, and your game animals? You won't have those any longer. It will never be the same. If you take their money, they will destroy everything in your forest. You might have that money for a while, but your children will never be able to survive with just that." And then I realized that if we gave them our land, we would become truly poor. So I decided to tell the adults in the community about my thoughts. "That's what will happen to us," I said. They heard me and replied, "Let's not take the money."

Toribio returned to the Texaco chief. The man listened to Toribio's report, but he said that if the Cofán did not take his offer, soldiers would come and remove them from the site by force. Toribio told him to go ahead and send the soldiers. In the following weeks, however, the soldiers never arrived. The situation remained calm. Later, the chief sent word that he wanted to talk to Toribio again. The Carmelites connected Toribio with a lawyer named Guillermo Ortiz who lived in Lago Agrio. Guillermo offered to assist Toribio in the meeting free of charge. When they got to the office, Texaco also had a lawyer. The lawyers began to speak among themselves. Guillermo said, "Why do you dislike the Cofán and what they need to live? If that's not the case, then you need to find them a big piece of territory so they can continue living the way they want." The Texaco chief was impressed by Guillermo. He said to Toribio, "All right, you're finally winning. Now you have your own lawyer." Reporting the statement made Toribio laugh. He said,

> Guillermo said to them, "Listen. This is what the Cofán want. They are people who have lived here a long time. They want to live well. All of you are sitting here in your nice office, with your nice air conditioning, and you're really comfortable. That's what the Cofán want, but for them that means living their own way. The forest makes them cool. It gives them fresh air to breathe. They want all that so they can live well. You must listen to them and have compassion for them." Then, the Texaco chief spoke, "Well, this lawyer has really beat me. I've decided not to bother you all any more. Right here, the problem will end for good." That's when we truly beat Texaco, when we truly stopped what they were doing in our community.

The other leaders who told me about the 1987 blockade confirmed Toribio's account. Deji stressed that the media were helpful allies. When a journalist asked him how many Cofán people were participating in the occupation, he said 250; the journalist told him to double the estimate to 500 to make the story sound better. Randy said Texaco's president of Ecuadorian operations contacted him in Quito. According to Randy, the president was "just an oil man" who had no idea how to handle the situation. CONFENIAE had complicated matters by helping the Cofán compose a list of demands that included such strange things as a "nursery for wild animals." The Texaco president did not know what was happening or what the Cofán were asking of him. He decided to give up. After all, it was already the end of 1987. In little more than two years, Texaco would cede its operator role to Petroecuador. It would leave the country entirely in 1992. Why go through so much trouble to open a new well it would not even be able to exploit for very long?

In late 2002, at the end of my doctoral research, I did a long series of interviews with Randy about Cofán history. During the sessions, I inquired about the 1987 blockade. When I asked what initiated the event and what effect it had, he replied,

> My take on it was that this group of people had just had enough. It was the last straw. They had their land taken away, their rivers taken away, all their hunting taken away, their ability to move around and go anyplace they want—it was all taken away. And the company was not even content with having eaten up all that. It wanted to take away the last little pittance they had. The biggest thing I remember about the whole thing was the attitude of "This is the last straw." That was the thing that stood out the most to me. It didn't take much cajoling to do it. How to do it, of course, was a different matter. They were receiving input from many sources, Toribio, for sure, and others of the leadership, although I can't remember who exactly that was at the time. . . . It definitely consolidated people against oil. That stance continues through today. There is a very strong base of resistance to any oil exploitation within the land. The worst thing that can be said about a Dureno leader is that he's accepting money from the oil company.

In the early 1990s, I became interested in working with the Cofán because of their reputation for total opposition to oil. As an undergraduate at the University of Illinois at Urbana-Champaign, I had become committed to the causes of tropical conservation and indigenous peoples' rights. In a course about the peoples and cultures of South America, Enrique Mayer, a Peruvian scholar of the Andes, introduced me to the issues. Within a year, I became the president of the Illinois Rainforest Action Group, an affiliate of the Rainforest Action Network. The organization supported the Cofán and other peoples of Amazonian Ecuador by publicizing the 1993 Texaco lawsuit and mobilizing for a boycott of the company. I was a participant in the campaign. I remember standing on the university quad and dumping a can of Hershey's chocolate syrup on the cement—meant to symbolize an oil spill—as I spoke through a megaphone about Texaco's deeds. A year later, in 1994, the Rainforest Action Network put out an action alert about the people of Zábalo's successful effort to remove Petroecuador from their territory. I found their accomplishment incredibly inspiring, and I wanted to figure out how they did it.

In late 1993, I had already begun working with Norman E. Whitten Jr., a University of Illinois anthropologist with a long history of collaborating with indigenous people in Amazonian Ecuador. In the fall of 1994, under Whitten's supervision, I was to head to Ecuador for a semester of study abroad, during which I intended to learn more about the campaign against oil. In a coincidence that still seems miraculous, one night in the summer before my departure, I sat down for dinner with my family in our suburban Chicago home. A CBS program named *America Tonight* came on the television. The episode featured the story of Zábalo's fight against oil. It focused on the intriguing figure at the center of the struggle, Randy Borman. As far as I can recall, it was the first time I had heard of Randy. Immediately, I was fascinated. A few months later, I was in Quito. I contacted Randy and did a long interview with him about his community's fight with Petroecuador. The conversation was the basis for my 1996 bachelor's thesis, "Reorganization and Resistance: Petroleum, Conservation, and Cofán Transformations." More than twenty years later, I am still writing about the same general issue.

In 1994, I imagined that the people of Zábalo were different from the people of Dureno, even though most of them originally came from Dureno. Beginning in 1979, Randy and a few Cofán friends started to travel downriver to hunt and work with tourists who wanted to see the Amazonian rivers, lakes, and forests. Five years later, they built houses and gardens at the remote location, which was close to the Peruvian border in an area with no roads, no oil wells, and no colonist farms. Most of the families who moved to Zábalo wanted to work on what Randy was already calling "community-based ecotourism." Just as important, though, was their desire to get away from the contaminated, depleted, *cocama*-filled lands near Dureno. I assumed that the families who decided to remain in Dureno had resigned themselves to an impoverished life in the oil zone. It was not until I arrived in Ecuador that I learned about the 1987 blockade. It occurred at a time when rainforest conservation was not a popular global issue. The first Dureno protest never received international media attention, unlike Zábalo's 1994 action.

When I began to think about doctoral research, I decided to focus on the Dureno Cofán's history with oil, including their 1998 decision to take over Dureno 1. I even titled my dissertation proposal "Dureno 1: The Presence of Oil in the Cofán World." Given security issues that prevented me from working near the Colombian border,[5] I had to postpone my Dureno project. By the time I began it more than a decade later, my thinking on oil had become more nuanced. Still, one of my central questions was why the Cofán chose to shut down Dureno 1 in the way and at the time they did.

People's memories of the event are much clearer than their recollections of the 1987 blockade. The best accounts come from the individuals who led the protest, including Toribio.[6] The Dureno 1 takeover had no single, immediate cause. The 1987 success strengthened the Cofán's confidence and resolve. Zábalo's successful 1994 protest convinced the people of Dureno that Petroecuador, which began to operate Dureno 1 in 1990, was vulnerable to Cofán protests. Moreover, the Ecuadorian environmental organization Acción Ecológica had become deeply involved with the community. Though based in Quito, the group embraced opposition to Ecuador's Amazonian oil industry as one of its central commitments. They knew the industry had hit the Cofán harder than any other indigenous people. They also knew the Cofán had a record of militant protest. The qualities made the Cofán the perfect people around whom to organize a symbolically powerful and culturally authentic resistance campaign.

———

FIGURE 6.4. *A mural in Lago Agrio outside
a Petroamazonas production facility*

In the year before the 1998 takeover, Acción Ecológica representatives engaged in long conversations with Dureno leaders to compose a list of Cofán demands concerning Dureno 1 and oil's larger effects on Cofán lives. Acción Ecológica wrote up and published the demands in a Spanish and A'ingae pamphlet entitled *El mejor lugar de la selva: Propuesta para la recuperación del territorio Cofán* (The best place in the forest: Proposal for the recovery of Cofán territory, in Spanish). The authors were listed as the Comuna Cofán Dureno and the Organización Indígena de la Nacionalidad Cofán del Ecuador. Toribio estimated that they printed as many as a thousand copies. Each had a glossy green cover with a photograph of Yori'ye wearing his feather crown. The publication featured cultural and historical information on Dureno as well as an overview of the community's relations with the oil industry, including the damages the Cofán had suffered.[7]

At the end of the pamphlet, the five points of the Cofán's central proposal are listed: close Dureno 1 and remove all infrastructure and wastes from the well site; declare a state of emergency for the Pisorié River and the Totoa Nai'qui River and close all sources of contamination into the waterways; restore the ecology of the Dureno 1 site, including the stream, river, platform, surrounding area, and road; recuperate Cofán territory by granting land titles for the communities of Sinangoé, Chandia Na'e, and Zábalo and amplifying Dureno's territory through land purchases; and compensate the Cofán with state funds to support Cofán development, health, and education initiatives.

Toribio said that before the Dureno 1 takeover, Acción Ecológica sent the pamphlets all over the country and the world. The organization made a point of giving them to Ecuadorian politicians. When they handed one to Jamil Mahuad, a man who would win the national presidency later that year, he told them he would support their proposal. After giving the booklet to every potential ally, journalist, and person in a position of power, they invited them all to Dureno 1 on the scheduled action date of October 12, Columbus Day in the United States and Día de la Raza in Ecuador. The takeover was not intended as a surprise attack. Rather, it was a political and media event designed to draw attention to the Cofán cause and to use public pressure and international sympathy to force the government to comply with Cofán demands.

On the morning of October 12, almost every man, woman, and child from Dureno went to Dureno 1. They were joined by people from other Cofán communities, leaders and supporters from other indigenous peoples, and nonindigenous allies. The Cofán wore traditional dress and carried spears and blowguns. There were hundreds of people. Soon, government officials began to arrive, mainly from Amazonian provinces. A helicopter flew in from the city of Coca with a contingent of military officers. Toribio, as president of the ethnic federation at the time, spoke to the assembled officials. "This is what we want and think," he said. "We have lived here since the old times. We have struggled to survive. This well is in our home. It's in our forest. It's on our land. It sends its wastes into our rivers and streams, into what we need to survive. It has contaminated our land. That's why we don't want it."

———

The Cofán kept spear-wielding "warriors" along the road to guard against incursions and to provide a stirring image for journalists to capture and disseminate. Dozens of collective and individual conversations occurred over the following weeks. They happened among Cofán people and between the Cofán and people from other ethnic groups. A Petroecuador official arrived and asked how he could help. He claimed that Dureno 1 was not even a good well any more; it was not producing much crude. The Cofán said if that was the case, the company should go ahead and shut it down. The Cofán also announced that if the company wanted to help, Cofán leaders had already given them their proposal.

The official replied that closing the well would be difficult. The company had installed a pumping system in it, but the mechanism was damaged, which was why production had dropped. The Cofán told him to close the well anyway, no matter what its condition. They said it had been on their land for more than twenty years without providing a single benefit to them. They did not just want compensation; they wanted the well to be gone forever. Some government officials stated that they wanted to help the Cofán acquire more and better land to live on, perhaps in a territory far upriver that had yet to be colonized. Cofán leaders replied that their proposal called for the amplification of Dureno's land, not the removal of the Cofán to a different location altogether. They had no interest in the officials' idea.

The Cofán stayed at the site for more than a month. They waited for President Jamil Mahuad to arrive, but he never did. People from all over the world sent funds to help buy supplies to support the Cofán in their action. Dureno residents also brought plantains and manioc from their gardens. Some hunted for meat in the nearby forest. Platoons of soldiers arrived to maintain order at the site. They stood on one side of the line the Cofán had drawn. They were dressed in battle fatigues, with machine guns at the ready. Journalists from Ecuador's top newspapers and television stations provided coverage of the event, as did a few international media sources. Eventually, a woman who said she was from the Ministry of Government arrived. She affirmed her commitment to help the Cofán, but she said the state could not close the well. She asked them when they would leave. Cofán leaders said they would never leave. It was their land, they proclaimed, and they had nowhere else to go.

Shamans played an important part in the takeover. Powerful *atesu'cho* from remote stretches of the San Miguel and Bermejo Rivers came to offer their aid. Alejandro and other Dureno shamans joined them. The visiting shamans could not mingle with people in the main camp; they were too strict about maintaining the prohibitions. They could not let potentially contaminated people feed them, give them *cui'ccu*, walk behind their backs, or cross their paths. Quickly, they said they began to feel sick. They decided to protect themselves by building a small camp and *yaje* house on a hilltop overlooking the well. There, they stood in their *ondiccu'je* and extravagant feather crowns, watching the action below. Every night, they drank *yaje*. Everyone could hear their chanting.

The soldiers became afraid of the shamans. They asked what the *ancianos* (old ones, in Spanish) were doing. People told them the men were *shamanes*. Ecuadorians of all backgrounds—indigenous or not—fear the malevolence of indigenous shamans, whom they sometimes call *brujos* (witches, in Spanish). The *atesu'cho* sent word that they had succeeded in contacting *tsanda* (thunder and lightning), a being they considered an *a'i*. *Tsanda* was their ally, they said. If they requested its help, it would strike the well site and kill the Cofán's enemies. Reportedly, the idea made its way to the soldiers and terrified them. Moreover, other Cofán participants told the soldiers that men with blowguns were hiding in the forest. Their darts would strike without sound or warning, the Cofán claimed. The poison on the dart tips would quickly enter the bloodstream and end the life of any person the projectiles reached.

Soon, some soldiers announced that they were not there to hurt the Cofán. Rather, they were there to support and protect them. A few even struck up friendships with Cofán protestors and shared liquor with them at night. One or two said they were not *blancos* (whites, in Spanish), but *indígenas*—Shuar or Napo Runa people. Their sympathies lay with the Cofán, they asserted, not with the government or the oil company.

———

In their memories of the Dureno 1 takeover, older people like Alejandro, Valerio, Lucia, and Laura portray the shamans as the true protagonists of the action. The *atesu'cho* decided to test their powers by transforming into *cocoya* who could descend below the earth and shut down the well through supernatural means. After many nights of drinking *yaje*, the shamans announced that they had "closed" or "dried" the well by placing a giant boulder over the oil deposit beneath it. No one in Dureno knew how they could do such a thing. But they trusted in the powers of the *atesu'cho*, to whom they had long turned for healing when no one in their own community could cure their ill.

The occupation went on for more than a month. Eventually, the government conceded; it announced it would shut down the well. Officials repeated the earlier comment that it was not producing much crude anyway, so there was no reason to keep it open. Perhaps the shamans were right about their success in drying up the oil. The more government officials thought about it, the less valuable Dureno 1 was, given its state of disrepair. Company workers came to remove the machinery and infrastructure. Down went the wellhead, the flares, and the separation tanks. The company also supposedly cleaned the pit. In truth, workers did little more than cover it with soil and sand. Oily runoff still emerged from the site and flowed into the stream, although there was much less waste than there was before.

After he finished the story, Toribio declared, "That's the way we fought at the Dureno 1 well—we struggled, fought hard, and finally closed it." Lucia summarized the action in different terms: "The old-time shamans entered Dureno 1, closed it up, and got rid of it. They came here and your ritual brother [Alejandro], too, drank *yaje* with them, closed the well, and discarded it for good." Even though the well was gone, the government never addressed the other Cofán demands. There was no real cleanup; contamination continued from other wells, pipelines, and production facilities; no funds were provided for Cofán health and development projects; ecological restoration never occurred; and the state did not buy or expropriate land to add to Dureno's territory.

I asked Toribio how people felt after the Dureno 1 action. Despite its ultimate shortcomings, Toribio said, everyone considered it a

FIGURE 6.5. *A spear that Roberto uses for fishing*

success. The Cofán had won. They had beaten the *companía*. Many thought Petroecuador would never return. Toribio told me that people from the upriver communities on the Bermejo and San Miguel Rivers where the powerful shamans live still ask when he will become the ethnic federation president again. His leadership impressed them. One day, they imagine, they might need him to deal with oil-related conflicts in their own communities.

The success also impressed the Cofán's allies. Members of Acción Ecológica told Toribio that people all over the world would hear about the Cofán. Outsiders would know that the Cofán are good and strong and that they *patsupa canse'fa* (acted fiercely and continue to survive). For years after the takeover, activists and tourists traveled to the community to hear about Dureno 1 and the Cofán fight against oil. Sometimes they came with Acción Ecológica, sometimes they came with other organizations, and sometimes they came alone. They wanted to meet and learn from the victorious Cofán. In Deji's words, the visitors said, "These Cofán are the ones who scared off the company. That's who the Cofán are. They are the ones who won."

Other indigenous people, too, arrived to speak with the people of Dureno. Acción Ecológica often served as their guides. They traveled from other parts of Ecuador and even from other countries. They wanted the Dureno Cofán to teach them how oil destroys people and the places they live. They also wanted to learn how the Dureno Cofán devised a way to overcome it. According to Arturo, Acción Ecológica introduced the community to visitors in the following terms: "These are the ones who truly dislike the *companía*. These are the ones who scared the *companía* and made it leave their territory. These are the only people who have ever done that." The Cofán were more famous than ever. Finally, they were celebrated for something they did—not something someone or something did to them.

On May 29, 1999, Acción Ecológica erected a large placard at the site of the closed well. It stood high above the ground on a thick metal pipe. It read, "A tribute to the Cofán people." With colorful paintings of anacondas on its sides, it announced the basic facts in bold, Spanish text:

The Best Place in the Forest
THE DURENO 1 WELL
Drilled by Texaco in 1969
Closed by the Cofán People on October 12, 1998
Depth: 10,300 feet
Accumulated Production: 2,500,000 barrels
GENERATED WASTES:
Formation waters: 1,000,000 barrels
700,000 cubic feet of burned gas
Crude spilled as part of well reconditioning: 6,000 barrels
Deforestation: 10 hectares
Contamination: Pisorié River, Aguarico River
AFFECTED ONES: The Cofán People

For nearly two decades after the Dureno 1 action, the oil industry failed to enter Dureno. Companies made requests, inquiries, and proposals, but the Cofán told them no. They were not interested in working with the *companía*. The *companía* had hurt them. It had killed them. In the future, its contamination would hurt and kill more of them. It had devastated the forests the Cofán depended on. Its roads brought people who forced the Cofán off their homeland. A few industry representatives tried to entice the Cofán with new promises, but the Cofán had no faith in oil. They knew the *companía* had always lied. They knew it always would. What had it ever given the people of Dureno? A few spoons, the Cofán laugh, recalling the 1969 encounter of Randy, his hunting partners, and Texaco workers at Dureno 1. No one except Randy remembers the bag of doughnuts the *companía* also gave the Cofán that day. Four spoons and some doughnuts—that was the *companía*'s reciprocity for two and a half million barrels of crude as well as the disastrous consequences of its extraction.

Two decades after they shut down Dureno 1, the Cofán have a more complicated perspective. None of them are looking forward to new wells, new roads, and new contamination. But they have grown wary of the environmentalists who claim to be their allies. When Martin accompanied me to Quito after my 2013 kidnapping scare, we decided to make use of the opportunity to speak to the Acción Ecológica director who was once so close to the people of Dureno. I will call her Claudia to protect her privacy. She agreed to talk to us at the organization's Quito headquarters. After a short tour of the space, she sat down with us in a conference room. Martin explained who I was and what we were working on.

Claudia seemed suspicious. Rumors had been circulating that Chevron was paying foreign informants to pose as journalists and anthropologists to gather information that would discredit people involved in the lawsuit. Although Claudia might have imagined I was a Chevron mole, it is more likely that she was simply tired of all the North Americans who come to Ecuador to write articles and books about oil's consequences. So few of them do anything meaningful for the people of Ecuador. Most complete their research, publish their accounts, and use the status they accrue to better their social and economic positions in their own countries.[8] As far as I know, Claudia had never worked closely with Martin. She had become somewhat distant from Dureno since the Cofán decided to allow seismic exploration on their land in 2013. By that year, Martin had been elected to leadership positions for both Dureno and the Cofán ethnic federation. But the Cofán leadership had done little to stop Dureno from working with the *companía*. They certainly were not calling on Acción Ecológica to aid them in a new resistance campaign.

Claudia spoke to us for hours. I intended our visit to serve as an introduction that would lead to a longer set of interviews. Because I did not have Claudia's consent to collect data on that day, I did not bring my digital recorder, and I took no notes. I wish I had. Claudia shared a fascinating account of the history of her relation with Dureno. She told us about the closing of Dureno 1. Strangely, she appeared to be speaking only to me; she paid little attention to Martin. At the end of the conversation, we shook hands, and I gave her a copy of my 2012 book about the environmental projects spearheaded by the people of Zábalo. She happily accepted it. Over the next two weeks, every email I sent her and every voice mail I left went unanswered. It appeared that Claudia had no interest in helping me write this book. Eventually, I returned to Dureno without the interviews I wanted.

My history of oil in Dureno would not include the voice of an actor who was essential to an important chapter of the story.

It is hard to determine what drove a wedge between Acción Ecológica and the people of Dureno. I hesitate to write too much about the issue because I sympathize deeply with individuals like Claudia. They have dedicated their lives to environmental conservation and indigenous rights. In Ecuador's political climate, they are at risk of government harassment and persecution. President Correa did not take kindly to people who attempted to stop existing oil operations or prevent the development of new ones. Activists may earn a small paycheck for their efforts, but they could probably earn much more with other, more secure jobs. They have told the world what is happening in Amazonian Ecuador, and they have brought attention to people in Dureno and other Cofán communities. Also, they do their best to keep the Ecuadorian government honest. Without their constant protest and publicity, it is likely that Ecuador's petroleum industry would extract crude in a manner even less clean and safe than it is now.

Nonetheless, I sympathize with the Dureno residents who are critical of environmental organizations, whether from Ecuador or other countries. Relative to the Cofán, the employees of the organizations occupy a much higher economic position. They make a living through their work, but they have never been able to offer significant economic resources to the Cofán, who need money as much as they need the forest. The *ecologistas* are able to justify their projects to donors thanks to Cofán accomplishments. Organizations like Acción Ecológica have definitely helped the Cofán, but Cofán labor, land, and lives were the main forces involved in the organization's Dureno campaign.

People wonder why the activists do not share more of their wealth with the community. Some Dureno residents dwell so much on the inequalities that they wonder whether Acción Ecológica's warnings about oil-related contamination were even true. Perhaps they are just liars, people think, like so many other *cocama* and gringos. Speaking about the organization's persistent interest in the Cofán's anti-oil stance, Laura stated, "They came to scold and counsel us so

———

FIGURE 6.6. *A tree in Dureno's forest interior*

many times, but they never helped us. They gave us nothing. So we asked ourselves, 'Maybe they are lying to us and somehow making money with our land?'" A young man laughed softly as he said it, but he phrased the issue in equally stark terms: "Perhaps they want us to prohibit the *compañía* because they do not want us to earn any money." For decades, *cocama* had told the Cofán similar things: "You people don't need money, you just need the forest and your culture." The outsiders who say such things are far wealthier than the Cofán, and they are visibly invested in Cofán choices. Outsiders often seem sad rather than happy when the people of Dureno acquire money. It makes sense for the Cofán to interpret Acción Ecológica's intentions in such terms, even if they do not reflect the real perspectives of activists like Claudia.

Most people report that after Dureno's 2013 decision to let BGP conduct seismic exploration on Cofán land, Acción Ecológica stopped visiting them. From the perspective of some individuals, the organization's support was much more conditional than it should have been. For other people, the organization became a threat to the community's well-being, and they were glad it stayed away. Word circulated that Acción Ecológica was funneling financial resources to the Dureno residents who did not want to let the company in. The alleged support exacerbated conflicts in Dureno. It meant more friction, more fights, and more division. It meant less reciprocity, less cooperation, and less goodwill. The great majority of Dureno residents are still certain that oil makes them suffer. But unhappiness has more than one cause. For the Cofán, fighting constantly with one's neighbors and even family members can be just as painful as having less food to eat and less certainty about one's health.

It is possible that the break between Acción Ecológica and the people of Dureno was due to the tension that Beth Conklin and Laura Graham describe in their 1995 article "The Shifting Middle Ground: Amazonian Indians and Eco-Politics." They assert that many environmental activists view Amazonian peoples according to the stereotypical image of "the ecologically noble savage." The outsiders have little knowledge of the actual perspectives, experiences, and objectives of people like the Cofán. Portraying native Amazonians as

———

natural conservationists attracts significant publicity for indigenous causes. But the assumption creates a form of coalitional politics that is all too fragile. As soon as Amazonians make choices that conflict with the image of ecological nobility, alliances and collaborations can crumble to the ground. Overnight, saviors of the rainforest become corrupt sellouts and outside support is replaced by outright condemnation.[9] To the best of my knowledge, neither Claudia nor other Acción Ecológica activists publicly criticize the people of Dureno for their willingness to rethink their relationship with oil. But many Dureno residents say that Acción Ecológica is interested in them only as opponents of the petroleum industry. They do not view the organization as a helpful ally in their attempt to negotiate a new form of coexistence with the *companía*.

There is also the oldest and deepest criticism: Acción Ecológica and other organizations are staffed by *cocama*, who have brought death and destruction to the Cofán for centuries. Hostility toward *cocama* even influences Cofán perspectives on the Chevron case. Lawyers filed the suit on behalf of thirty thousand inhabitants of Amazonian Ecuador, the majority of whom are *cocama* settlers. Just like the Cofán, the nonindigenous colonists have suffered high rates of contamination-related illness. To think that *cocama* suffering is equivalent to Cofán suffering makes little sense to most Dureno residents. To imagine that compensation from the suit would help the *cocama* more than the Cofán is an even more unpalatable thought. Deji told me how hard it is for the people of Dureno to see *cocama* as their allies in the fight against oil:

> The *cocama* came here on the oil roads. The *cocama* can't say, "We, too, have been contaminated by oil." They are the ones who came here and contaminated everything! Only we Cofán can say, "Yes, we are the poor ones, the suffering ones. We are the ones who are the true inhabitants of this land. We are the ones who have been damaged by the *companía*." The *cocama*, and even the Napo Runa, came here on roads the *companía* built. They can't say they have been damaged by oil. Like us, the Siona can say it. But it's just the two of us. We are the only ones who truly suffer here.

———

The *cocama* are everywhere in Cofán territory. They are settlers, priests, and activists. They also work for petroleum companies, including the one that entered Dureno's territory to search for oil in 2013. Perhaps the new *cocama* workers would be different from the ones who drank with Cofán men, raped Cofán woman, possibly killed a Cofán chief, and brought virtually nothing to the Cofán except trauma, disease, and dispossession. That was the bet the people of Dureno made when they voted to suspend their opposition and allow the *companía* onto their land.

•

CHAPTER 7

THE POSSIBILITY OF COEXISTENCE

By March 2013, BGP was everywhere in Dureno. When I arrived at the beginning of June, the forest floor was littered with yellow and orange cables. The equipment ran over streams, through gardens, and past homes. Trees near seismic trails were marked with painted numbers, and color-coded pieces of tape hung from branches. By July, everyone was hearing the loud booms of the underground explosions. Some people even felt the earth shake beneath their homes. All non-Cofán BGP employees—who were *cocama*, Afro-Ecuadorian, and Napo Runa—slept and ate at the company camp on the Pisorié River, near the southeastern edge of Dureno's territory. During the day, they arrived in canoes at the community's main port and walked past people's homes and gardens toward the forest interior. While we were hunting one afternoon, Alejandro and I bumped into two seismic workers in the deep forest. They showed us a map of the dense grid of trails they had cut over Dureno's territory.

FIGURE 7.1. *Alejandro holding a map of BGP's seismic trails in Dureno. Photo by Michael Cepek.*

Although they had opportunities, few Dureno men decided to make trails and lay cables alongside the non-Cofán workers. The work was too hard, they said, and it did not pay enough, at $380 a month. Instead, community members chose to work mainly as camp guards and *motoristas* (transporters of workers in canoes). Five men, including Alejandro and Deji, worked as guards; as many as forty-five worked with canoes. The guards earned $450 a month. Their work was easy; all they did was sit at the camp and watch BGP's equipment. Staying at the camp for twenty-two days at a time could be boring, but the company fed its workers well. Deji laughed that he gained so much weight working for BGP that all his pants no longer fit. For months after the work ended, he had nothing to wear but a pair of shorts.

Depending on the size of the canoe and motor, BGP paid the *motoristas* as much as $2,000 a month. The money spread through social networks. Canoe owners received the payment, but they used it to hire friends and family members to drive their boats and labor as *punteros* (point men) who sit in the front of canoes to watch for obstructions in the river. BGP also paid the community's elected leaders $300 a month to work as monitors. Ostensibly, they were responsible for making sure the company complied with environmental rules. In practice, the leaders used the funds to travel to Lago Agrio to meet with BGP officials and discuss company operations.

The work flooded Dureno with money. Even more significant was the compensation the community received. In exchange for the Cofán's vote to allow seismic exploration on their land, BGP agreed to give a $1,000 payment to each Dureno resident who was fifteen or older. The company also agreed to buy a $2,000 outboard motor for each household. Some families, though, decided to use the $2,000 as a partial payment for a larger or better motor or to buy other commodities such as chainsaws, weed whackers, gas stoves, and refrigerators. As per the agreement, the $2,000 was designated for durable goods. Dureno residents could do whatever they wanted with the $1,000. Many used it to pay off debts. Others bought food, clothing, cell phones, or school materials. Some put part of it in a Lago Agrio bank. To the dismay of their parents, a number of young men spent most of it on beer. Alejandro and Lucia used the money to buy a $1,500 fiberglass canoe and a bicycle for Roberto. With the $2,000, they paid for most of a fifteen-horsepower Yamaha motor.

By the end of July, BGP had completed seismic exploration, and the income disappeared. Later in 2013, the community signed an agreement with Petroamazonas for other oil-related work: reopening Dureno 1, extending an existing well platform twenty meters across the community boundary onto Cofán land, and constructing Dureno 2, a well that replaced the old Guanta 12 that once sat at the far edge of the platform, outside Dureno's territory. The new operations did not provide significant work opportunities, but the community negotiated the purchase of eight pickup trucks as compensation. They immediately began renting the trucks back to Petroamazonas, which paid Dureno approximately $11,000 a month for them. According to the Petroamazonas agreement, the income would last for at least three years. In addition, Petroamazonas agreed to pay for truck-driving courses for five Cofán men, who might eventually become *compañía* employees. It also offered partial university scholarships for twelve community residents and full university scholarships for three. Furthermore, it arranged for a medical team to visit Dureno each month.

Initially, most community members did not want to cooperate with either BGP or Petroamazonas. They were resentful about past oil-associated damages and fearful of new ones. They also assumed the companies would never give what they promised. The *compañía* was a liar, they said, and it always would be. But this time the companies complied with their agreements. Moreover, both BGP and Petroamazonas worked in a manner that was far better than in past oil operations. BGP's seismic trails were forty-five centimeters wide rather than three meters; the company agreed to cut down no large trees or useful species; it compensated the community when it destroyed valuable plants by mistake; it built its camp far from the main settlement; it replanted trails and its camp site with useful tree species; it offered employment to all Cofán individuals who wanted it; it prohibited workers from consuming alcohol or drugs; and it agreed to fire any workers who propositioned Cofán women or failed to treat any Cofán people, including those who worked for BGP, with respect. Petroamazonas's wells, including the reopened Dureno 1, were different from past wells. Most importantly, the company collected all waste liquids in secure holding tanks and shipped them offsite for reinjection into abandoned wells or other forms of safer disposal. Officials of both companies met repeatedly with elected leaders and the broader community to discuss their plans and alter them according to Cofán feedback.

Perhaps most significantly, in early 2012 the Ecuadorian government agreed to build a millennium community in Dureno. Cofán people interpreted it as partial compensation for all the harms oil had brought to them since the 1960s. It would include a high-quality cement and bamboo house for each family, new schools, and improved infrastructure for potable water, a sewage system, and Internet and satellite TV connections for families willing to pay a monthly fee. In total, the work and compensation brought roughly $10 million to

---

Dureno over three years, far more than the four spoons and bag of doughnuts Texaco gave to the Cofán at Dureno 1 in 1969.

Although rumors about the oil-related work had emerged by 2012, I was surprised when changes actually started happening. I was also upset. Like so many nonindigenous outsiders with activist inclinations, I did not want the Cofán to give in to the petroleum industry. I, too, had romantic notions about Cofán people's noble, unwavering opposition to unsustainable development, environmental destruction, corporate power, and government pressure. As an anthropologist, however, my job was to do my best to understand why people were doing what they were doing, to comprehend the logic behind their actions rather than to criticize their choices or tell them to make different ones. I soon learned that although many individuals were happy with the changing relations to oil, most of them still harbored doubts and fears. Oil's renewed appearance in Dureno also generated intense conflicts that threatened to rip the community apart.

Even though petroleum companies and the Ecuadorian state appear to be interacting with the people of Dureno in new ways, no one is sure what the consequences of the *compañía*'s reappearance will be. People might be entering a mutually beneficial relationship with the petroleum industry, they might end up returning to their previous oppositional stance, they might become more antagonistic then ever, or their perspectives might fragment in ever more profound and incompatible ways. In a sense, the worst possible outcome would be a deep split in Dureno concerning how to deal with oil and the challenges that accompany it. Not only will division prevent the Cofán from confronting problems with the necessary degree of coordination and solidarity; it will create a sense of discord that will make Dureno increasingly unable to sustain the calm and peaceful lifestyle that most Cofán people desire.

If Toribio was one of the individuals most responsible for cultivating Dureno's opposition to oil, Eduardo Mendua played an even more important role in reversing the community's anti-oil stance. He was elected president of Dureno in December 2011, and he took office in January 2012. Almost immediately after assuming a leadership role, he began discussions with the government to organize the building of the millennium community. He had his first meeting with BGP in March 2012 and his first talks with Petroamazonas in February 2013. Although other Dureno leaders and the larger community eventually became part of the discussions, Eduardo made them happen. Even more importantly, he framed them in ways that were convincing to individuals who had long been hostile to oil, though not everyone believed him. To put it lightly, he became a divisive figure for both Cofán people and the nonindigenous activists who remained interested in what oil was doing to the Cofán and their territory.

I signed my original research agreement with Dureno in 2011. At the time, Roberto Aguinda was president of the community. I had been friends with Roberto for more than ten years. He worked with Randy Borman at the Foundation for the Survival of the Cofán People, and he was an enthusiastic participant in my dissertation fieldwork. When I returned to Dureno to begin investigations for this book in 2012, I learned that a new individual had become president. Consequently, I had to sign a new version of the agreement. I had never met Eduardo, but I had heard worrisome things. People said he was very smart, very forceful, and very critical of gringo researchers and nonindigenous *ecologistas*.

My longtime collaborator Martin helped to mediate the conversation. Surprisingly, it went smoothly. Eduardo agreed to approve my project as long as there would be significant community benefits. I was thankful that my research grant allowed me to provide adequate reciprocity, including decent payments for interviewees ($10 an hour) and research assistants ($500 a month), concrete goods (two desktop computers, one laptop, a digital projector, and an Internet connection), and a commitment to give all book royalties to Dureno and all data to the Cofán ethnic federation for a planned digital archive. My agreement also stipulated that Martin would be a true collaborator in the design and implementation of the project. Martin worked alongside me on interviews, economic diaries, and data analysis. One of my obligations was to help train him to be an anthropologist capable of doing his own studies. During my research, he completed an anthropology degree through a distance program with the University of Cuenca in highland Ecuador.[1]

———

I did not do an interview with Eduardo until 2013, but I learned a lot about him the previous year. He was only twenty-nine at the time. People told me his nicknames: "Otavalo," the name of a highland indigenous group, because Eduardo used to wear his hair long in the style of many Andean natives; "Negro" (black man, in Spanish) and "Singo" (black person, in A'ingae), because of Eduardo's relatively dark skin and intense demeanor;[2] and "Shamán," which no one could explain to me. Today, Eduardo has short, spiked hair. He has a broad face and a thick, powerful body. He has the physique many Cofán people find most attractive: strong but plump. Lucia told me that some of Eduardo's relatives fatten themselves with *cocama* injections they buy in Lago Agrio, an interesting but improbable idea. Apart from a purchased furniture set, Eduardo's house is modest. When I went to visit him and his wife, Fabiola Ortiz, he was often lounging in a hammock, shirt off and waving a towel at himself to cool down. His mother is Florinda Vargas. His father, Vijirio, died in the 1990s, possibly due to oil contamination.

Eduardo has an impressive mind. He did not finish high school, but a year in Ecuador's army allowed him to perfect his Spanish. He told me he has always been an autodidact. He spent much of his childhood reading newspapers and watching television news programs. Over time, he accumulated a wide circle of intellectual confidants: indigenous leaders, progressive *cocama* lawyers, and Spanish-speaking academics. They gave him books and engaged him in intense conversations. Unlike many Dureno residents, he is attuned to the ever-shifting landscape of Ecuadorian politics. He can comment with authority on the country's 2008 constitution, its international treaties, and its federal budget.

Although Eduardo speaks A'ingae very quickly, I can easily under-stand him because he inserts so many technical Spanish terms into conversations. They are often Latinate words with English cognates, such as *autonomía* and *biodiversidad*. At times, he appears to use a creole language all his own. For example, one day he told me, "Tse tsu ashaen, va proceso. Ña va cuna imágenma atte: áfaye, in'jañe, tsoñe, planteaye, generaye, enfrentaye, discutiye pa'ccoma" (And then it began, this process [Spanish]. I saw this new image [Spanish]: to speak, to think, to do, to outline and propose [Spanish], to generate and produce [Spanish], to confront and deal with [Spanish], to dispute and debate [Spanish] everything).

People like Toribio and Randy are extremely intelligent and capable leaders who speak in a slow, deliberate, and calm manner. Eduardo is fast, loud, and sometimes reckless. He exudes energy and strength, and he is quick to anger. He is more than happy to engage in debates with people who do not see eye to eye with him; he is extremely confident but seems too impatient to spend much time entertaining disagreements. In meetings, other Dureno residents sometimes respond critically to his points. He replies in a tone that lets others know the conversation is over and the matter is settled. Based on my observations, it appears that Eduardo does not aim primarily to silence opponents. Rather, it seems as if he simply cannot bear to waste time by listening to arguments he has already heard, understood, and—if he has deemed them valid—integrated into his own positions.

I learned a lot about Eduardo from his mother, Florinda. She was one of my favorite collaborators. Like a few Dureno elders, she is a *foño'pa*, a woman who always wears her traditional dress. She uses a pencil to draw thick black lines on her brow, whose hairs she plucked out long ago. She crafts beautiful ornaments. One day, I saw her sitting in her hut making a woman's necklace with entirely traditional materials: palm fiber, forest seeds, and plumes from toucans and macaws. The latter came from Zábalo; there are no macaws left in Dureno. She did not even use glass beads, which the Cofán have had for centuries. Although it was not intended for sale, I asked her if I could buy it. She said yes. It now hangs in my living room, where I admire it every day.

Florinda is something of a naysayer and a curmudgeon, but a sly smile usually accompanies her sarcastic remarks. During my research, it was easy to talk with her about anything, history, oil, or community gossip. She was always eager to give me the dirt on anyone. Probably, it was because others have slung a decent amount of dirt at her over the years. Her father was Imbiquito, a Shell employee and Shuar native who came to Dureno from southern Ecuador in the 1940s. For a long time, everyone in Dureno disliked Imbiquito. He drank too much manioc beer and viciously beat his Cofán wife. Yori'ye decided to punish Imbiquito by ordering other men to restrain him so Yori'ye could whip him with tapir hide. Fortunately, Imbiquito learned his lesson and changed his ways.

Florinda's brothers were also violent; one was stabbed to death in Lago Agrio during a fight with a *cocama*. Florinda herself has no such reputation, but some people told me she was briefly married to a *cocama* hide trader in her youth. Her Shuar genealogy and alleged affection for *cocama* men made her a bit of an outsider. She eventually married Vijirio, a Cofán man from Colombia. As a widow, she now lives alone. Alejandro and Lucia laugh about the romance she is rumored to have struck up with Mauricio Mendua, a Zábalo elder and distant relative of her dead husband. Mauricio was married to Yori'ye's daughter, who died of stomach cancer less than a decade ago. As two individuals who possibly lost spouses to petroleum contamination, Florinda and Mauricio would make a telling couple. Their stories would let the world know just how deeply oil's historical damages continue to impact Cofán lives.

Some people suggest that Eduardo, too, is influenced by the Shuar blood that runs through his veins. The Cofán view the Shuar as fierce, violent people. They are widely known for vendetta warfare and head shrinking, two practices they gave up long ago. Florinda herself sees no negative qualities in her son. She is a staunch defender of all he has done in Dureno. She smiled coyly as she told me how smart he is. She laughed and said she has no idea how he got his *tsove* (head), which is *nánitssi* (complete). He did not finish school, Florinda admitted, but he has *rande in'jan'cho* (big thoughts). She claimed that *cocama* talk to her son and wonder how he knows all he knows. Even as a child, Florinda recalled, Eduardo was an *injama'pa* (thoughtful and intelligent person).

According to Florinda, Eduardo was solely responsible for bringing the *companía* back to Dureno. He was the one who made people understand that the *cocama* had never given them anything in exchange for the destruction they had caused. He was also the one who convinced them it was time to use the petroleum industry to make

FIGURE 7.2. *Florinda Vargas (left), Eduardo Mendua (second from left), Fabiola Ortiz, and Eduardo's and Fabiola's children*

their lives better. She knows some people disagree with Eduardo, but she dismisses their perspectives. She does not hesitate to call them envious, stupid, and wrong.

I have a warm but complex relationship with Eduardo. We enjoy each other's company, and he loves to tell me about his political philosophy and vision for the community. I am certain he knows I do not agree with everything he says. One of the things I find most compelling about him is his willingness to confront the Cofán's enemies. He speaks well of many nonindigenous politicians, but he despises most of the *cocama* who have invaded Cofán territory. He defiantly proclaims that because the Cofán way of life is superior to the *cocama* way of life, it will never disappear. If a young person leaves Dureno to work or study, he is certain they will return. If an outsider tells him the Cofán are less intelligent than other Ecuadorians, he laughs in the person's face and says most Cofán people speak at least two languages. "How many languages do you mestizos speak?" he snaps with a caustic smile.

A number of people told me about an incident that indicates Eduardo's uniqueness. For many years, the Cofán had entered young women into the annual competition to become the *reina* (queen, in Spanish) of the parish to which Dureno belongs. The event takes place in the *cocama* town, also named Dureno, on the other side of the Aguarico River. Each year, no matter how beautiful and well prepared the Cofán contestant was, she lost. After Eduardo became president in 2012, he worked with a Dureno woman to train her for the competition. He taught her how to speak well in Spanish and walk properly in both a formal dress and a bathing suit. She was very nervous. According to everyone who witnessed her performance, she did extremely well. Even the *cocama* appeared to be impressed. Reportedly, everyone knew she would win.

When a *cocama* official identified a *cocama* contestant as the winner, Eduardo was enraged. Fully sober, he ran onto the stage, ripped off the winner's crown, threw it on the ground, and angrily lectured the *cocama* who were there. He prohibited them from ever crossing the river to attend a Cofán party or seek healing from a Cofán shaman. If they did, he warned, they "would not survive." Casual *cocama* visits to Dureno diminished for a couple years. In more than two decades of working with the Cofán, I cannot think of a single other person who would engage in such a fearless, aggressive act in the face of hundreds of *cocama* men, especially on *cocama* land. At this point, Eduardo has a reputation that extends far beyond Dureno. No *cocama* would make the mistake of calling him a worthless, lazy *indio*. No matter how well Cofán people's humorous, self-effacing demeanor meshes with my own, I find Eduardo's unconventional boldness inspiring. The Cofán will need more leaders with his attitude if they hope to overturn the structures of domination that have plagued them for centuries.

I recorded only one formal interview with Eduardo. I usually do spot transcriptions of interviews; I summarize much of the discourse in English and compose exact A'ingae transcriptions only of particularly significant segments. In Eduardo's case, almost every word was valuable; I translated nearly everything. He acknowledged that many other Dureno residents say bad things about him: that he commands people too much, that he does not listen to others, that he is too wealthy, and that he is secretly taking *companía* bribes in order to make the community more favorable to the petroleum industry. He laughingly dismissed the accusations. In 2009, he said, he began constructing and selling fiberglass canoes. He used his outgoing personality to build relationships with indigenous politicians, who favored him for municipal and provincial contracts. He told me he made $50,000 in one year, not much less than what I made at the time. We laughed that even though I am a gringo with a PhD and a university professorship, we were economic equals. In 2013, he supplied canoes and other equipment for the cleanup of an oil spill on the Coca River. The work netted him almost $800,000 in contracts, although I do not know how much he profited from them.

Eduardo admits that he already has a lot of money. So why, he asks, would he seek bribes from the *companía*? He has a personal accountant, a man with a *cocama* father and a Cofán mother who lives in Lago Agrio and hails from the community of Sinangoé.[3] He said he offers to show his financial records to anyone. He claimed his economic opportunities are not the result of corruption. Rather, they are the fruits of his hard work and constant search for contacts who can expand his influence and bring more benefits to Dureno. Eduardo even has his own pickup truck to facilitate his travels. His Cofán allies compare him favorably to past leaders in many ways, but they consistently mention one trait: they say that other *na'su* spent most of their time "sitting" in the community, whereas Eduardo is constantly "standing," "walking," and "traveling" to other lands in search of resources to bring back to Dureno.

Unlike some indigenous leaders, Eduardo strongly supported Ecuadorian President Rafael Correa, who held office from 2007 to 2017. Many Dureno residents told me that Eduardo is also a personal friend of Jorge Glas, Correa's former vice president. Correa is a self-proclaimed Christian socialist. His critics condemned him for demagoguery and an overreliance on oil money, but his multiple reelections and relatively high approval ratings marked him as one of the most successful leaders in Ecuadorian history. His fans point to the way he used oil revenues to better the lot of the country's poor with social welfare programs and investments in infrastructure and public education. Eduardo claimed that Correa should favor the Cofán because they are a *pueblo comunista'faya* (a communist people, a Spanish phrase with A'ingae suffixes). From his perspective, with a strong leader they can be like the *chinondeccu* (Chinese people), one people with one *in'jan'cho* (way of thinking and desiring). In fact, he argues, they were like that in the past due to the cohering power of Yori'ye:

> In the old times, we had a great shaman, a great leader. He knew how to call game. He knew how to cure people and keep them healthy. He knew how to do everything. Now, we can have that again. We need to strategize well and work with the government. We need to negotiate well and create a solid structure here. If we do a good job planning what to do with our land and lives, our leaders here in Dureno can have the same kind of power Yori'ye had.

Eduardo told me he wants nothing more than to unify and *armaye* (to arm, in Spanish with an A'ingae suffix) the Cofán. He wants them to resist the *cocama*, to improve their quality of life, and to protect their land. He explained that a return to Cofán well-being is actually in line with the nationalist vision that Correa advanced. In a sense, Eduardo wants the Cofán to participate in the national leftist project by beating the *cocama* at their own game. If they find ways to make a living without leaving Dureno, Eduardo asserted, Cofán people will have *seguridad de trabajo* (security of work, in Spanish). If they find ways to strengthen their own medical system while increasing access to Western care, they will have *seguridad de salud* (security of health, in Spanish). If they find ways to protect their natural resources while devising new subsistence strategies, they will have *seguridad alimentaria* (food security, in Spanish).

The phrases were part of Correa's political discourse, his vision of what *buen vivir* (good living) means for all Ecuadorians. Eduardo has no trouble articulating Correa's ideas with long-standing Cofán values to create a hybrid vision for Dureno's development. It is certainly no traditional Amazonian ideal, but it is definitely compelling. Eduardo's ambition is contagious. I think he knows how much he impresses me, which is perhaps why he has never spoken against my presence or research. During my last visit in 2016, he even asked for my advice on how he could write a book about his philosophy as a Cofán leader.

Like all Cofán people, Eduardo is no fan of Chevron. He, too, can list the ways the *companía* damaged Cofán people and their way of life. But he contends that Ecuador's contemporary petroleum industry is a different beast. He points to the differences between the way Texaco conducted seismic explorations and the way BGP did. In addition to Petroamazonas's sizable compensation to the community, Eduardo notes its superior technology, especially its waste disposal system. If seismic testing indicates additional crude reserves in Dureno, Eduardo is convinced the Cofán can work with Petroamazonas to extract oil in a relatively clean, safe, and beneficial manner. The people of Dureno have yet to decide whether to allow Petroamazonas to drill new wells on their land, but Eduardo has already begun discussions with the company. Any agreement he brings to the community must be approved by a majority vote.

In 2014, Eduardo told me the Cofán's most basic demands for any

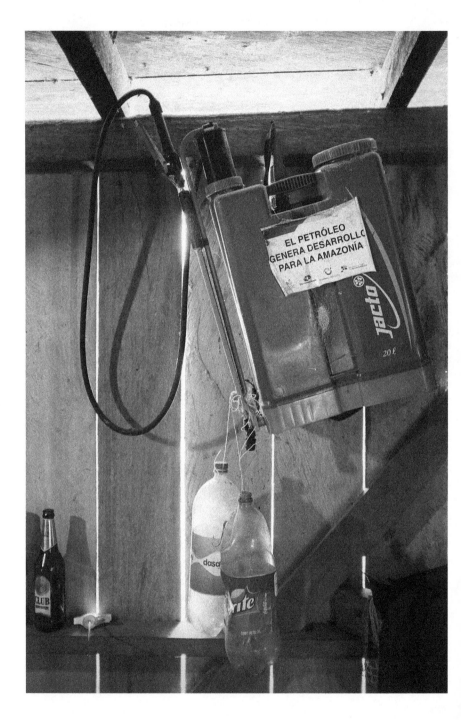

FIGURE 7.3. *A government-issued pump that Alejandro uses to spray insecticide and herbicide, with a sticker that reads, "Petroleum generates development for Amazonia"*

new oil drilling on their land. First, Petroamazonas must construct no new roads that link Dureno to outside transportation networks. Instead, the company must move all its equipment using a barge to cross the Aguarico River. From there, a small road would start and stop on Cofán land. It would head to new oil platforms but not connect to the highway system. The Aguarico would continue to serve as a barrier to *cocama* incursions. Cofán control of the barge would give them additional income and act as a pressure point they could use to paralyze company operations and force the industry to work in agreed-upon ways. Second, Petroamazonas must build only two drilling platforms on community land. Each must be far from Dureno's main settlement. Eduardo knows the company has the technology and resources for directional drilling, a method that allows ten or more wells to be drilled at underground angles from a single point toward different parts of a crude deposit. The new technology would mean safer, cleaner extraction with less deforestation, fewer flares, fewer roads, and a maximally contained waste stream.

Eduardo acknowledged that the Cofán will demand a form of oil production that costs more than simpler techniques. But he is convinced the community has the power to push for what it wants. Also, he said the Cofán can negotiate more substantial financial benefits, perhaps a royalty on each barrel produced. Eduardo even imagines creating a Cofán petroleum services company. Cofán engineers and ecologists would staff and run the business. Eduardo told me he had spoken with Canadian native people who were directly involved in petroleum production. Eduardo explained that with more knowledge and command of the technology, the Cofán could gain even more riches from oil while making sure it does little to no damage to their land and health.

In general, Eduardo wants the Cofán to take control of the institutions that others use to profit off them. The Cofán already have their own canoe manufacturers and grocery store, but he envisions Cofán transportation companies, Cofán law firms, and Cofán medical clinics. He wants the Cofán to do all the *cocama* do but do it better and accrue the lion's share of the rewards. He has no fantasies that oil will last forever. Based on his readings and conversations, he estimates

—

that Ecuador's crude reserves will disappear in two to three decades. That is why, he told me, his real dream is to protect Dureno's forest and build a high-class tourism complex in the community. With money earned from oil, he said the Cofán would be able to create a refuge of biodiversity that people from all over the world would pay to visit. They would stay in luxurious, Cofán-owned accommodations, and they would learn from Cofán experts about Cofán culture, territory, and ecological knowledge. He estimated the community would need at least $8 million to create the business. He predicted they could accumulate that much or more from their temporary alliance with the petroleum industry.

Eduardo insisted that now is the time to act. No one can be sure whether a future administration would be as cooperative or trustworthy as Correa's. If they wait, they will risk gaining nothing from a potentially right-wing president who would ignore their demands, strip them of their resources, and offer nothing in return. They have had plenty of experience with such *cocama* politicians in the past.

The people of Dureno had few reasons to believe in oil when Eduardo began talking to the *companía* in 2012 and 2013. They also had few reasons to trust Eduardo as a new *na'su*. In many ways, Cofán society is radically egalitarian. Cofán people do not share everything, but as soon as a person accumulates more resources or power than his or her neighbors, others immediately assault them with gossip and insult. The "bad talk" typically enrages its target. It can even provoke leaders to abandon their positions. As the Cofán say, people often *fi'ttiye* their *na'su*; the word's most direct translation is "to kill," but it also means "to speak badly about" or "to dislike intensely." People depended on Yori'ye's unique powers, but they also distrusted and berated him. Behind his back, they called him a fool, a demon, and a jaguar. They also criticized him for being lazy; they said he spent all day in his hammock and got up at night only to drink *yaje* or manioc beer. Contemporary leaders suffer the same fate. I do not know a single *na'su* who has not been accused of wrongdoing, immorality, or some other unsavory quality.

Almost always, people gossip about a leader's unfair enrichment. A leader's resources and skills in the outside world are essential to negotiating the challenges of that world. Without the ability to move among *cocama*, a contemporary *na'su* would not be able to advocate for his people. When Deji was community president, people accused him of maintaining covert relations with *cocama* businessmen and stealing community money. People still gossip about Randy's allegedly ill-gotten resources even though he is no longer an ethnic federation leader. I have seen no proof of Cofán leaders' corruption, but I have not looked for it, either. As an outsider, it is not my place to criticize elected Cofán representatives. As some Dureno residents claim, Eduardo could be taking money from the *companía*. But he denies it. I have no reason to disbelieve him, although many Cofán people do.

When Eduardo introduced the idea of allowing seismic exploration on Dureno land, the community split in half. Those who trusted him and were in favor of the idea were *in'jansundeccu* (likers). Those who wanted nothing to do with oil were *chi'gasundeccu* (haters). The schism emerged along family lines. As it increased in intensity, it began to break families apart. Many people told me about a community meeting in 2013 during which residents debated whether to work with BGP. The *in'jansundeccu* stressed the compensation, work opportunities, and superior technology the company would use. Although some *chi'gasundeccu* mentioned environmental destruction, *cocama* abuse, and future well drilling, their most inspired criticism focused on the rumor that the company was paying Eduardo to ensure community acceptance. People were angry at the idea that Eduardo was making money off them. The argument got so intense that two adult sisters began screaming at each other, then started punching each other. People had to pull them apart. The incident left a deep impression on all who witnessed it. Never had such vitriol emerged among the people of Dureno. For a while, one group of *chi'gasundeccu* said they wanted to break off and form their own community. They refused to work with the oil industry or be represented by Eduardo.

Some people blame Acción Ecológica for exacerbating the conflict. A persistent story began to circulate. According to most versions, the organization approached a young Dureno man named Jorge (a pseudonym) to mobilize the community against BGP. Jorge had long been opposed to oil. He also worked with many environmental and indigenous rights organizations. As a onetime community president, he, too, suffered accusations of corruption. People gossiped that he took donations meant for Dureno and spent them on himself. Despite the rumors, Acción Ecológica continued to trust him. Jorge and Eduardo used to be good friends. Reportedly, Jorge told Eduardo that Acción Ecológica would pay them each $500 a month to organize community workshops aimed at strengthening the Cofán's anti-oil stance. Eduardo told Jorge he already had money. "I don't want to become rich," Eduardo supposedly said. "I want everyone to have work and money."

Whether he was paid by Acción Ecológica or not, Jorge began to spread misinformation about Eduardo and his "promises." He said BGP and Petroamazonas were lying. He said the millennium community would never be built. He said the *companía* was giving Eduardo tens of thousands of dollars in exchange for negotiating smaller compensation agreements for the community. Soon, the conflict was not about oil at all. It was about the fight between Jorge and Eduardo and their families and allies. Although he denies it, Eduardo reportedly made a death threat against Jorge. Jorge attempted to get Eduardo arrested, but he failed.

As people slowly learned that BGP and Petroamazonas would comply with their agreements, the fighting subsided. For much of 2013 and 2014, though, Dureno was a mess. People hated each other, insulted each other, and even physically attacked each other. Neighbors "killed" neighbors, siblings "killed" siblings, and children and parents "killed" one another. "Tisupanuccu zucco'fa," Martin said— "We got caught up in a huge problem." Toribio spoke out against the fights oil was causing. "We argued so much among ourselves," he told me. "We began to hate each other. We stopped helping each other. When that oil money emerged, it really damaged us. It damaged everyone."

The fighting also divided generations. At first, most young people wanted the company to enter, and most old people did not. The youth began to ignore or belittle elders, whom they mocked as "cute little old ones." The rupture even began to take on ethnic dimensions. The anti-oil contingent said the pro-oil side was not truly *a'i*, not truly Cofán. Like Eduardo, the *chi'gasundeccu* said, the people in favor of the *compañía* were the children of a Shuar invader. Or they were the offspring of *cocama*, *singo*, or Napo Runa men who had impregnated Cofán women. Eduardo tried to stop the fighting, but he also intensified it. He determined the order in which people would receive the payments and motors from BGP. According to many reports, the people who supported him got the money and goods first. Those who supposedly lied about him had to wait. Eventually, everyone received their share of the compensation. Not even oil's most vociferous opponents, including Toribio, ended up refusing the benefits.

Initially, Alejandro was one of the *chi'gasundeccu*. He did not trust Eduardo. He thought Eduardo might have been working with the *compañía* to enrich himself. He also thought Eduardo might have been lying about the payments, the outboard motors, and the work opportunities. In addition, he worried about the rivers and the forest, the fish and the game. But he felt he was too inarticulate to say much during the heated community discussions. Instead, he stewed in his house. Hearing the vicious gossip made him miserable. When he recalls the period, he uses a gesture to describe his reaction to the disputes. He sits up, stares straight ahead, and waves his hands around his ears and face in a movement that evokes a chaotic whirlwind. All of the words flew by his head and drove him crazy, he said. He was angry and worried; he could not sleep. The sicknesses caused by oil could be horrible, but the tension it provoked could be just as bad. Alejandro began to dream of building a house far up the Pisorié River where he could live alone. It would be quiet, he said, distant from the noisy, aggravating, and painful conflict that had taken over the community.

The tension lingered for a long time, but the people of Dureno eventually voted to allow BGP to conduct seismic exploration and to let Petroamazonas reopen Dureno 1 and redrill Dureno 2. People cite multiple reasons for their decision to allow oil back into the community. For many, the conflict had become too damaging. Former *chi'gasundeccu* decided to end the problem by surrendering to the *in'jansundeccu,* who had begun to outnumber them. Eduardo devised a particularly ingenious argument to appeal to elders, many of whom wanted to keep the *companía* out. He told them the compensation was mainly for them. They were too old to find good work, he reminded them, and they did not speak Spanish well enough, either. Unlike the young people, the elders were too tired to garden, hunt, and fish for all their food. Eduardo said he wanted to give them money so they could eat and live.

Eduardo told the elders the young should not be the only ones to profit from the old people's historical efforts. The elders were the ones who struggled to cut Dureno's boundary trails, secure its land title, and protect it from *cocama* incursions. If anyone should get money, it should be them. The implicit message was that the young people would let the company in after the elders died. Consequently, they would reap all the rewards. The argument made sense to old people. It revolved around familiar ideas of fairness, equality, and reciprocity. Alejandro hated oil, but Eduardo's words convinced him. When I asked why he finally sided with the pro-oil faction, he said,

> The elders said they didn't want to die without receiving anything. Many old ones have already died and not gotten any money. We were the ones who struggled so hard to cut the boundary trails. We did that, but many of us have died without receiving a cent. People talked about that. Then I, too, became lost. I told them, "Well, if you all want to do that, I'll do it, too. I won't live much longer. Maybe it would be better if I get some benefits, too—if I receive something so I can buy food to eat before I die." I said that, and then we all agreed to let the *companía* enter. Everyone thought hard about it, and we did it. That's how it happened. Before, I really wanted to prohibit the *companía* from our land. My heart still wants that, but we decided to let the *companía* in.

There were additional reasons. People knew there were oil wells on all sides of Dureno. They also knew companies could drill more along the community's boundaries. With directional drilling, the wells could extract the crude from beneath Dureno without actually being in Dureno. Consequently, the oil would be gone and the Cofán would receive none of the benefits. Pollution from spills and flares, however, would continue to cross the boundaries in air, rivers, and contaminated fish and game. Many people argued that allowing the *compañía* to operate within Dureno would paradoxically create a better environmental situation. Not only would the Cofán receive work, money, and benefits; they would have far more power to monitor and influence company operations. In the event of unfulfilled promises or irresponsible actions, the Cofán would be able to halt work through small-scale protests that are much easier to justify and orchestrate on their own land. In short, saying no to oil would mean no benefits and heightened damages. Saying yes would mean more resources, more control, and a less damaging extraction process.

Some Dureno residents also agreed with Eduardo that they should take advantage of the political moment. President Correa offered a stick and a carrot. Although he claimed to side with Ecuador's progressive social movements, he lashed out at many indigenous and environmental organizations. If people took to the streets and engaged in what some deemed violent acts of protest, Correa labeled them *terroristas* and sometimes imprisoned them.[4] During his time in office, there were serious clashes between the military and indigenous protestors. People died. One of Correa's central mottos was "Con diálogo, todo. Con fuerza, nada" (With dialogue, everything. With force, nothing). Cofán people no longer believe they can block roads and take over oil wells. Earlier administrations responded peacefully to such acts of resistance. Correa was different. With Correa's ally Lenín Moreno now in office, the Cofán are afraid they would end up in jail—or dead—if they were to repeat the 1987 and 1998 actions. Some even fear the government would revoke their land title and evict them from their territory.

Correa's carrot was increased participation in development. Through negotiations, Eduardo has shown the people of Dureno that an honest dialogue with state and corporate officials offers substantial benefits, including the ability to shape the process of petroleum exploration and extraction. Most Cofán people no longer believe they can say no to oil, but they do believe they can say how it will

—

FIGURE 7.4. *Alejandro in the second floor of his house*

be extracted. Perhaps they are naive, but they contend they might have the power to decide whether a new road gets built through Dureno, whether oil wastes enter their environment, and whether well platforms are built close to their homes. Correa's administration convinced them that negotiations bear real fruit. They have seen the results in the operations of BGP and Petroamazonas.

In 2013 and 2014, the people of Dureno found even more reasons to cooperate with the petroleum industry. Many observed that work and compensation decreased interhousehold theft and the conflicts it caused. With money from oil, young men had no reason to steal. Some people also asserted that additional income allowed them to use their forest in a more sustainable way. If they could buy more of their food, they said, they would not have to overexploit Dureno's dwindling natural resources. Consequently, their children and grandchildren would have the opportunity to maintain hunting and fishing as central parts of the Cofán way of life. Finally, some people argued that having the *companía* on Cofán land would allow young people to stay in Dureno. Ambitious youth would not have to search for jobs in Lago Agrio or other cities. Instead, they would be able to remain with their Cofán friends and family members. They would continue to speak A'ingae every day, to marry other Cofán people, and to have Cofán children. Ironically, in other words, the oil industry might allow them to ensure the future of their culture.

After I completed my main period of fieldwork for this book in 2014, I told many of my activist friends in Ecuador and the United States about Eduardo's vision for community enrichment and empowerment. They seemed deeply skeptical. Although they wondered whether Eduardo was corrupt and power hungry or was misrepresenting the people of Dureno, I think something more fundamental was at play. As Jessica Cattelino argues in *High Stakes: Florida Seminole Gaming and Sovereignty* (2008), many Westerners believe that indigenous people must be poor in order to be "authentic." From their perspective, she writes, material wealth automatically leads to indigenous cultural decline. In other words, a rich Indian is not really an Indian at all, at least not for long. Eduardo and the people of Dureno certainly would disagree with such a characterization. They see no reason to remain impoverished. They identify many ways that increasing their access to material resources, including money, will help them to maintain rather than cause them to lose their cultural distinctiveness.

Although the overt conflict between Dureno's pro-oil and anti-oil factions ended for the time being, many people remain torn about the *compañía*. The words of the *in'jansundeccu* make sense to former *chi'gasundeccu*, but doubts and animosity linger. During interviews, some of my collaborators seemed optimistic one moment and anxious and fearful the next. Alejandro listed the benefits the recent agreements had brought. Then, he laughed and said, "But maybe we'll all just get cancer and die." When I asked Deji what might become bad if Petroamazonas drills new wells in Dureno, he replied, "From my perspective, nothing bad will come of it. More money will make things better. But when that runs out, things might become even worse. Or maybe some horrible illness will emerge. I really don't know." Emeregildo told me that if they negotiate well, the people of Dureno will have money and food for years. Then, he laughed and concluded, "But we'll receive other things, too. First we'll receive contamination. Then we'll receive sickness. And then we'll receive death. Those are the things we'll truly receive." Laura claimed that people do not really know what will happen if Petroamazonas drills new wells: "Without thinking, we just brought the *compañía* back in. And now we're in the process of punishing ourselves even more. That's just the way we Cofán are." She laughed and said, "People want the money. It doesn't really matter to me. I'm old and will die soon anyway."

Many people said they were afraid of the potential contamination and possible disappearance of fish and game. Others expressed uncertainty regarding their ability to persuade the *compañía* to pursue the kind of development they want. Some told me Petroamazonas might decide to ignore Cofán demands and put wells close to Cofán houses. The company might decide it is too expensive to work without direct road access to new platforms. No one in Dureno wants new roads or a sea of oil wells on their land, especially if they are close to their homes. Recently, Petroamazonas erected a drilling rig on the other side of the Aguarico, directly across from the main settlement

FIGURE 7.5. *A cocama worker in Dureno's millennium community*

but outside Dureno's boundaries. It operated for months, creating a racket that kept people up at night and caused temporary hearing problems among children. The idea of having ten or twenty platforms right next to people's homes is unacceptable. They would expose Dureno residents to overwhelming noise, noxious fumes, and the threat of direct contamination. Moreover, they would drive animals far away, making hunting even more difficult than it is now.

Some people fear that additional oil development might lead to even greater levels of conflict. Deji worries that easier access to new roads would break families apart. He explained that Dureno's relative isolation actually helps families deal with their problems. The possibility of easy flight could mean that husbands could leave wives or vice versa after minor disagreements. Silvio likewise explained that oil money would make social relations even more tenuous. If men and women have enough money to survive without each other, they will have little reason to solve their domestic disputes. Instead, they could leave the community to live on their own or begin families with non-Cofán people. A new road network would also make it easier for non-Cofán people to enter Dureno. Valerio mentioned the "thieves" and "murderers" who would come from Colombia to ravage the community. Deji said that *cocama* and Napo Runa people would enter to seduce and impregnate young women. That is what happened, he reminded me, in the population centers of Totoa Nai'qui and Pisorié Canqque, which are much easier for outsiders to reach given their proximity to roads and settler farms.

Emeregildo and Toribio have been two of the Cofán's most dedicated anti-oil activists. Neither is happy with the recent turn of events. Emeregildo is known globally as a critic of Chevron; Toribio enjoys a reputation as an enemy of the entire petroleum industry. Emeregildo described his fears to me. When I asked whether the people of Dureno were still able to prohibit the petroleum industry from entering their land, he replied,

With the way the president here [Eduardo] has made us lose ourselves, it has already begun, and now we can longer stop the *companía*. We've already let the seismic company in. Now, the seismic work is done, and soon they will come in and begin drilling for oil. If we had decided against allowing seismic exploration, we'd have a much better chance of protecting ourselves from oil development. But now, with the seismic studies already completed, they have seen how many drilling sites there are. With that, they will soon begin to enter and do even more.

I asked Emeregildo what Chevron officials would think now that the people have allowed the *compania* to enter the community again. He replied,

I'm really afraid of that. Chevron has never stopped trying to figure out a way to beat us, even though we've already won the case against them. They're always looking for a way. They pay attention to which communities have decided to work with the *compania*. Their spies are traveling all throughout this land. They're just waiting for someone to say, "No, the petroleum industry doesn't really contaminate anything." If someone says that, they'll be doing Chevron a big favor. Then, Chevron will try to criticize and discredit what we have said about them. They'll say the people behind the lawsuit were lying about oil the whole time. They'll say the Cofán are actually working with the *compania*. And then we'll lose everything we've accomplished. They're always waiting for us to say things like that, to make mistakes. They're doing all they can to find that information.

Toribio shared Emeregildo's fears, but he placed more emphasis on the social damage even a good relationship with the petroleum industry could cause. He was worried that easy money and easy work would destroy the Cofán as a people. He explained,

This is what I think about the *compania*. Now, we are living by selling our land to the *compania* [receiving financial benefits for company operations]. And that is bad from my perspective. Why? It's teaching us to be lazy. We just sit here and receive the money. We don't have to do anything for it. We don't have to work in the forest. We don't have to grow and sell manioc or corn or plantains. Now, some people in Dureno have no gardens. They just receive the money and buy plantains in Lago Agrio. Because of that, it will become even worse here in the future. People won't want to work. They will all be lazy. They will steal from the people who have finished school, found a job, and struggled to make a little bit of money and buy a few things. They'll get angry at those people. They might try to kill them and take what they have. That's what will happen here. They'll start acting like *cocama*, like thieves and killers. Many people here will become *cocama*. It will be bad.

As a defender of Eduardo and a contrarian by nature, Florinda disagreed with the dire warnings of such people as Emeregildo and Toribio. She described their fears in ways that make those concerns seem silly or insignificant. When I asked her about the possibility of new wells appearing on Dureno land, she laughed. As usual, she replied with a bit of interesting dark humor. In response to a specific question about the possible emergence of new contamination-related illnesses, she gave me a short lecture on the existential condition of all people, Cofán or otherwise:

How would any new illnesses emerge? Things have always killed us. Even in the old times, we couldn't live without dying. We died then, too. And that's what it's like now. When someone dies, they die. Alejandro's older sister is dead, but I'm still alive. Recently, many elders have died. That's just the way it is. That's what I think. You're going to die. There's no way for you to live forever. No. We all have to die. No one can live truly well.

I was still thinking about the dismal predictions I recorded in 2013 when I returned to Dureno in 2016. But at least two important things had changed. First, the global price of oil collapsed in the fall of 2014 and had yet to recover. The Ecuadorian government had stopped drilling any new wells, including in Dureno. Second, Eduardo lost the December 2015 election for Dureno's presidency. By a very narrow margin, a man named Silverio Criollo became the new community *na'su.* Silverio is a little older than Eduardo and not the same kind of leader. Although he has some medical training and works as Dureno's unofficial doctor, he has no computer, email, or Facebook page. His Spanish is much weaker than Eduardo's, and he does not have as wide a social and political circle. He is also much poorer.

Silverio has a more cautious stance toward the petroleum industry. Many of his closest relatives spoke out against BGP and Petroamazonas during the 2013 community conflicts. Many never stopped criticizing Eduardo and the decision to begin a different relationship with oil. Nevertheless, Silverio said he would continue to work with the *compañía* if the majority of people wanted him to maintain the relationship. But he will certainly not be the same kind of pro-oil *na'su* Eduardo was. He will never be able to convince anyone to give up their deep-seated thoughts on the matter. And it is entirely possible that Eduardo will win the next election and continue Dureno's prior developmental path if the price of oil rebounds and an oil-friendly national administration remains in power.

I never got a solid answer for why Eduardo lost. Some people said community residents had become sick of his commanding ways. Others said he had become less and less respectful of elders and their concerns. Perhaps most importantly, in 2015 he and his brother had gotten drunk at a community party and caused a conflict. His brother got into a fight with one of Silverio's relatives and beat him up badly. Eduardo was not the main aggressor, but he was involved in the incident. The event did not reflect well on him, his family, or his allies. Eduardo's brother became sick a few months later. A rumor circulated that Silverio's grandfather—a shaman who was also the father of the man Eduardo's brother had fought—had attacked Eduardo's brother. A shaman in a different Dureno population center identified Silverio's grandfather's *davu* in Eduardo's brother. After spending a lot of money on shamanic and Western treatments for his brother, Eduardo allegedly went to the offending shaman and demanded $500 in compensation. He had spent at least that much money on his brother's recovery. Most people said the old man would never pay, nor should he. I do not know if the shaman denied or confirmed the allegation. Shamans are like that; they do not want to be blamed for attacks but are happy that people consider them powerful enough to commit them.

Despite losing the election, Eduardo appeared to be in relatively good spirits. Over the previous two years, he seemed worried in our email conversations. He said that Petroamazonas reportedly wanted to construct six new platforms in Dureno, triple the number Eduardo first imagined. But the crash of the oil market meant the company had put all new operations on hold. Eduardo laughed and said that the reopened Dureno 1 was a bust. Its daily output was far less than Petroamazonas had predicted. Nonetheless, Petroamazonas continued to rent the community's trucks, and people continued to get their food allotments. Perhaps the old shamans really had succeeded in drying up the oil during the 1998 protest.

The biggest reason for Eduardo's good mood in 2016 was that the millennium community was finally under construction. Despite the oil crash and Ecuador's resulting budgetary crisis, the government remained committed to fulfilling its promise. The Quito construction firm it contracted had cleared many hectares of land and moved a number of households and gardens to build the complex at the western edge of Dureno's main population center. Dozens if not hundreds of workers, many of them Cofán, were laying sewage pipes, building a potable water system, and erecting 108 homes. It was an impressive sight. The houses had solid cement foundations and piers, bamboo walls, and roofs made of a green plastic-like material that would supposedly keep the structures cooler than metal roofs, which can make buildings unbearably hot. Although the houses sit in straight lines on small stone thoroughfares, the planners were careful to leave large trees between them to add to their aesthetic appeal.

The structures look like the large, high-end tourist cabins I have seen at jungle resorts. The resemblance is intentional. Eduardo and other Dureno leaders were able to work with the architects on the designs. The dense arrangement of houses evokes a small city but an indigenous Amazonian city that is at least somewhat in tune with its forest surroundings. The complex will not conflict with the luxury tourism business Eduardo hopes to create. If anything, the new houses look more "authentically indigenous" than the enclosed, wood-plank, metal-roofed houses in which most Cofán people now live.

People were excited about the millennium community. It was actually happening, and it looked good. Many Dureno residents, including Alejandro, were making a fair wage working on the complex. Others were earning money feeding and housing *cocama*, *singo*, and Napo Runa workers. When I visited, there were no reports of *cocama* abuse. Everyone seemed to be on good terms. At Dureno's main river port, the contractor had erected a huge billboard that read, "Oil promotes 'good living' in your community! Construction of the Project 'Millennium Community Cofán–Dureno.' Dureno Parish, Sucumbíos Province. Duration: 480 days. Our *patria* [homeland, in Spanish] forever!"

When I wrote this chapter in late 2016, the millennium community was still under construction. I regularly checked its progress through the pictures my Dureno friends posted on their Facebook pages. Even though Ecuador's financial situation had not improved, my contacts assured me that the government would not leave Dureno until it completed construction. Despite their optimism, however, people did harbor doubts about the new housing complex. Would the homes be too close to each other, leading to conflict among families? Would the hollow bamboo walls become infested with wasps, rats, and giant cockroaches? Would the houses be too far from people's gardens, making traditional work routines difficult? Would the government end up asking people to pay for it all, even though it promised it would not?

During a conversation about the millennium community, Martin told me a funny story about his grandmother. When the provincial government finally extended power lines across the Aguarico River to Dureno around 2000, many old people did not realize they would have to pay for electricity. They thought it was one more resource that was naturally there, just like the trees they used for firewood. When Martin's grandmother received her first power bill, she was enraged. She grabbed her machete, walked to the cement pole to which the power line was attached, and began hacking at its base as if it were a tree. Martin laughed hysterically at her reaction. But his point was

———

FIGURE 7.6. *Alejandro and other Cofán men working on Dureno's millennium community*

serious: the people of Dureno do not yet know what the ultimate costs of the millennium community will be.

Everyone told me there was no signed agreement for the construction of the complex. It was simply done *tayopi'su shacane*, "to repay the oldtime debt" the petroleum industry had accrued for harming the Cofán in so many ways. Nonetheless, the most politically astute Dureno residents realize it will be hard to say no to oil now that the resource has paid for the millennium community, which might cost more than $10 million when it is finally complete. Fighting the oil industry is becoming harder and harder for the Cofán of Dureno. They have battled oil before. Against the odds, they have beaten it, even if their victories were temporary. They might be able to beat it again. Or they might not even want to or have to. In Dureno, oil's future is uncertain, just as it is everywhere else. Whether the substance emerges from a piece of land depends only partially on the people who own, control, and occupy that land. Global political-economic shifts determine the commodity's fluctuating price, which is often far more important than the power of a community or a nation-state to determine whether oil remains in the ground.

In an email exchange during the writing of this chapter, Martin told me that the *compañía* had paused its work in Dureno. "Petroamazonas has put everything on hold," he wrote. "The price of oil is very low right now. I hope it stays that way forever." During most of my research, Martin had worked alongside Eduardo to enable oil to flow from Dureno. For personal and political reasons, however, he had become critical of both Eduardo and the petroleum industry. Alongside his father, Emeregildo, Martin began to work for an international environmental organization.[5] Martin reclaimed his original position, that despite the benefits Dureno had received, oil was trouble for the Cofán, and it was best to stay as far away from it as possible.

CHAPTER 8

•

LIFE IN OIL

I n Dureno, oil is anything but a simple matter. Even in a family as small as Alejandro's, there are different senses of what life was like before and after the *companía* came and forced the first drops of *simpe'cha'a* from the ground. Alejandro pines for the old days of powerful shamans and plentiful game. He longs for the calm rivers and forests through which he once moved freely. Lucia misses the satiation, health, and strength she knew as a child. But she does not miss the warring *atesu'cho* and the *cocoya* they let loose to terrorize everyone; she had much to fear in the days before oil, too. Roberto has never known a world without oil. He smiles in wonder when his parents tell him how much meat they used to eat. He loves the idea of living without schools, jobs, and stomachaches. But he would be extremely sad to give up some of his possessions, especially his smartphone.

Oil cannot be blamed for all the bad things Cofán people have

FIGURE 8.1. *A dog on Dureno's riverfront*

experienced over the past fifty years, but it certainly played a large part in making them happen. To understand oil's complex consequences in Dureno, we need to open our minds about what the substance is, not just for the Cofán but for all people. At a global level, oil appears in paradoxical ways. Although the petroleum industry and its products are central to modern life, their immense scale and utter incalculability make them hard to pin down.[1] Because oil is everywhere and in everything—land, air, water, cars, clothes, medicine, food, bodies, economy, politics—it can seem invisible, even absent.[2]

When we ponder the relatively recent appearance of oil in Dureno, it is tempting to think it should be easy to see because, in the most basic sense, it seems like "matter out of place," the phrase that Mary Douglas proposed in 1966 as a cross-cultural definition of "pollution" or "dirt." Oil is supposed to characterize life in the modern West, not in indigenous Amazonia. The arid deserts of West Texas and the Middle East are the spaces most commonly associated with the substance's extraction. When they imagine oil in eastern Ecuador, activists, journalists, and the broader public expect its destructiveness to be exceedingly clear. In Amazonia, there is so much pristine life to spoil. Oil can assault the thousands of plant and animal species that cover the lightly populated tropical landscape. Oil can devastate the bodies and cultures of native peoples whom Westerners cannot help but view as new, fragile, and unwilling members of the modern world. The imagery supports a sense of intuitive anger and undeniable tragedy. But it occludes more than it reveals.

To understand the place of oil in Cofán life, it is helpful to conceptualize the substance as a "quasi-object," a term proposed by the philosopher and anthropologist of science Bruno Latour. He writes that quasi-objects are things that are simultaneously "real as Nature, narrated as Discourse, collective as Society, existential as Being."[3] Although oil is definitely a material thing, it exists in other ways, too. It is wrapped up with people's words, thoughts, and actions as they envision its underground existence, enable its rise to the earth's surface, and ensure its movement through pipelines, tankers, refineries, and retail outlets to support the daily lives of billions of people. As it passes between, around, and through them, it composes the bonds that tie people together and force them apart. As an ensemble of materials, words, and relations, oil is never stable. It starts as one set of things and becomes another. No matter how broad its reach, oil is finite and tenuous. It is too unwieldy and volatile to have a fixed essence.

Oil always operates in a matrix of social, natural, and conceptual conditions that shape its power and form. Those conditions are particular to certain places, times, and peoples. The geographer Matthew Huber argues that oil is the central component of the lifestyles of suburban North Americans, who recruit the commodity into their projects for self-made, entrepreneurial lives.[4] The anthropologist Fernando Coronil outlines how oil created the natural body of the Venezuelan state, whose leaders mobilized petroleum and its wealth to make modernity magically appear for the citizenry.[5] The political theorist Timothy Mitchell suggests that whereas coal power offered workers numerous opportunities to paralyze the economy and press their claims, the shift to oil sustained a less promising infrastructure for the pursuit of democratic politics.[6] In all these cases, oil existed in different forms and did different things.

The same is true in Dureno. In the first chapter of this book, I characterize Cofán life in oil in two ways. I call it a subtle, ambivalent, and contradictory condition and a form of slow, confusing, and ultimately unknowable violence. From certain angles, oil looks like it has completely destroyed the Cofán and tossed them into the waste bin of history. From other viewpoints, it seems as if Cofán people have so successfully survived oil's assault that it did virtually nothing to them or that it only added one more chapter to the story of violence, sickness, and dispossession they already knew. From still other perspectives, Cofán people appear to be mobilizing the substance to create a more promising space for themselves in the contemporary world. By delving into the many-sided quality of Cofán experiences with oil, I hope to have remained true to the nuances I detected in my ethnographic research. I also hope that I disrupted common understandings of the simplicity of the Cofán-oil encounter and provided a solid empirical basis on which to discuss the culpability of the petroleum industry and Cofán demands that it compensate them for their losses.

So what is oil in Dureno? What transformations did it initiate, and what shapes might it take? First, it is important to note that it is the same thing in Dureno as it is nearly everywhere in the world. It exists in an expanding collection of commodities that are central to Cofán life. Although many Cofán people have clear memories of paddling and poling dugout canoes, none want to return to the days before they had gasoline-powered motors. The technology allows them to travel far and fast with little effort. It has been key to their ability to maintain their lifestyle in a transformed environment. With gasoline, they can hunt and fish at locations distant from Dureno's central settlement and return the same day. With so few resources remaining close to their homes, they would have had to abandon their subsistence practices long ago were it not for oil-powered mobility. But motors are just one element of the object world petroleum sustains in Dureno. There are the same kinds of clothes, foods, medicines, power sources, televisions, stereos, and other commodities that characterize life around the globe. Although the Cofán's possession of such goods depends on their fluctuating access to money, they appreciate each and every one of them.

Oil has many other manifestations in Dureno. One of its most important consequences was a radical transformation of people's understanding and experience of the material world. As Deji explained to me, the idea of toxic contamination—a form of dirtiness that harms and kills—was unknown to Cofán people before crude saturated their lives. Oil became a strange set of things: a swarm of visible and invisible substances that killed not because they were sent by supernaturally empowered enemies but because of their basic physical properties. In complex and confusing ways, the materials transformed rivers, forests, rains, skies, fish, and game. The natural world became a hostile force.

Shamans could injure people with mysterious objects, but oil wastes were a different kind of weapon. The antagonistic substances entered Cofán bodies, where they hid for years until they revealed themselves in such enigmatic forms of suffering as *cáncer*. Illness and death became truly material phenomena. Their social genesis was no longer detectable through supernatural investigation. Consequently, oil appeared as a new form of bodily being. Cofán flesh became susceptible in new ways. It harbored new kinds of objects and forces. It became inscrutable to Cofán sensation and expertise. Oil's unpredictable ways of doing harm opened the Cofán to a new kind of medical knowledge that surpassed Cofán abilities at the same time as Western medicine's limits became apparent. Scientists and doctors, too, are unsure what oil becomes in the bodies of Cofán people. Nonetheless, most experts seem certain that its effects are not good.

Oil also appeared as a physical infrastructure and a social invasion. *Cocama* workers cleared land for platforms, camps, and roads that led to towns and cities. The newcomers moved through villages and forests; many built homesteads and stayed. They became farmers, ranchers, merchants, and land speculators. The infrastructure they constructed set the stage for the Cofán's near-total dispossession. Nonindigenous settlers have colonized many parts of Amazonian Ecuador, but the oil industry's power and resources made Cofán territory's transformation extremely rapid and far-reaching. Before the people of Dureno could blink, oil was emerging from their land and settlers were claiming and destroying their territory.

The Cofán domain shrunk. People's treasured ability to wander freely and enjoy the abundance of the forests and rivers belonged to the past. So, too, did their power to respond to tension, conflict, and the deaths of their leaders by leaving their old communities and forming new ones on unoccupied land. Oil covered Cofán territory with paralyzing fear and violent relations. Cofán people did not know how or why it was happening. They hoped it would not last, but it did.

In the forests that remained, oil initiated other transformations. Many anthropologists argue that relations between Amazonian peoples and nonhuman beings do not occur as encounters between thinking subjects (people) and mute objects (animals and plants). Instead, they suggest that the forest itself is a deeply social space. According to a number of ethnographic studies, native Amazonians communicate with animals in complex ways, especially while hunting.[7] Cofán people's knowledge and appreciation of nonhuman capacities is undeniable, but it was only after the petroleum industry brought *cocama* into their forests that hunting became an inescapably intersubjective endeavor. Even lone Cofán hunters had to contend with the violent newcomers who had populated their land. Cofán people became attuned not only to the tracks, movements, and calls of their prey but to the barking dogs and angry shouts of belligerent *cocama* landlords, who had become the forest's new *na'su*. Whereas Cofán shamans periodically communicated with supernatural owners of game animals, hunting outside Dureno's boundaries made clashes with violent masters a constant, nerve-racking, and terrifying predicament. Hunting was always about killing, but it had finally become an exchange in which the Cofán were as much prey as predator.

Oil shaped the forest in other ways, too. No matter how much their territory has changed over the past five centuries, the forest's basic existence was never in question. After the petroleum industry began operations, Cofán people confronted a new possibility: the end of the forest itself. Larger and larger sections of the Aguarico River basin were denuded. Pastures, farms, palm-oil plantations, oil-processing

FIGURE 8.2. *Laura Mendua and her husband,*
Silvio Chapal, poling a canoe up the Dureno River

facilities, roads, and towns replaced the landscape the Cofán knew. As they walk along Lago Agrio's bustling streets, elders can still point to the places where they hunted woolly monkeys and collected medicinal plants. The memories remain, but the environment in which the images were created is gone. In a striking lesson, oil taught the Cofán that the forest exists because humans allow it to.

As the forest shrank, the activities that occurred within it began to diminish. Buying and eating began to replace hunting, fishing, gardening, and gathering. There was more wage labor, more time in schools, and more dependence on the market. Even in Dureno, the forest has become emptier of what the Cofán need to survive. Each year, people have less reason to spend time in it. The Cofán still consider themselves forest dwellers, but the foundation of that identity is becoming increasingly tenuous.

By emptying the forest and loosening people's ties to it, oil promoted tense social relations within the village. Less game means less meat, and less meat means less sharing and less interhousehold cooperation. The need to buy food rather than harvest it means that people need more money. The financial stress causes many residents to spend more time working for a wage, which leaves them less time and energy to help each other build a house or weed a garden. The need for money also motivates people to help others only if paid to do so. The declining circulation of food and labor threatens the sense of peaceful well-being that has made Dureno such an appealing place to live, especially in comparison to the violent, atomistic lifestyle that the Cofán associate with *cocama*.

The unstable social relations make it difficult to deal with inequality. When the prospect of unequal, unfair enrichment reared its head during the reentry of oil companies in 2013, the community almost broke apart. Instead of directing their animosity at *cocama*, the people of Dureno began to dislike each other. They even attacked each other. Other anthropologists have commented on oil's ability to sow discord in Amazonian Ecuador.[8] Division can be an intentional corporate tactic to stifle opposition or an unplanned by-product of new work, new money, and new outsiders meddling in community affairs.

Although oil's presence in Dureno is characterized by an overwhelming and confusing negativity, the commodity has supported countervailing processes of empowerment. The anti-oil protests of the 1980s and 1990s were essential moments in Cofán mobilization. They brought the Cofán into contact with outsiders who taught them how and why to take collective action. The people of Dureno discussed problems, debated solutions, and decided to act together to confront their enemies. Oil's role in the process amplified Cofán concerns and accomplishments. Journalists and activists became invested in Cofán struggles because the Cofán's adversary was one of the world's great environmental villains. Theirs was a David and Goliath story with appealing elements, including colorful natives and a remote, Edenic setting. Soon, people around the world heard the word "Cofán" for the first time. They donated money, made visits, pressured governments, organized speaking tours, called for boycotts, and spread Cofán words and images to the farthest corners of the earth. Although Cofán people's roles in the campaigns were often scripted, the very fact of their involvement extended their political capacities in profound ways.

The Cofán's fame as oil's enemy was also constraining. The negotiations between the people of Dureno and the petroleum industry in 2013 recast them as untrustworthy, acculturated sellouts. But the tarnished image seemed insignificant relative to the possible benefits of a new alliance with the Ecuadorian state. As historical victims of oil, the Cofán called for the construction of the multimillion-dollar millennium community. Under the leadership of Eduardo, the people of Dureno positioned themselves as willing partners in a national leftist project that sought to better livelihoods by extracting more and more crude. The miraculous appearance of oil wealth—finally within the Cofán's reach—spawned ambitious dreams of advancement. Eduardo envisioned an $8 million tourist complex funded by oil revenues that he intended to use to protect the forest, promote Cofán expertise, keep people in Dureno, and ensure sustainable income for all community residents. Following Eduardo's lead, people felt their power grow as they negotiated with oil companies to gain wealth and shape the process of exploration and extraction. Eduardo even imagined creating a petroleum services company that would be

———

owned and run by Cofán people. The idea might appear far-fetched, but it reflects a new sense of oil as a potential engine for political and economic improvement.

The cascade of changes raises the question of what Cofán culture is, such that oil could destroy it. The most basic issue is the physical survival of Cofán people, many of whom either have died or will die because of oil-related illnesses, especially cancer. Equally obvious assaults were the early rapes of women and the death of Yori'ye. The people of Dureno deem the latter event especially destructive. It meant the disappearance of the last great *na'su*, a leader who could cure their sick, kill their enemies, repel their assailants, solve their disputes, and fill their bellies with fish and game. The death of Yori'ye marked the end of a certain mode of Cofán being. People still drink *yaje*, and elders like Alejandro still cure their neighbors, but the days when shamanism provided life's basic structure are likely gone for good.

Randy Borman once told me that given all the crises the Cofán have faced over the past five centuries, the only two constants in their history have been the forest and their language. If those remain, he suggested, Cofán people will remain. For the moment, the language is strong. Even in Dureno, A'ingae is the near-universal tongue. The forest is another matter. Inside the community's boundaries, it continues to stand, but it provides less and less. It is a tiny remnant of what the Dureno Cofán used before Texaco arrived. Although Randy and other leaders are working hard to augment the Cofán's landholdings, most of their homeland has been settled and farmed. Cofán people might be able to reclaim some of it, but the odds are not good. Moreover, it will be difficult to ensure the ecological integrity of the lands they still use. By contaminating, clearing, and opening their forests to outsiders, the oil industry has damaged the very basis of Cofán life. It also threatens the Cofán's future, specifically, their ability to interact with their homeland in old and new ways to produce additional generations of hunters, fishers, farmers, researchers, park guards, tour operators, and environmental activists—anything that could help them maintain their flexible relation with the forest, their language, and each other.

According to the statements on the Amazon Post, a Chevron-funded website that presents "Chevron's Views and Opinions on the Ecuador Lawsuit," Chevron denies all allegations that it has harmed the peoples and environments of northeastern Ecuador, including the Cofán and their homeland. In Chevron's words, "All of the legitimate evidence presented to the Ecuadorian court demonstrates that former Texaco Petroleum Company operations present no risk to residents' health and have not resulted in any significant impact to groundwater, drinking water, biodiversity, or indigenous culture."[9] Chevron concludes, "The scientific evidence clearly shows that the assertions of harm in Ecuador made by the plaintiffs' lawyers and their supporters have no merit."[10]

Although I would not frame the damage claims in the same ways the plaintiffs' lawyers did, I find the idea that Chevron harmed neither the peoples nor the environments of northeastern Ecuador absurd. Chevron responds to the allegations with a variety of arguments: there are insufficient medical records to support claims of contamination-related illnesses and deaths; the company claims that its own tests of water sources and forest environments show no oil-related damages (although tests conducted by the plaintiffs' team paint a different picture); and the population of most indigenous peoples actually increased after Texaco began its work in 1964. Chevron does admit that the Cofán have faced serious problems since the 1960s, but it attributes nearly all of them to colonization and the resulting transformation and expropriation of Cofán land. It asserts that although Texaco brought in the workers and built the infrastructure, the Ecuadorian government is to blame because it asked Texaco to help carry out its long-term plan: populating the country's Amazonian provinces with nonindigenous people.[11]

With regard to more subtle processes of cultural change, Chevron blames the SIL, including the Borman family. In his official response to the Ecuadorian verdict, Chevron's paid anthropological expert Robert Wasserstrom writes, "The missionaries proceeded to modify traditional patterns of settlement, kinship, social organization, marriage, subsistence, religion, etc. Missionary activity continued through the 1990s and is largely responsible for the 'loss of their [indigenous peoples'] cultural identity and integrity.'"[12]

My account of the Borman family's legacy—life-saving medical interventions, health care training, A'ingae literacy, Dureno's land title, and Randy's territorial recuperation efforts, which occurred before and after his parents left Dureno—should make clear that I see little merit in Wasserstrom's argument concerning the missionaries who worked with the Cofán in the second half of the twentieth century. As to the colonization of northeastern Ecuador, lawyers, historians, and political scientists can debate who is legally, ethically, and causally responsible. It is not my area of expertise. Nonetheless, no one would argue that the large-scale transformation of Cofán territory would have occurred when and how it did were Texaco not involved.

Chevron's other arguments do not hold up to the evidence presented in this book. Although the Cofán population has been increasing since the 1920s, the end of the Capuchin missions and the entrance of modern health care workers, including Bobbie Borman, were the main causes. Moreover, a simple increase in population does not mean that no medical or cultural damages occurred. In the decades after Texaco arrived, many Cofán people died at a young age, many more suffered through serious illnesses, and all watched their way of life change in painful ways.

As I did fieldwork for this book, I was struck by the sheer magnitude and consistency of the testimonies I collected concerning the cultural, ecological, and medical transformations that occurred as Texaco's operations shaped the land around Dureno. I have no doubt that oil contaminated the Cofán's air, water, and food. I am certain its wastes damaged Cofán bodies. The people of Dureno did not have access to the doctors who could have reported their illnesses and discovered the causes of their deaths, but that does not mean pollution did not harm them. Even though Chevron was able to produce test results that it claims cast doubt on the current contamination of Texaco's old work sites, it never did significant studies of the company's environmental and health impacts in the 1960s, 1970s, and 1980s, when its operations were most destructive.

I have no idea how to calculate the harm oil did to the people of Dureno or how much money would adequately compensate them for their losses. For an anthropologist, the questions are strange and uncomfortable. Cofán people have suffered in so many ways: the fear, conflict, illness, deaths, rapes, and loss of so much land that would have supported their culture and given them the freedom to transform their way of life according to their own visions of self-determination. It is hard to describe, let alone quantify, such privation while admitting a basic fact: as a people, the Cofán are still here. Oil did not destroy them. Their lives might not be exactly as they want them, but they are filled with humor, joy, and purpose alongside suffering, sorrow, and pain.

Writing those words fills me with ambivalence. I doubt this book provokes the sense of unambiguous tragedy that accompanies simpler depictions of the Cofán-oil encounter. On the basis of everything I have seen and heard in Dureno, it is clear that Cofán people continue to enjoy their way of life, battered as it is. They continue to negotiate their challenges with determination and substantial success. Despite my better-than-dismal perspective on their prospects, I believe they deserve compensation. After serving as the primary engine of the Cofán homeland's transformation, Chevron owes the people of Dureno a lot. The Ecuadorian government has at least begun to admit its role in causing Cofán suffering; its construction of the millennium community was an important first step. What has Chevron admitted? According to its own statements, nothing.

Rather than focus on the factual matters of its past operations in northeastern Ecuador, Chevron has chosen to respond to the Ecuadorian verdict, which now stands at approximately $9.5 billion, by criticizing its opponents. With hundreds of attorneys working on its behalf, it has succeeded in convincing US judges that the plaintiffs' lawyers used fraud and intimidation to win the case. Some of their accusations are compelling. They involve bribery, falsified evidence, ghostwritten reports, and even a ghostwritten Ecuadorian judgment. But to many of the allegations, the plaintiffs' lawyers respond in ways that I also find compelling. In addition, they point to two important facts: the plaintiffs struggled from 1993 to 2001 to hold the case in the United States to make it as corruption-free as possible, while Texaco successfully argued that the case should be held in Ecuador; and on the eve of the US corruption trial, Chevron gave up all claims

FIGURE 8.3. *Roberto on the Aguarico River*

for monetary damages so it would not have to face a jury verdict. A clearly sympathetic judge decided the case from the bench. Chevron never had to convince a panel of twelve impartial citizens that corruption was the reason it lost in Ecuador.

I am not a lawyer, an environmental scientist, or a public health specialist. I am an anthropologist, and my job was to listen to the Cofán's side of the story. Before I began my research, few non-Cofán people had made significant attempts to do that. As I resided in their community, watched their lives, and heard their words, the people of Dureno convinced me that oil has harmed them in profound and painful ways. They also convinced me that they are still here, learning and fighting. They have managed to survive amid oil's destruction, and they will continue to do so until the world finds a way to meet its needs without removing the crude that lies beneath the land that the Cofán call home.

ACKNOWLEDGMENTS

Many people helped me write this book. First and foremost, I wish to thank the members of the indigenous Cofán nation of eastern Ecuador. I began to work with Cofán people as an undergraduate student in 1994, and I have returned to Cofán territory for academic and applied projects nearly every year since then. Getting to know people in the communities of Dureno, Zábalo, Duvuno, Sinangoé, and Chandia Na'e has been an immense privilege. Without their constant instruction and goodwill, my life would be very different—and much less rewarding.

No Cofán people were more important to the writing of this book than Alejandro Criollo, Lucia Quenamá, and Roberto Criollo. They have been compassionate hosts, wise teachers, and great friends. In Dureno, Martin Criollo and Deji Criollo acted tirelessly as coordinators of the research activities that made writing possible. Randy Borman, too, offered essential advice, insights, and logistical support. Although I worked with dozens of Dureno residents, the following individuals were especially helpful collaborators: Roberto Aguinda, Toribio Aguinda, Felipe Borman, Silvio Chapal, Emeregildo Criollo, Eduardo Mendua, Laura Mendua, Valerio Mendua, and Florinda Vargas. In addition to Alejandro and Lucia, my other *combandeccu* and *inisendeccu* provided emotional and material support: Juanito Aguinda and Carmeza Lucitante, Hugo Lucitante and Sadie Lucitante, and José Portilla and Vertina Lucitante. Bub and Bobbie Borman, too, were helpful sources of cultural and historical information.

———

For very little in return, Bear Guerra offered to work with me to produce the photographs that depict what my words cannot. Together with his wife, Ruxandra Guidi, he has become an intellectual confidant, an inspiring collaborator, and a true friend, and I hope we can work together on many future projects. At the University of Texas at San Antonio, Jason Yaeger and Dan Gelo secured me the time and resources to write. Also at UTSA, a group of graduate students offered to read my drafts and help me improve the manuscript: Christina Frazier, Chris Jarrett, Clint McKenzie, Jess Reid, and Sarah Townsend. Leah McCurdy did a fabulous job of composing the maps that appear in the book. Outside of UTSA, Amelia Fiske, Michael Goldhaber, Judith Kimerling, Paul Kockelman, and Norman E. Whitten Jr. offered deep readings and critical insights that made the book much stronger than it otherwise would have been.

At the University of Texas Press, Casey Kittrell has been a superb editor, and I look forward to continuing our collaboration. He somehow convinced an extraordinary set of scholars—Juliet Erazo, Doug Rogers, and Mary Weismantel—to bring their immense energy and intellectual resources to the review process. In Quito, Claire Nicklin and Andrew Reitz have been gracious hosts at the beginning and end of all my research trips. In the United States, I have been lucky to work with the other members of the board of the Cofán Survival Fund: Kendall Baker, John Himmelfarb, Susan Himmelfarb, and Tom Waterer. Other individuals were important allies as I did fieldwork and wrote: Scott Anderbois, Mitch Anderson, Lucas Bessire, David Bond, Dominic Boyer, Luiz Costa, Clark Erickson, Paja Faudree, Carlos Fausto, Matthew Ford, Laura Graham, James Greene, Cymene Howe, Cameron Hu, Donald Moncayo, Jeremy Mumford, Francine Strickwierda, and Laurel Spellman Smith. I could not have written the book without the funding provided by the Wenner-Gren Foundation for Anthropological Research (Grant #8518), the American Council of Learned Societies, and the University of Texas at San Antonio.

The death of Terry Turner in 2015 was a tremendous emotional and intellectual blow. Alongside my other dissertation adviser, Manuela Carneiro da Cunha, Terry did so much for me. I never would have written this book without his mentorship, which continued long after I finished my PhD. Thankfully, I continue to learn from Terry's family: Jane Fajans, Allison Fajans-Turner, and Vanessa Fajans-Turner. As I wrote, I thought frequently of the Fajans-Turner family. I hope Terry would have been happy with the way this book turned out.

In Chicago and San Antonio, my parents, John and Charleen Cepek, and brother, John Cepek, were tremendous sources of support. Unfortunately, before this book was published, my father died of a traumatic brain injury suffered while on vacation in Europe. His death has had a profound impact on me, and it has left me more determined than ever to make this world a more just place for all its residents. He was a great example of how one can use one's own life to make the lives of others better.

In San Antonio, I wish to give special thanks to the nurses and doctors who saw me through a life-threatening illness in 2015. Without the care of William Davis, Gregory Freeman, Nathan Hales, Richard Newman, and Burton Shaw, I never would have been able to start, let alone finish, the writing process. Just as important as their examinations and surgeries, though, was the love of my wife, Amy Rushing. She sat by my side for nearly two months and took care of me after I got out of the hospital and began to write. Together with our dogs, Dannie, Paco, and Osa, she has given me the home I always wanted and the strength I always needed. I owe her everything.

NOTES

CHAPTER 1: BLACK WATER

1. In this book, I use the A'ingae spelling system created by Bub and Bobbie Borman, a missionary-linguist couple who began working in Dureno in the 1950s. The system is similar to that for Spanish with a few important differences, most of which are reflected in the word *cui'ccu*: the use of an apostrophe to signal a glottal stop, double consonants to signal aspiration, and *u* to signal a vowel similar to the English "u" but with unrounded labialization. In addition, placing an *n* or *m* after a vowel signals nasalization.

2. "Oil Spill in Cofán Territory," video, 2:50, published on YouTube by Luis Narvaez, July 3, 2014, https://www.youtube.com/watch?v=ZGFr5H6Dry0.

3. In their study of industrial pollution in Argentina, the sociologist Javier Auyero and the anthropologist Débora Swistun describe how government, corporate, medical, media, and scientific officials send mixed messages concerning the nature and consequences of contamination. They describe the sometimes unintentional practice as the "labor of confusion" (Auyero and Swistun 2009). The phrase is a fitting label for what occurred in Dureno after the 2014 spill.

4. I take the phrase "slow violence" from the English professor and environmental critic Rob Nixon, who uses it to describe forms of harm that occur gradually and even invisibly (2013). Nixon's concept is similar to what the sociologist Thomas Beamish writes of as "crescive troubles," pollution-related problems that accumulate slowly and are typically ignored (2002).

5. With this phrase I intend to capture anthropology's two primary

---

concerns over the past century: its conceptualization of people as radically different others that Michel-Rolph Trouillot identifies as the discipline's historical dedication to the "savage slot" (2003) and its conceptualization of people as beings subjected to violence and trauma that Joel Robbins describes as anthropology's current fixation on the "suffering subject" (2013). A good example of a recent work attuned equally to the otherness and suffering of lowland South America's native inhabitants is Lucas Bessire's *Behold the Black Caiman* (2014).

6. There are many sources that report on Texaco's operations in Ecuador as well as the ongoing legal conflict with Chevron. The book that began the controversy was *Amazon Crude* (1991), which the environmental lawyer Judith Kimerling wrote to make the world aware of the links between oil production, environmental destruction, and human rights abuses in Amazonian Ecuador. Chevron has released many court documents and online publications that provide its perspectives on the central environmental and legal issues; most can be found on theamazonpost.com, a website the company maintains. For research and opinions that come from the plaintiffs' legal team and allies, the most useful sites to consult are chevrontoxico.com, stevendonziger.com, and thechevronpit.blogspot.com. Two books have appeared that accept the US courts' controversial conclusion that the Ecuadorian judgment was tainted by fraud and bribery: *Law of the Jungle* (Barrett 2014) and *Crude Awakening* (Goldhaber 2014). For some of the most even-handed coverage of the legal issues at play, consult lettersblogatory.com and search for the terms "Lago Agrio," "Chevron," and "Ecuador." The site elicits perspectives from observers partial to both the plaintiffs and the defendants. One of its managers, Ted Folkman, provides his own critical but balanced perspectives.

7. Doug Rogers has written a useful survey of the anthropology of oil (2015b). He divides the literature into works on the "temporalities of oil" and works on the "materialities of oil." This book fits roughly into the latter category. Many publications inside and outside of anthropology explore the relationships between oil, history, power, and contemporary forms of viewing and inhabiting the world. For some of the best books, I recommend *The Prize* (Yergin 1991), *Crude Existence* (Reed 2009), *Carbon Democracy* (Mitchell 2011), *Lifeblood* (Huber 2013), *Oil Culture* (Barret and Worden 2014b), *Peak Oil* (Schneider-Mayerson 2015), *The Depths of Russia* (Rogers 2015a), and *Oil Wealth and Insurgency in Nigeria* (Adunbi 2015).

8. Said 2003, xix.

CHAPTER 2: DURENO

1. Ecuador's oil industry actually began in 1911 with the drilling of a well on a peninsula along the country's Pacific coast. Nevertheless, the industry is now based squarely in its Amazonian region, from which the great majority of the country's crude comes. Royal Dutch Shell attained rights to explore there in 1937, but it did not reach Cofán territory until the 1940s. It drilled two exploratory wells before it left Ecuador, both to the south of the Cofán homeland.
2. After I got married, my wife began to use the same set of terms for Lucia, Alejandro, and Roberto. Alejandro and Lucia address her as Inise, and Roberto addresses her as Opi'su Chan, "carrying mother."
3. Among sources that do provide useful information on pre- and postcolonial Cofán history are Borman 2009; Friede 1952; Kohn 2002; Newson 1995; Robinson 1979.
4. Wasserstrom 2014.
5. Borman et al. 2007, 73.
6. Cabodevilla 1997; Wasserstrom, Reider, and Lara 2011.
7. Sahlins 1974, 30.
8. In her doctoral dissertation (1999), the biological anthropologist Lori Fitton provides a large amount of data on the health conditions of the Dureno Cofán. Her information, though, is now more than twenty years old. The economic and environmental situation in Dureno changed radically between the mid-1990s and the mid-2010s, when I did field research for this book.
9. For information on the medicinal plants the people of Dureno use, see Cerón 1995 and Pinkley 1973.
10. Three anthropologists (Castillo 1999; Fitton 1999; Robinson 1979) and one ethnobotanist (Pinkley 1973) wrote doctoral dissertations about Dureno. I have found Scott Robinson's historical research to be the most useful aspect of these works for my own investigations with Cofán people.
11. Kane 1995, 183, 192, 194.
12. Tidwell 1996, 86–87, 106, 107.
13. Boudin 2009, 182–189.
14. Walker 1996.
15. Berlinger 2009.
16. The essential source on anthropology's colonial origins and politics is Talal Asad's *Anthropology and the Colonial Encounter* (1973).
17. The Cofán Survival Fund (www.cofan.org) is a US nonprofit organization whose sole mission is to raise funds for the Fundación

Sobrevivencia Cofán (FSC, Foundation for the Survival of the Cofán People), a Cofán-directed Ecuadorian foundation committed to protecting, managing, and conserving Cofán territory.

CHAPTER 3: THE DEATH OF YORI'YE

1. People disagree about how Yori received his nickname. A few young people told me that *yori* is an A'ingae word that means "to crouch," which is how Yori'ye often held himself. As usual, older people say the young ones are mistaken. "Yori," the elders reported, was actually the name of a mestizo river trader who exchanged manufactured goods for Cofán forest products. Deji, my main research assistant, said that the "mestizo Yori" got into trouble with Ecuadorian or Colombian soldiers. Perhaps he ran up an unpayable debt. Or he might have killed someone. When the soldiers finally found him, his many daughters stood between him and the authorities. They fought off the soldiers and protected their father from imprisonment. Yori'ye, too, was blessed with a large group of daughters. Deji said he called himself Yori because outsiders would never be able to capture him, just as they were never able to capture his namesake.

2. By the time I began working with Cofán people, few individuals had clear memories of Yori'ye's paternal grandfather, who was a central figure in Cofán history. Most people did not even know his name. Today, the people of Dureno typically refer to him as Tetete Du'shu, "child of Tetete people." Marylette "Bub" Borman, a missionary-linguist affiliated with the Wycliffe Bible Translators/Summer Institute of Linguistics, arrived to work in Dureno in 1954. In his genealogical records, Borman recorded Yori'ye's grandfather's name as Aniseto. He wrote that Aniseto was a "Tetete child captured by Hernando Quenamá de Santa Cruz" and that people called him Angotura. Angoteros is the name of a community on the Napo River below the point where it meets the Aguarico in present-day Peru. There is little doubt that Aniseto spoke a Western Tukanoan language when he was captured, which probably occurred in the second half of the nineteenth century. Oral history suggests that he was ten or eleven at the time. The rest of his family was killed in a raid by other indigenous people. He took his captor's last name, which is how the appellation entered Cofán society. The outsiders brought him to a school managed by priests in highland Ecuador. There, he learned Spanish. After he grew up, the priests returned him to his homeland so he could serve as a go-between with church and government

authorities. Given the earlier conflict, the site of his capture was still too dangerous. In order to avoid it, he moved upriver, where he married a Cofán woman. No one knows how he learned A'ingae, but he definitely spoke it alongside Spanish and Western Tukanoan. He also carried a silver-capped cane that marked his government position. Yori'ye acquired the cane after Santos passed away. When Yori'ye died, his son Aurelio took the cane.

3. I have written extensively about Randy Borman (Cepek 2009, 2012, 2014). Aware that Dureno's small resource base would not be able to support its residents for long, he led a group of Cofán people to leave Dureno and establish the downriver community of Zábalo in the 1980s. Earlier, he served as an elected leader at Dureno. In the 1990s, he became the president of the Cofán ethnic federation. Today, he manages the Foundation for the Survival of the Cofán People, the key actor in securing Cofán rights to more than four hundred thousand hectares of eastern Ecuador.

4. Some missionary families affiliated with the SIL had a more negative impact on the people with whom they worked. Multiple sources attest to the deleterious consequences of the institution as a whole (Colby and Dennett 1995; Hvalkof and Aa 1981; Stoll 1983). In 1996 Randy Borman published a paper on the perspectives and activities of his parents; it provides important historical information on Dureno.

5. Alejandro's brother Atanacio told me about his travels to the San Miguel River as a youth. The Cofán there were particularly strict about the prohibitions. They were always hungry; they ate practically nothing. They almost completely segregated themselves from young women. They held their noses as women passed and kept their activities separate. "They lived by suffering," Atanacio said. But their difficult ways kept them clean. They had tremendous strength, energy, and discipline, which were essential to their quests.

6. Alejandro's seventy-year-old nephew Lorenzo, himself a skilled *yaje* drinker, described Yori'ye's abilities to me: "Yori'ye could transform into everything. Into macaws, into jaguars, into everything. Everything he had seen, he could become. He would come and go, come and go. He would chant and speak to the *canttini'cco a'i* (river cane people), and they would arrive. He went to them and returned with them. He had a piece of river cane. Even though there were no holes in it, he played it as a musical instrument. And then he smashed it, making a loud noise—but it was left undamaged! Then, another person took it back from him and hung it up. Then, he chanted again. He left and returned.

He left and spoke to the *sata a'i* (spear people). And when he returned, someone had sharpened his spear. They walked over and gave it to him. He played it as if it were a musical instrument, too. Then he smashed it, making a loud noise. But nothing happened to it—there were no holes in it! He would play sugarcane as if it were a musical instrument. That's how he transformed into a collared peccary and made the collared peccaries come. He would take his large plug of cured tobacco and play that, too. That's how he made the tobacco *na'su*, the tobacco *cocoya*, arrive. Yori'ye would go and return as the tobacco *cocoya*. He would speak as the *cocoya*, grunting in a deep, deep voice. The next day, you would look at the tobacco he played, and it was just regular tobacco! Yori'ye played everything. Everyone saw it—not just those who were inebriated with *yaje*. All who gathered saw him play those objects. It was amazing. We thought about it all the time."

7. The *yaje* people are essential extensions of shamanic power, but they are a source of danger, too. If they have befriended a person and given him their clothing, ornaments, and weapons and that person makes a mistake and breaks a prohibition, the *yaje* people become angry with and disgusted by the person. Their gifts depart from the person's body, inside of which they were kept. The afflicted person loses power, suffers illness, and sometimes dies.

8. Cofán people recognize many more types of jaguars than do Western scientists.

9. My assistant Deji told me another story about Yori'ye's anger and violence. Deji's mother, Elsira, came to Dureno from Colombia as an unmarried youth with her friend Otiria. Otiria met Deji's father, Enrique, and wanted to marry him. But Yori'ye disapproved. He told Elsira to marry Enrique and Otiria to marry Aurelio, Yori'ye's son. Elsira agreed but Otiria refused, and she returned to Colombia. Later, Elsira went to Colombia to buy cloth with Enrique and his brother. They met Otiria and told her to come back to Dureno and marry Aurelio. She refused again. Her mother, too, said that Otiria would never marry Aurelio. Elsira, Enrique, and Enrique's brother returned to Dureno and told Yori'ye that both Otiria and Otiria's mother would not allow the marriage. Yori'ye was enraged. According to Deji, Yori'ye drank *yaje*, transformed into an anaconda, and swam to Colombia. Otiria's younger brother saw a creature's head in the river. Thinking it was a game animal, he asked Otiria to paddle him to the middle of the river so he could spear it. When they approached the animal, they saw that it was an anaconda. It rose from the river and knocked Otiria

———

overboard. A man heard her scream, but by the time he dove into the water and swam to her, it was too late. She had drowned. People in Colombia knew the anaconda was Yori'ye, and Yori'ye never denied it. None of Otiria's kin were naive enough to attempt revenge. They knew Yori'ye would kill them, too.

10. Bub Borman flew from Limoncocha to Dureno to see Yori'ye's corpse before it was buried. He said that Yori'ye's mouth and nose appeared to be filled with stale vomit, and that the bruises on his neck could have been caused by the tightly wound beaded necklaces he was wearing. Bub was unable to make a definitive pronouncement on the cause of Yori'ye's death, though.

11. Brown 1989.

CHAPTER 4: THE *COCAMA* ARRIVE

1. Other anthropologists have asked me why Cofán people use the term *cocama* for non-native Spanish speakers. A large downriver indigenous group that occupies the main channel of the Marañon River (in Peru) is known as the Cocama-Cocamilla. Randy Borman, in a personal conversation, suggested that Cofán people once maintained trade relations with the Cocama-Cocamilla. He said the Cofán probably began calling nonindigenous people *cocama* after non-native Peruvians displaced and outnumbered the indigenous population of the area. Randy's idea, though, is just an educated guess.

2. Rosaldo 1993.

3. The harm that *cocama* traders did to Cofán people has become an important political issue. Chevron's lead social expert during their trial in Ecuador was an anthropologist named Robert Wasserstrom. He established a consulting firm based in Houston that provides services to energy companies (terra-group.net). Since 2011, I have had many conversations with Wasserstrom about the history of Cofán territory. He is a skilled researcher whose team has done important archival work, and some of his writings are published in academic journals.

   Wasserstrom's articles' underlying message is that Chevron is not responsible for the tragedies that have befallen the Cofán and neighboring indigenous groups. Many activists and journalists suggest that the Cofán lived in a pristine, isolated, and ahistorical state when Chevron (then Texaco) arrived in their territory in 1964. The idea, of course, is absurd. Wasserstrom has successfully debunked the misrepresentation of Cofán history, an easy task for scholars familiar with the literature. Instead of blaming oil companies for the problems northeastern Ecuador's native inhabitants have faced over the past fifty years, Wasserstrom stresses the role of two other actors: the Ecuadorian government and the SIL. For a summary of Wasserstrom's points, see the document "Lack of Evidence in the Sentencia of Cultural Damages Caused by Petroleum Activity," which is available for free online; Wasserstrom 2011.

I disagree with many of Wasserstrom's arguments. I am not qualified to determine who bears ultimate responsibility for building the roads, pipelines, and oil wells in ways that led to the invasion and destruction of Cofán territory, although most Cofán people blame Chevron. I am more qualified to dispute one of Wasserstrom's subtler arguments, that the *cocama* rubber collectors who came to Cofán territory in the late nineteenth and early twentieth centuries so radically transformed Cofán society that they nearly destroyed it. The implication of Wasserstrom's claim is that the consequences of Texaco's operations pale in comparison to the impacts of the *cocama* who made Cofán people gather rubber. In other words, during the twentieth century, Wasserstrom suggests, oil companies were the least of the Cofán's problems.

The people of Dureno acknowledge that their parents and grandparents periodically worked rubber. They have no oral history, however, of the massive social disruption and forced or semiforced labor that Wasserstrom outlines in his work, which is perhaps more a depiction of the Colombian situation. Wasserstrom admits that the Cofán did not suffer the outright slavery and massacre that the rubber economy brought to the lower Putumayo River, as Michael Taussig describes in *Shamanism, Colonialism, and the Wild Man* (1987). Wasserstrom does suggest that a large proportion of the Ecuadorian Cofán simply "disappeared" with the rubber bosses. For the remainder, he asserts, life was largely a matter of recovering from "fifty years of debt servitude"; 2014, 536–537.

My collaborators in Dureno stressed how few goods the *cocama* gave in exchange for Cofán products. Yet, their stories do not reflect the social devastation that Wasserstrom attributes to the rubber economy, at least in the twentieth century. After all, Wasserstrom bases his work entirely on the existing literature and an analysis of missionary and government archives. He has done no direct research with Cofán people. Most of them would have no interest in collaborating with an anthropologist paid by Chevron.

Instead of recounting their exploitation and coerced labor at the hands of rubber bosses, the Dureno Cofán place much more emphasis

---

on the violence perpetrated by priests and soldiers as well as the disastrous effects of epidemics. They provide vivid accounts of events, sites, and individuals that Wasserstrom did not detect in his archival research. For example, he makes no mention of the school staffed by Capuchin priests near the mouth of the Dureno River. Nor does he acknowledge the possibility that some Cofán families simply refused to cooperate with either priests or rubber traders—options my collaborators recounted in detail. The great majority of my informants stated that their parents and grandparents labored in the company of *cocama* merchants only when it suited them. More frequently, they worked on their own, in their spare time, gathering products that they traded to the *cocama* who periodically visited their communities.

One could argue that my Cofán collaborators are either confused or mistaken, that they have forgotten what the rubber economy did to them, or that they simply do not remember their family members who disappeared because of the rubber collectors—despite the many tragic events and destructive forces they do remember and speak about. As an anthropologist who has worked with Cofán people for more than two decades, I prefer to give more credence to their testimony.

4. Cepek 2012, 210–212.
5. The Josephine priests who came after the Capuchins were reportedly much kinder, and people gradually lost their fear of them. The Carmelites who worked later in upriver Cofán territory and on the San Miguel River were apparently motivated by a more progressive ideology. They organized medical efforts and cultural documentation projects on behalf of Cofán communities. They even provided material and logistical support to Cofán protests against the oil industry.
6. For detailed information on the building of the oil infrastructure, and especially the construction dates of certain wells and other structures, I have found these sources to be particularly helpful: Baby, Rivadeneira, and Barragán 2004; Gordillo 2005; Kimerling 2006; Martz 1987; Schodt 1987.
7. I have not been able to find conclusive corroborating information for many of these dates, which should be considered estimates.
8. The *cocama*, black *cocama*, and Napo Runa to whom Rufino refers came with Texaco or on its roads. The Shuar man was Imbiquito Vargas, who originally worked for Shell and ended up marrying a Cofán woman and having Cofán children. He belongs to a different category than the others. Although most people recognize the non-Cofán ancestry of these people's descendants, the children are largely accepted as

regular community members. They speak and act as Cofán individuals, and few people question their Cofán-ness unless they commit violent acts that make people recall the ethnic difference of their parents or grandparents.

9. Most of the *cocama* who married into Totoa Nai'qui eventually left their Cofán wives. Only one continues to live there.

10. Some of these names—for example, "Criollo"—clearly derive from Spanish, and none have specific meanings in A'ingae. Like many peoples around the world, the Cofán probably had no last names before Westerners such as missionaries and government census takers began entering their territory and trying to keep track of them for purposes of control and/or taxation. Cofán people associate the names I list with Cofán family lines. A child takes his father's last name first and his mother's last name second. Women do not change their last names upon marriage. The idea seems bizarre to them, as it would make the marriage appear to be incestuous. The Cofán consider marrying an individual who shares either one's maternal or paternal last name to be improper, although some couples have broken the rule.

CHAPTER 5: DAMAGED WORLD

1. Kimerling 1991, 59, 65, 67. Suzana Sawyer (2015) describes the conflicting forms of scientific research employed during the Ecuadorian phase of the Chevron trial, in which lawyers and expert witnesses disagreed about what makes petroleum wastes potentially harmful to human health.

2. Kimerling 1991, 59–73.

3. Hurtig and San Sebastián 2002, 2004; San Sebastián, Armstrong, and Stephens 2002; San Sebastián et al. 2001; San Sebastián and Hurtig 2004.

4. Paz y Miño et al. 2008.

5. Kelsh, Morimoto, and Lau 2009.

6. Lago Agrio Legal Team, n.d., "Summary of Independent Health Evaluations of Area of Ecuador's Rainforest Where Chevron Operated from 1964 to 1990," Chevron Toxico, http://chevrontoxico.com/assets/docs/cancer-summary.pdf.

7. Checker 2005.

8. The difficulties are also nearly insurmountable for relatively well-off communities close to major metropolitan centers in more developed countries, as Dan Fagin brilliantly describes in *Toms River* (2013).

---

9. Unfortunately, Bobbie died a few months after our conversation.
10. Committee on Natural Disasters et al. 1991.
11. One man told me that the medicinal plant species that grew along the shoreline of the Pisorié River eventually disappeared because of oil contamination in the waterway.
12. The technical name for the procedure is endoscopic CO_2 laser cricopharyngeal myotomy.
13. I borrow the term from Auyero and Swistun 2009.

CHAPTER 6: PROHIBITION AND PROTEST

1. In A'ingae, people only use the plural nominal suffix (*-ndeccu*) to refer to multiple humans. Every other object in the world is treated as a singular entity, a "mass noun" like "sugar" or "flour," substances that require a unit ("five pounds of flour") to be pluralized. Even though most Cofán people recognize that there are different *companía* and that each is composed of many humans, they never pluralize the noun. Consequently, it is difficult to discern whether they are discussing one or more corporate entities in any single statement about the *companía*.
2. The Cofán ethnic federation has undergone many name changes. First, it was the Asociación de Comunidades Indígenas de la Nacionalidad Cofán. Second, it was the Organización Indígena de la Nacionalidad Cofán del Ecuador. Third, it was the Federación Indígena de la Nacionalidad Cofán del Ecuador; under that name, it achieved a legal status with the government in 2001. Just a few years ago, Cofán leaders changed its name once more, to the Nacionalidad Originario A'i-Kofán del Ecuador. At the same time, Cofán leaders began to write and speak of themselves in political contexts as "A'i-Kofán" rather than as "Cofán," although the shift has not stuck with most Cofán people. *A'i* means "human being" or "Cofán person" in A'ingae. "Kofán," of course, means "Cofán." But the word does not appear to derive from A'ingae. Randy Borman suggests that the word was created by Spanish conquerors when they descended the eastern Andean foothills in the sixteenth century and encountered A'ingae-speaking people. Those people referred to the uppermost branches of the Aguarico River as the "Cofa Na'e" (Strong River or Important River). When the Spanish managed to ask the A'ingae speakers who they were, they probably replied "Cofa Na'e'su A'i" (People of the Cofa River). Apparently, the Spaniards rendered the phonetically complex phrase into the much simpler *cofanes*.
3. We did compose and sign the agreement, but I was unable to fulfill its

terms. In 2000, I received a Fulbright grant to do dissertation research in Dureno in 2001 and 2002. But weeks before I was scheduled to arrive in Dureno, the US State Department decided the area was unsafe for a gringo. Plan Colombia, a US-funded effort to stop coca cultivation in Colombia, had just begun. The violence raged on the other side of the border. Drugs, arms, refugees, and militant factions were crossing into Ecuadorian Cofán territory. The State Department, which controls the Fulbright program, decided that I could continue to work in Ecuador only if I remained far from the border. A few conversations with Randy Borman convinced me that it would be interesting to study what he and the Foundation for the Survival of the Cofán People were up to in Quito. I arrived there to begin work in January 2001. I lived with Randy, his family, and Cofán students who were studying in Quito schools. I also began to learn A'ingae. After six months, I decided that Zábalo was far enough from the trouble zone to be safe, so I spent my next year there learning about Cofán culture and conservation projects. I returned to Quito for the last six months of my dissertation research. Although I was not supposed to go to Dureno while collecting data for my dissertation, I did travel there in 2002 to meet Alejandro and Lucia and to help them with the process of adopting Roberto.

4. By the end of 1987, the exchange rate was 280 *sucres* to one US dollar, according to Country Data, http://www.country-data.com/cgi-bin /query/r-3939.html. The rate would have made Texaco's offer equivalent to more than $500,000—about $2,000 for each Dureno resident at the time. The number sounds extraordinarily high given my cursory knowledge of the history of company-community negotiations in Amazonian Ecuador. Of course, it is possible that the Texaco chief was lying to Toribio; he certainly did not offer the Cofán a signed agreement. It is also possible that Toribio misremembered the number.

5. See note 3.

6. An extremely important actor in the Dureno 1 takeover was Ramón Yumbo. At the time, Ramón was president of Dureno. He was probably the best Spanish speaker in the community. His father was an early Napo Runa migrant to Cofán territory. Ramón has always identified as Cofán, but he only speaks Spanish, even though everyone speaks to him in A'ingae and he understands perfectly. I have talked to Ramón many times. During my research for this book, he was hardly ever in Dureno's central settlement. He is a resident of Opirito, a different population center. I tried to contact him to arrange at least one interview, but he was unresponsive. I imagine he had already grown tired of gringo

researchers. Perhaps he knew I was on good terms with Dureno's president at the time, with whom Ramón was involved in a conflict.

7. The publication also includes an account of the *coancoan*, a supposedly sacred underground being threatened by oil drilling. I provide a more detailed discussion of the *coancoan* in Cepek 2016.

8. Judith Kimerling is a notable exception. She has spent years living in Ecuador and collaborating with indigenous peoples on issues related to oil development. Apart from her academic work, she serves as international legal counsel for an alliance of indigenous Waorani communities who are committed to protecting their territory from oil development. In 2007 she received the Field Museum's Parker/Gentry Award for Excellence in Conservation/Environmental Biology. In 2011 she was awarded the Albertson Medal for Sustainable Development. I have spoken with her about a future collaboration between ourselves and Cofán and Waorani people concerning the possibility of devising an adequate compensation structure for indigenous inhabitants of Amazonian Ecuador who have been harmed by oil development.

9. Conklin and Graham 1995.

CHAPTER 7: THE POSSIBILITY OF COEXISTENCE

1. I worked alongside Martin in 2012 and 2013, but Deji replaced him as my primary research assistant in 2014. Martin's oldest son had become involved in a community conflict. Because the son was still an unmarried member of Martin's household, community leaders decided to sanction Martin's entire family as punishment for the son's wrongdoing. The decision meant that Martin could no longer obtain community benefits, including a salary for working on my project. Fortunately, Deji proved to be an excellent replacement. I felt sorry for Martin. The loss of income was hard on his family. We continue to communicate by email, and I hope to work with him again in the future.

2. People use the word *singo* to describe individuals who have strong desires for or attachments to certain people or objects. For example, Alejandro calls himself a *ccumba singo* (a person who really loves tobacco). People call a womanizer a *chamba singo* (a person who always pursues women). I am not sure why Afro-Ecuadorians and Afro-Colombians are associated with strong desires. In some Cofán communities, people do tell stories about black men who raped Cofán women in the distant past; Cofán people mention this when they note the frizzy hair, broad noses, and dark skin characteristic of some

Cofán family lines. In general, though, the Cofán are not particularly antagonistic toward *singo*. They certainly do not dislike them more than *cocama*.

3. Eduardo's accountant is Luis Narvaez, the same man who helped me produce the video about the 2014 oil spill and upload it to his YouTube channel. In addition to being an accountant, he has a small media-production business in Lago Agrio.

4. Becker 2011, 57–58.

5. The organization is the Ceibo Alliance, a joint effort of ClearWater and the Leonardo DiCaprio Foundation. DiCaprio began the effort with a $3.4 million donation; "DiCaprio Foundation to Award $15 Million for Environmental Causes," *Philanthropy News Digest*, January 21, 2016, http://philanthropynewsdigest.org/news/dicaprio-foundation-to-award-15-million-for-environmental-causes.

CHAPTER 8: LIFE IN OIL

1. Appel, Mason, and Watts 2015.
2. Barret and Worden 2014a.
3. Latour 1993, 90.
4. Huber 2013.
5. Coronil 1997.
6. Mitchell 2011.
7. Descola 1996; Kohn 2013.
8. Sawyer 2004.
9. "The Facts: Chevron in Ecuador and Plaintiffs' Strategy of Fraud," *Amazon Post*, n.d., http://theamazonpost.com/fact-sheet/the-facts-about-chevron-in-ecuador-and-the-plaintiffs-strategy-of-fraud/ (accessed May 3, 2017).
10. "Environmental Claims against Chevron in Ecuador: The Facts," *Amazon Post*, n.d., http://theamazonpost.com/fact-sheet/facts-behind-the-environmental-claims-against-chevron-in-ecuador/ (accessed May 3, 2017).
11. Ibid.
12. Wasserstrom 2011. Wasserstrom makes his case in more detail in three articles he co-authored, all of which can be found on the *Amazon Post* website: Southgate, Wasserstrom, and Reider 2009; Wasserstrom and Bustamante 2015; Wasserstrom and Southgate 2013.

GLOSSARY

a'i: Human being or Cofán person

ai'pa: Potentially friendly non-Cofán indigenous person, usually an individual belonging to the Siona or Secoya ethnic group

Amisacho: Historical Cofán village that became Texaco's base camp and the city of Lago Agrio

atesu'cho: One who has learned, usually a powerful shaman

aya: Spectral shade or malevolent spirit that emerges from a person after he or she dies

canse'pa: A person's life force, susceptible to capture by malevolent spirits and enemy shamans

cocama: Nonindigenous Spanish speaker

cocoya: Demon or malevolent supernatural agent

cui'ccu: Beverage made from water and mashed plantains or bananas

davu: Rock-, glass-, or bone-like object that is one of a shaman's most important weapons

Duvuno: Contemporary Cofán community upriver from Dureno on the Aguarico River

Lago Agrio: Provincial capital of the Ecuadorian province of Sucumbíos

Napo or Napo Runa: Indigenous Kichwa-speaking people who began moving into Cofán territory in the late nineteenth century

na'su: Chief, leader, master, or owner

ondiccu'je: Long tunic that is the traditional form of male Cofán dress

simpe'cha'a: Word used to refer to crude oil before Cofán people knew what it was

Sinangoé: Contemporary Cofán community near the headwaters of the Aguarico River

---

singo: Afro-Ecuadorian or Afro-Colombian person

Tetete: Now-disappeared indigenous people who spoke a Western Tukanoan language, wore no clothes, lived in the forest interior, and sometimes attacked and stole from Cofán people

yaje: Cofán people's most important hallucinogenic drink, known to many Westerners as ayahuasca (*Banisteriopsis caapi*)

yoco: Stimulating caffeinated beverage made from a forest vine (*Paullinia yoco*)

Zábalo: Contemporary Cofán community downriver from Dureno on the Aguarico River

WORKS CITED

Adunbi, Omolade. 2015. *Oil Wealth and Insurgency in Nigeria*. Blooming-
ton: Indiana University Press.

Appel, Hannah, Arthur Mason, and Michael Watts. 2015. "Introduction:
Oil Talk." In *Subterranean Estates: Life Worlds of Oil and Gas*, edited
by Hannah Appel, Arthur Mason, and Michael Watts, 1–26. Ithaca, NY:
Cornell University Press.

Asad, Talal. 1973. *Anthropology and the Colonial Encounter*. New York:
Humanities Press.

Auyero, Javier, and Débora A. Swistun. 2009. *Flammable: Environmental
Suffering in an Argentine Shantytown*. Oxford, England: Oxford
University Press.

Baby, Patrice, Marco Rivadeneira, and Roberto Barragán. 2004. *La Cuenca
Oriente: Geología y petróleo*. Quito: Petroecuador.

Barret, Ross, and Daniel Worden. 2014a. Introduction to *Oil Culture*,
edited by Ross Barret and Daniel Worden, xvii–xxxiii. Minneapolis:
University of Minnesota Press.

———, eds. 2014b. *Oil Culture*. Minneapolis: University of Minnesota Press.

Barrett, Paul M. 2014. *Law of the Jungle: The $19 Billion Legal Battle over
Oil in the Rain Forest and the Lawyer Who'd Stop at Nothing to Win*.
New York: Crown.

Beamish, Thomas D. 2002. *Silent Spill: The Organization of an Industrial
Crisis*. Cambridge: MIT Press.

Becker, Marc. 2011. "Correa, Indigenous Movements, and the Writing of a
New Constitution in Ecuador." *Latin American Perspectives* 38 (176):
47–62.

Berlinger, Joe, dir. 2009. *Crude*. Film. New York: First Run Features.

Bessire, Lucas. 2014. *Behold the Black Caiman: A Chronicle of Ayoreo Life.* Chicago: University of Chicago Press.

Borman, Randall B. 1996. "Survival in a Hostile World: Culture Change and Missionary Influence among the Cofán People of Ecuador, 1954–1994." *Missiology* 24 (2):185–200.

———. 2009. "A History of the Río Cofanes Territory." In *Rapid Inventory No. 21: Ecuador: Cabeceres Cofanes-Chingual,* edited by Corine Vriesendorp, William S. Alverson, Álvaro del Camp, Douglas F. Stotz, Debra K. Moskovits, Segundo Fuentes Cáceres, Byron Coronel Tapia, and Elizabeth P. Anderson, 222–227. Chicago: Field Museum.

Borman, Randall B., Corrine Vriesendorp, William S. Alverson, Debra K. Moskovits, Douglas F. Stotz, and Álvaro del Campo. 2007. *Rapid Biological Inventories No. 19: Ecuador: Territorio Cofan Dureno.* Chicago: Field Museum.

Boudin, Chesa. 2009. *Gringo: A Coming-of-Age in Latin America.* New York: Scribner.

Brown, Michael. 1989. "The Dark Side of the Shaman." *Natural History* 89 (11): 8–10.

Cabodevilla, Miguel Angel. 1997. *La selva de los fantasmas errantes.* Pompeya, Ecuador: Centro de Investigación Cultural de la Amazonía Ecuatoriana.

Castillo, Gina E. 1999. *Looking for the Papers That God Forgot: An Ethnography of Environmental Change.* PhD diss., York University, North York, Canada.

Cattelino, Jessica. 2008. *High Stakes: Florida Seminole Gaming and Sovereignty.* Durham, NC: Duke University Press.

Cepek, Michael L. 2009. "The Myth of the Gringo Chief: Amazonian Messiahs and the Power of Immediacy." *Identities: Global Studies in Culture and Power* 16 (2):227–248.

———. 2012. *A Future for Amazonia: Randy Borman and Cofán Environmental Politics.* Austin: University of Texas Press.

———. 2014. "A White Face for the Cofán Nation? Randy Borman and the Ambivalence of Indigeneity." In *Performing Indigeneity: Contemporary and Historic Displays of Indigeneity in Public Spaces,* edited by Laura R. Graham and Glenn Penny, 83–109. Lincoln: University of Nebraska Press.

———. 2016. "There Might Be Blood: Oil, Humility, and the Cosmopolitics of a Cofán Petro-Being." *American Ethnologist* 43 (4): 623–635.

Cerón, Carlos E. 1995. *Etnobiología de los cofanes de Dureno.* Quito: Museo Ecuatoriano de Ciencias Naturales.

Checker, Melissa. 2005. *Polluted Promises: Environmental Racism and the Search for Justice in a Southern Town*. New York: New York University Press.

Clifford, James. 1988. *The Predicament of Culture: Twentieth-Centure Ethnography, Literature, and Art*. Cambridge, MA: Harvard University Press.

Colby, Gerard, and Charlotte Dennett. 1995. *Thy Will Be Done: The Conquest of the Amazon; Nelson Rockefeller and Evangelism in the Age of Oil*. New York: HarperCollins.

Committee on Natural Disasters, Commission on Engineering and Technical Systems, Division on Engineering and Physical Sciences, and National Research Council. 1991. *The March 5, 1987, Ecuador Earthquakes: Mass Wasting and Socioeconomic Effects*. Vol. 5 of *Natural Disaster Studies*. Washington, DC: National Academies Press.

Conklin, Beth, and Laura Graham. 1995. "The Shifting Middle Ground: Amazonian Indians and Eco-Politics." *American Anthropologist* 97:695–710.

Coronil, Fernando. 1997. *The Magical State: Nature, Money, and Modernity in Venezuela*. Chicago: University of Chicago Press.

Descola, Philippe. 1996. *In the Society of Nature: A Native Ecology in Amazonia*. Cambridge, England: Cambridge University Press.

Douglas, Mary. 1966. *Purity and Danger: An Analysis of Concepts of Pollution and Taboo*. London: Routledge.

Fagin, Dan. 2013. *Toms River: A Story of Science and Salvation*. New York: Bantam.

Fitton, Lori J. 1999. *Is Acculturation Healthy? Biological, Cultural, and Environmental Change among the Cofán of Ecuador*. PhD diss., Ohio State University, Columbus, Ohio.

Friede, Juan. 1952. "Los kofan: Una tribu de la alta Amazonia colombiana." Paper read at Proceedings of the Thirtieth International Congress of Americanists.

Goldhaber, Michael D. 2014. *Crude Awakening: Chevron in Ecuador*. New York: RosettaBooks.

Gordillo, Ramiro. 2005. *El oro del diablo? Ecuador: Historia del petróleo*. Quito: Corporación Editora Nacional.

Huber, Matthew. 2013. *Lifeblood: Oil, Freedom, and the Forces of Capital*. Minneapolis: University of Minnesota Press.

Hurtig, Anna-Karin, and Miguel San Sebastián. 2002. "Geographical Differences in Cancer Incidence in the Amazon Basin of Ecuador in Relation to Residence Near Oil Fields." *International Journal of Epidemiology* 31:1021–1027.

———. 2004. "Incidence of Childhood Leukemia and Oil Exploitation in the Amazon Basin of Ecuador." *International Journal of Occupational Environmental Health* 10 (3): 245–250.

Hvalkof, Soren, and Peter Aa. 1981. *Is God an American? An Anthropological Perspective on the Missionary Work of the Summer Institute of Linguistics*. Copenhagen: International Work Group for Indigenous Affairs.

Kane, Joe. 1995. *Savages*. New York: Knopf.

Kelsh, Michael A., Libby Morimoto, and Edmund Lau. 2009. "Cancer Mortality and Oil Production in the Amazon Region of Ecuador, 1990–2005." *International Archives of Occupational and Environmental Health* 82 (3): 381–395.

Kimerling, Judith S. 1991. *Amazon Crude*. New York: Natural Resources Defense Council.

———. 2006. "Indigenous Peoples and the Oil Frontier in Amazonia: The Case of Ecuador, ChevronTexaco, and *Aguinda v. Texaco*." *International Law and Politics* 38:413–664.

Kohn, Eduardo. 2002. "Infidels, Virgins, and the Black-Robed Priest: A Backwoods History of Ecuador's Montaña Region." *Ethnohistory* 49 (3): 545–582.

———. 2013. *How Forests Think: Toward an Anthropology Beyond the Human*. Chicago: University of Chicago Press.

Lago Agrio Legal Team. N.d. "Summary of Independent Health Evaluations of Area of Ecuador's Rainforest Where Chevron Operated from 1964 to 1990." Chevron Toxico. http://chevrontoxico.com/assets/docs/cancer -summary.pdf.

Latour, Bruno. 1993. *We Have Never Been Modern*. Cambridge, MA: Harvard University Press.

Martz, John D. 1987. *Politics and Petroleum in Ecuador*. New Brunswick, NJ: Transaction Books.

Mitchell, Timothy. 2011. *Carbon Democracy: Political Power in the Age of Oil*. London: Verso.

Newson, Linda A. 1995. *Life and Death in Early Colonial Ecuador*. Norman: University of Oklahoma Press.

Nixon, Rob. 2013. *Slow Violence and the Environmentalism of the Poor*. Cambridge, MA: Harvard University Press.

Paz y Miño, C., A. López Cortéz, M. Arévalo, and M. E. Sánchez. 2008. "Monitoring of DNA Damage in Individuals Exposed to Petroleum

Hydrocarbons in Ecuador." *Annals of the New York Academy of Sciences* 1140:121–128.

Pinkley, Homer V. 1973. *The Ethno-Ecology of the Kofan Indians.* PhD diss., Harvard University, Cambridge, MA.

Reed, Kristen. 2009. *Crude Existence: Environment and the Politics of Oil in Northern Angola.* Berkeley: University of California Press.

Robbins, Joel. 2013. "Beyond the Suffering Subject: Toward an Anthropology of the Good." *Journal of the Royal Anthropological Institute* 19:447–462.

Robinson, Scott S. 1979. *Towards an Understanding of Kofan Shamanism.* PhD diss., Cornell University, Ithaca, NY.

Rogers, Douglas. 2015a. *The Depths of Russia: Oil, Power, and Culture after Socialism.* Ithaca, NY: Cornell University Press.

———. 2015b. "Oil and Anthropology." *Annual Review of Anthropology* 44:365–380.

Rosaldo, Renato. 1993. *Culture and Truth: The Remaking of Social Analysis.* 2nd ed. Boston: Beacon.

Sahlins, Marshall. 1974. *Stone Age Economics.* Chicago: Aldine Transaction.

Said, Edward. 2003. *Orientalism.* 25th anniversary ed. New York: Penguin.

San Sebastián, Miguel, Ben Armstrong, Javier Córdoba, and Carolyn Stephens. 2001. "Exposures and Cancer Incidence near Oil Fields in the Amazon Basin of Ecuador." *Occupational Environmental Medicine* 58:517–522.

San Sebastián, Miguel, Ben Armstrong, and Carolyn Stephens. 2002. "Outcomes of Pregnancy among Women Living in the Proximity of Oil Fields in the Amazon Basin of Ecuador." *International Journal of Occupational Environmental Health* 8 (4): 312–319.

San Sebastián, Miguel, and Anna-Karin Hurtig. 2004. "Oil Exploitation in the Amazon Basin of Ecuador: A Public Health Emergency." *Pan American Journal of Public Health* 15 (3): 205–211.

Sawyer, Suzana. 2004. *Crude Chronicles: Indigenous Politics, Multinational Oil, and Neoliberalism in Ecuador.* Durham, NC: Duke University Press.

———. 2015. "Crude Contamination: Law, Science, and Indeterminacy in Ecuador and Beyond." In *Subterranean Estates: Life Worlds of Oil and Gas,* edited by Hannah Appel, Arthur Mason, and Michael Watts, 126–146. Ithaca, NY: Cornell University Press.

Schneider-Mayerson, Matthew. 2015. *Peak Oil: Apocalyptic Environmentalism and Libertarian Political Culture.* Chicago: University of Chicago Press.

Schodt, David W. 1987. *Ecuador: An Andean Enigma.* Boulder, CO: Westview.

Southgate, Douglas, Robert Wasserstrom, and Susan Reider. 2009. "Oil Development, Deforestation, and Indigenous Populations in the Ecuadorian Amazon." In *Meetings of the Latin American Studies Association.* Rio de Janeiro, Brazil: LASA.

Stoll, David. 1983. *Fishers of Men or Founders of Empire? The Wycliffe Bible Translators in Latin America.* London: Zed Books.

Taussig, Michael. 1987. *Shamanism, Colonialism, and the Wild Man: A Study in Terror and Healing.* Chicago: University of Chicago Press.

Tidwell, Mike. 1996. *Amazon Stranger.* New York: Lyons and Buford.

Trouillot, Michel-Rolph. 2003. *Global Transformations: Anthropology and the Modern World.* New York: Palgrave Macmillan.

Walker, Christopher, dir. 1996. *Trinkets and Beads.* Film. New York: Faction Films.

Wasserstrom, Robert. 2011. "Lack of Evidence in the Sentencia of Cultural Damages Caused by Petroleum Activity." At Docslide.US, http://docslide.us/documents/expert-report-robert-wasserstrom.html.

———. 2014. "Surviving the Rubber Boom: Cofán and Siona Society in the Colombia-Ecuador Borderlands (1875–1955)." *Ethnohistory* 61 (3): 525–548.

Wasserstrom, Robert, and Teodoro Bustamante. 2015. "Ethnicity, Labor, and Indigenous Populations in the Ecuadorian Amazon, 1822–2010." *Advances in Anthropology* 5:1–18.

Wasserstrom, Robert, Susan Reider, and Rommel Lara. 2011. "Nobody Knew Their Names: The Black Legend of Tetete Extermination." *Ethnohistory* 58 (1): 421–444.

Wasserstrom, Robert, and Douglas Southgate. 2013. "Deforestation, Agrarian Reform, and Oil Development in Ecuador, 1964–1994." *Natural Resources* 4 (1): 31–44.

Yergin, Daniel. 1991. *The Prize: The Epic Quest for Oil, Money, and Power.* New York: Simon and Schuster.

INDEX

Page numbers in *italics* represent people, places, and topics mentioned in captions.

burning of waste, 106, 128, 144–149, 157, 173

caimans, 142–143
cancer: author's experience with, 159–160; carcinogens, exposure list, 127–128; Cofán experiences of, overviews, 152–153, 156–163; from drinking contaminated water, 135, 138, 156–157; prevalence of, 9–10, 38; studies, 128–130
canoe-building businesses, 35, 41, 207
canse'pa (life force), 78, 83
Capuchin missionaries, 24, 63–64, 97, 100–101
carcinogens, toxic chemical list, 127–128
Carmelites, 97, 174, 258n5
Cascales, Ecuador, 60
Catholic Church: missionary efforts of, 24, 63–64, 97, 100–102, 174, 243–244, 258n5; radicalization of, in Latin America, 174
Cattelino, Jessica, 220
ccopa chango (shit hole), 2
Ceibo Alliance, 123
Chaco, Ecuador, 39
Chapal, Nancy, 122
Chapal, Silvio, 114, 118–119, 124, 156, *238–239*
chavapa añe (buying and eating), 34
Checker, Melissa, 129–130
Chevron: arguments/position on responsibilities of, 162, 242–246, 256–257n3; Emeregildo's fears for future, 225; legal actions against, 12, 14, 51–52; studies funded by, 129. *See also* Texaco

Chiga (God, sun), 120
Chiga ttevaen'jen (the writings of God), 102
China National Petroleum Corporation, 18, 86
Christian groups. *See* Catholic Church
cleansing rituals, 38, 70, 71, 78
cleanup effort, employment in, 8
ClearWater organization, 148
Clifford, James, 53
clothing and dress: modern influences on, 120; *ondiccu'je* (traditional tunic), 18, 46, 95, 119, 120, 124–125; ornamentation, 18–19, 30, 70, 80; traditional, 18, 95, 122, 124, 203
cocama (nonindigenous Spanish speakers), *93*; Cofán fears of, 87, 90–92, 96, 115–119, 169–170; cultural impact of, 92, 94–96, 119–120, 122–123, 256–258n3; and disease, 87, 96–97; influx of during oil exploration, 103, 107; as interlopers in Cofán struggles, 194–195
cocoya (malevolent supernatural agents/demons): attacks from, 38–39, 77–78, 158; and blood contamination beliefs, 67; and Cofán beliefs, 35; and hallucinogenic visions, 71, 74, 75; and shaman transformation, 64, 74
Cofán ethnic federation, 21, 171
Cofán-ness: concept of, 43, 45–47, 50–53; and cultural preservation, 119, 122. *See also* acculturation and "noble savage" image; Cofán people; cultural identity
Cofán people: Aguarico River

settlements, contemporary, 26–27, 30; Alejandro as personification of, 18; character and nature of, 212–213; fatalism of, 158–159; historical profile, 170; naïveté of, in early oil days, 111–114; naming conventions among, 259n10; origin of name, 260n2; precolonization settlements, 60; profile and demographics, 21–22, 24–25. *See also* community

Colombia: Cofán communities in, 21–22; dangers of, 260–261n3

colonization programs, modern, 107

community (Cofán): *comuna* status, granting of, 115; divisions in, over oil company involvement, 212–217, 221, 224–226, 240; enrichment and empowerment visions related to, 211–212, 241–242; and fears of future disruption and contamination, 220–221, 224–226; income of, from collective sources, 41; modernization and increasing tensions in, 41–43, 240

companías (petroleum companies in general), 166–167

Comuna Cofán Dureno, 182

Confederación de las Nacionalidades Indígenas de la Amazonía Ecuatoriana (CONFENIAE), 176–177, 178–179

congenital defects. *See* birth defects and oil pollution

Conklin, Beth, 193–194

consumer culture, evolution of, 235–236, 240

contaminación, 133

contamination beliefs/concepts: regarding petroleum pollution, 132–133, 233, 236; reproductive blood, 60, 67, 69–70, 132–133

Coronil, Fernando, 234

Correa, Rafael, 11, 208, 209, 217

Cortez, Elias and Ermilo, 79–81

"crescive troubles," 250n4

Criollo, Alejandro, *3, 16, 37, 177, 197, 218–219, 230*; background and character of, 17–19; and concern over community conflict, 215; as personification of Cofán, 18–19, 46–47; reflections on past by, 232; as shaman/healer, 35, 83–85, *161*; and Yori'ye, 59

Criollo, Atanacio, 60, 81, *95*, 101

Criollo, Deji, *32–33*; activism of, 173–174; on agreement with oil companies, 221; and Cofán land claims, 114–115; family of, 124–125; on precolonization conditions, 31

Criollo, Elsira, 124–125

Criollo, Emeregildo: activism of, 173–174; on cancer, 153; on *cocama* as untrustworthy, 112–113; cultural losses feared by, 224–225; deaths of sons, 151–152; and rights activism for Cofán, 122–123; water pollution experience of, 134

Criollo, Enrique, 102, 124–126

Criollo, Fernando, 57, 77, 84, 102

Criollo, Lucia, 232

Criollo, Manuel, 124–125

Criollo, Martin, 90; activism of, 231; leadership roles of, 190; sanctions against family of, 262n1; university degree of, 201

"Reorganization and Resistance:
Petroleum, Conservation,
and Cofán Transformations"
(Cepek), 180
reproductive blood and contamination beliefs, 60, 67, 69–70,
132–133
research methodology, 14
restoration and cleanup, Dureno 1
takeover, 183, 186
ritual and tradition. *See* traditions
and rituals
road construction, 104–106, 167,
173–179, 181, 211
Robbins, Joel, 251n5
Rodriguez Lara, Guillermo, 114
Rogers, Doug, 251n7
Rosaldo, Renato, 92
Royal Dutch Shell, 17, 79, 102
rubber industry, 24, 257–258n3

Sahlins, Marshall, 31
Said, Edward, 15
saline fluid in waste pits, 143
sanctions (personal), community-
imposed, 43
sanitation issues, 38, 144
San Miguel River, 21, 60, 97,
100–101
San Sebastián, Miguel, 128
Santa Cecilia settlement, 63–64, 97,
100, 103
Savages (Kane), 50
scholarship on Cofán cultural
change, 50–53
schools, 97, 100, 122, 199
seclusion practices and reproductive blood, 60, 67, 69–70
Secoya people, 30, 61
seismic exploration: 2013 agreement

on, 167–168, 190, 193, 215–217;
analysis of, 86–87, 103–104; and
cocama colonization, 107; trails
cleared for, 103, 196, *197*, 199
seje'pa (medicine/poison), 133
separation process, 104, 127, 128,
173, 186
se'piye (prohibiting/protesting), 169
sewage and garbage pollution, 38,
144
sexual aggression of *cocama*, 87,
110–111, 117, 119, 195
shamans/shamanism: Ai'pa,
learning from, 62; and calling of
game, 66, 76–77; and cleansing
(internal) rituals, 38, 70; competition and violence among,
59, 83–84; *davu* as weapon for,
72, 74, 84, 85; deaths of and
myths about, 64, 83; dreams and
visions, 42, 66, 72, 74, 75, 77, 83,
84, 91; in Dureno 1 takeover, role
of, 185–186; fear of, 185; healing
and health practices of, 35,
38–39, 77–79, 83–85; income
from, 40; mistrust/fear of,
20–21, 92; stereotyping of, 85;
Toribio's interest in, 172; tradition of, and cultural identity, 10,
58, 242; training practices of,
62; violence of, 59, 63, 75–76,
110, 170. *See also* transformation
in shamanism; Yori'ye
Shell. *See* Royal Dutch Shell
"Shifting Middle Ground, The"
(Conklin and Graham), 193–194
Shipicco (Cockroach; Ermilo
Cortez)), 79–80
shombe (wooden club, "property of
the vagina"), 170

CPSIA information can be obtained
at www.ICGtesting.com
Printed in the USA
LVHW030328250821
696016LV00002B/12